Remembering Paris in Text and Film

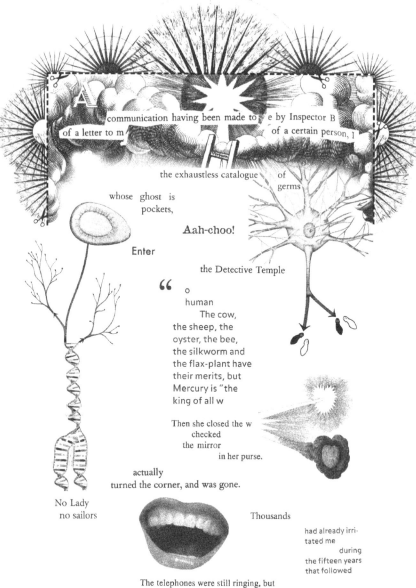

Remembering Paris in Text and Film

EDITED BY
Alistair Rolls and Marguerite Johnson

Bristol, UK / Chicago, USA

First published in the UK in 2021 by
Intellect, The Mill, Parnall Road, Fishponds, Bristol, BS16 3JG, UK

First published in the USA in 2021 by
Intellect, The University of Chicago Press, 1427 E. 60th Street,
Chicago, IL 60637, USA

Copyright © 2021 Intellect Ltd
Paperback edition © 2023 Intellect Ltd
All rights reserved. No part of this publication may be reproduced,
stored in a retrieval system, or transmitted, in any form or by
any means, electronic, mechanical, photocopying, recording, or
otherwise, without written permission.
A catalogue record for this book is available from
the British Library.

Copy editor: MPS Limited
Cover designer: Aleksandra Szumlas
Cover image: Christelle Gonzalo
Frontispiece image: 'A Communication', (Edwards 2014: [7])
Production manager: Georgia Earl
Typesetter: MPS Limited

Hardback ISBN 978-1-78938-418-5
Paperback ISBN 978-1-78938-760-5
ePDF ISBN 978-1-78938-419-2
ePUB ISBN 978-1-78938-420-8

To find out about all our publications, please visit our website.
There you can subscribe to our e-newsletter, browse or download our current
catalogue and buy any titles that are in print.

www.intellectbooks.com

This is a peer-reviewed publication.

Contents

Acknowledgements	vii
Introduction: Remembering in Paris and Paris as Remembering	1

1. Charles Baudelaire's *Paris Spleen*: Re-presenting Paris — 21
Alistair Rolls

2. Baudelaire and the Classical Tradition: Virgil, Ovid and Sappho in Paris — 39
Marguerite Johnson

3. Sappho in the Salons — 59
Marguerite Johnson

4. Memory, Modernity and the City in Agnès Varda's Paris Films — 77
Felicity Chaplin

5. Looking (Back) at the Moon in Parisian Cinema — 92
Alistair Rolls

6. *Breathless* in Paris — 108
Christopher Falzon

7. As Sedate as Swans: The Parisian Side of Jean-Paul Sartre's *La Nausée* — 127
Alistair Rolls

8. 'La forme d'une ville/Change plus vite, hélas! [...]': Translation and the Changing Modes of Urban Cognition — 150
Clive Scott

9. Paris, Capital of the Australian Poetic Avant-Garde: Christopher Brennan's 'Musicopoematographoscope', John Tranter's 'Desmond's Coupé' and Chris Edwards' 'A Fluke' and *After Naptime* — 165
David Musgrave

CONTENTS

10. Forms of Remembrance in the Sculpted Verse of Louise   187
Colet, Anaïs Ségalas and Some of their Male Contemporaries
Daniel A. Finch-Race and Valentina Gosetti

Contributors   211
Index   215

Acknowledgements

As will be touched on in our editors' introduction below, this book has its origins in two interdisciplinary undergraduate courses that Marguerite and Alistair ran at the University of Newcastle, Australia in 2018. Paris was the hook used to bring together staff and students from various streams of the Humanities; our interests and the focus of our discussion included modernity, nostalgia and reception. This idea that the urban experience that Paris presents to us today is necessarily alive with the ghosts of the past, and of course the oxymoronic tension of such lively ghosts, morphed into the present volume with its theme of remembering.

We should like to thank the following people for the part that they played in this journey: all our contributors, who have been so supportive and professional throughout; our colleagues at the University of Newcastle who helped bring the courses to life, including Rebecca Beirne, Hamish Ford and M. B. Kirchen; our undergraduate students, whose interest and generous feedback encouraged us to pursue the idea of this book; Marguerite's amazing postgraduates Tanika Koosmen and Adam Turner, who generously attended the tutorials and shared their thoughts with us and the students; and, finally, the team at Intellect, especially Tim Mitchell and Georgia Earl but also the anonymous reviewers whose positive and detailed feedback was very much appreciated.

The cover image was supplied by Alistair's colleague and friend Christelle Gonzalo. Christelle is *inter alia* one of the foremost authorities on legendary author and Parisian identity Boris Vian (on whom a chapter in this book was considered); she is also an archivist, historian and owner of the antiquarian bookshop Sur le Fil de Paris, which is located on the rue de l'Ave Maria, in the 4th arrondissement, just across the Seine from the Île Saint-Louis and thus just a short distance from where this image was taken. The photograph is entitled 'La Cité depuis les tours de Notre-Dame'; it dates from around 1860. The photographer is unknown. We are extremely grateful to Christelle for finding this photograph, which is a beautiful embodiment of remembrance, and for allowing us to use it here.

Introduction:
Remembering in Paris and
Paris as Remembering

Alistair Rolls and Marguerite Johnson

Baudelaire, I think of you!

'Andromaque, je pense à vous! [Andromache, I think of you!]' (Baudelaire 1998: 172 [173]). So begins 'Le Cygne [The Swan]', Baudelaire's famous lament on the pace of change in the Paris cityscape under Haussmann's programme of urban renewal. This is a poem about Paris; it is an immediate and visceral response to the changes of the fabric of the city as it changes before the poet's eyes. Its present tense captures this act of thinking *in medias res*. And yet, the object of these thoughts, we are told, is Andromache, not Paris. If Andromache and her grief, her past, are provoked by Baudelaire's use of the present, then the Paris in which the poet is located, and on whose streets we readers are invited to position ourselves, is also and at the same time a metaphor and thus rendered absent to self. The disjuncture of this first line is metonymic of the poem, which is the site of Baudelaire's signature chiasmata as much as it is of Haussmann's urbanization; it is also, we argue, metonymic of Paris itself. To think of you is also, almost, *not* to think of you; that is, by thinking of Paris, I also think of Andromache. To think of Paris, in this framework, is to understand metaphorically what is before one's eyes, or to hold under tension what is present and what is past, what is 'real' and what is legend. At the same time, if we reverse the polarity, the very writing of poetry (with its metaphors and artistic devices of a timeless past, or of the past as timelessness) is undermined here – as the poem takes shape – by the presence of the real world. The city's refusal to settle on a given form (one metaphor gives way to another and another), that is, to hold its shape long enough for us to take it in and account for it, is embodied by this taking shape of a poem that itself eschews self-coincidence.

For the purposes of the present volume, which will think of Paris through various lenses, this tension is the stuff of remembrance. Paris causes us to remember itself as other, and we create Paris through memory. As we observe above, by thinking of Paris, the poet also thinks of Andromache and this dual or even potentially multi-layered system of remembrance is not only a marker of Baudelaire's responses to the city but also a common inscription of French literature and art. It is also present in historical / 'historical' memory, as in Gilles Corrozet's 1532 travelogue and urban history, *La Fleur des antiquitez de Paris* (*The Flower of Antiquity of Paris*). Therein, Corrozet includes the legendary genealogy that situates Paris as the second Troy (something later not lost on Baudelaire), composing a guidebook that 'creates a legible sense of place' (Hodges 2008: 136). Elizabeth Hodges reminds us of Pierre Nora's *Les Lieux de mémoire* (*Realms of Memory*), in which he traverses 'the interrelated categories of place, memory and history' (Hodges 2008: 142).[1]

Furthermore, this is a city that has long been a site of remembrance (long enough perhaps for us to consider it, timelessly, to have always been so). This explains Baudelaire's thinking of Andromache, who, as a model of grief, is herself remembering. The past is not just remembered (as something complete) therefore; rather, it is reconstructed, recalled as a site of remembrance. The result for Baudelaire is something of a chicken-and-egg situation, which is captured by the reference to the poet's 'mémoire fertile [fertile memory]', which is said to be seeded by thoughts of the mythical figure (1998: 174 [175]). In fact, the speaker's memory is at once inseminated by Andromache and always already fertile at the time when he walks across 'le nouveau Carrousel [the modern Carrousel]' (1998: 174 [175]). Does Andromache (as a metaphor for Paris) make him remember, or does Paris become a metaphor, and thus Andromache – as thoughts form into a poem (about the non-taking of form) – because he was, in the pre-diegetic instant before conjuring his first word, remembering? It seems crucial that this conundrum not be resolved. '[L]a forme d'une ville [the form a city takes]', he says, changes more quickly than the mortal heart (1998: 174 [175]). Certainly, it is not the simple fact of Paris's continuous, and rapid, changing of form that causes the poet to remember, for it appears equally true that the poet's remembrance renders him unable to settle on a stable poetic form for the city, hence the disruption of metaphor, which gives rise to a chain, or bedraggled procession, of metaphors. Metaphor itself ends up disrupted and dragged through dusty (de)construction sites. Memory here is simultaneously about settling on shapes and shapes' refusal to settle; this is remembrance as undecidability, and thus, to draw on Shoshana Felman's famous defence of textual/critical ambiguity (1977), as an attempt at salvation.

If resistance to form, perhaps we might call it a classical form, is the result of urban renewal, it is equally important that form is nonetheless taken, and no less classical a form than that of Andromache. The shock of modernity breaks forms, but it does not break with the past; the remembrance of the past may well deform, but it also creates forms. In the absence, the death even, of clear metaphor, we stand witness to the creation of metaphors, whose ragged shapes are nonetheless noble enough. For Ross Chambers, this poem has time, its progress and the futility of resistance to that progress, at its core (2015: 77–88, 150–53). For the purposes of this book, all this memory work, in which Baudelaire revels, is intimately bound up with the city. In 'Le Cygne', to follow our chosen model, Paris is both present, on the site of what will become for future generations the Louvre museum, and elsewhere, in the mythical time, or timelessness, of Troy (think of Corrozet's creation of a legendary royal lineage for Paris as he traverses the ancient ruins of a Roman city).

The chapters in this volume tend to settle on one side or the other of Baudelaire's memory puzzle. Some will respond to texts that are 'about Paris', reading the various acts of remembrance at work in them; others will use various forms of remembrance to see Paris in texts. We will follow Baudelaire's thoughts of Andromache backwards, looking for his memories of learning the Classics, seeing in the poetics of modernity a site of what we recognize today as the Classical Tradition (or Classical Reception). We will also follow the telescopic chain of metaphors of 'Le Cygne' to its logical end-point, which is, paradoxically enough, a refusal to end. The unnamed 'others' to which the final words of the poem refer take us out of the present and into the future, just as the explosion onto the page of 'Andromache' allows us to glimpse a possibility of remembrance in the space before. When we read, for example, Jean-Paul Sartre's *La Nausée* (*Nausea*) and construct that text in, as and through Paris, it is, we argue, because our literary patrimony is already rich with thoughts of Baudelaire (see Chapter 7). To think of Baudelaire when one reads a later text, a text by another author, is an act of Parisian remembrance and intertextuality. This is possible, not because it all began with Baudelaire; instead, it is possible because 'Le Cygne' is always already an intertext (it is a Parisian response to the Classics) and an act of autodifferentiation, and indeed of deconstruction (Paris is both a place of form *and* formlessness, of physical destruction *and* mental construction).

Paris, memory and tradition

As much of this volume is concerned with Paris and memory/history, the presence of what we call 'tradition' is a strong and important one. We understand 'tradition' as the embedded text – the old text within the new one – and what this literary importation does, or what it means in a new context. But, we take the term 'text' as a broad one; for us, herein, it may be something written (which it quite often is), painted, built, reviled, politicized, imaginary and imagined, or otherwise. Here is, for example, Martin Scorsese's *Hugo*, discussed in Chapter 5 as a tradition based on Georges Méliès's cinema, which itself carried embedded within its own praxis a tradition of Parisian theatre. This tradition, which flows through Méliès's films into Scorsese's, considers memory as a nostalgia for a lost, somewhat magical age. Paris is at the centre of both filmic texts, as it is in other films, such as Jean-Luc Godard's *À bout de souffle* (*Breathless*), discussed in Chapter 6, which may be interpreted as the act of recording Paris for posterity – as Chris Falzon writes: '*Breathless* is a kind of documentary of Paris, capturing the everyday life of the city, and this in turn frames and sets into relief the film's cinematic artifice'. Chapters 2 and 3 also look at the concept of artistic tradition, through the lens of what is called the Classical Tradition, which has morphed into Classical Reception since the end of the 1990s (see Hardwick 2003; De Pourcq 2012). In these contributions, tradition is understood as both antiquity and memory. By antiquity, we acknowledge the western equation of antiquity with Greece and Rome and the hegemony of elite education systems that kept the memory alive. Think Parisian schoolboys swatting over Robert Estienne's *Dictionarium latinogallicum*, first published in 1538. Think of the young Charles Baudelaire as the son of a skilled Latinist, who created an illustrated *Latin Vocabulary* for his young students, the sons of the Duke de Choiseul-Praslin (Lloyd 2008: 9). Think also of 'La Voix [The Voice]':

> Mon berceau s'adossait à la bibliothèque,
> Babel sombre, où roman, science, fabliau,
> Tout, la cendre latine et la poussière grecque,
> Se mêlaient. J'étais haut comme un in-folio.
> [My cradle rocked below the stack of books –
> That Babel of instructions, novels, verse
> Where Roman rubbish mixed with Grecian dust,
> I was no taller than a folio.]
>
> (Baudelaire 1993, 1857: 312–13)

Here, memory is inextricably tied to books, to Classical texts expressly, as well as to the poet's own poetry. In this sense, to read Baudelaire reading Paris is not only to embed the man-child in his Parisian nursery but also to recognize the child-man as future poet. His intimate engagement – even, relationship – with Greek and Latin literature, expressly poetry, bares the mark of his anti-romantic sensibility when it comes to invoking the voices and the figures of antiquity. The size of a folio, the fledgling Baudelaire – even at such a young age – sees the Classics as Roman rubbish and Grecian dust, as ephemeral and vulnerable to silly aggrandizement, yet inherently sad and precious at the same time. He sees antiquity as anything but romantic. He sees them as he sees Andromache. Our use of 'Le Cygne' as one leitmotiv of this collection is also to reference Baudelaire as another leitmotiv, and he too is a benchmark, a guide, for these poets. He is French literary reception, memory and nostalgia.

The voices of a Classical past also immerse themselves in the creation of a fantasy Paris in symbiotic union with a Grecian antiquity. Here, we also have female poets, Natalie Barney and Renée Vivien rebuilding Sapphic/sapphic enclaves on the West Bank.[2] Baudelaire's longing for an old Paris amid the shock of a new one shows poets like Barney and Vivien that an imaginary Classical past is both a poetic technique and a way of life. Both women, but particularly Vivien, translated the fragments of Sappho, which demonstrates another approach to establishing, maintaining and communicating memories of antiquity in a Parisian setting. In this sense, the act of translation is as much about the physical site of the process and its history as it is about the particular tradition being excavated. What a translator like Vivien wants to 'say' about Sappho is inextricably tied to Vivien in Paris. In the same way, translators of Baudelaire are as attuned to the Haussmannization of Paris as they are to the French words on the page awaiting transformation (an old text about to be made anew). This is encapsulated in the words of Clive Scott, in Chapter 8: 'Within the understanding of literary criticism as an institutional discipline, Reading works with History to assess and interpret the literary work within a given context and set of literary affiliations, within, that is, what we might roughly call a tradition.'

Paris (and the) intertext

What we are discussing here is a sense of tradition as something to be made. Likewise, remembering is an act of putting back together (re-membering not only as opposed to, but also as a kind of, dis-membering), of drawing on our memories imaginatively in order to remake the past in our own (present) image. To this extent, tradition, reception and translation function like forms of intertextuality. For intertextuality, too, is a writerly phenomenon insofar as, however much the text prompts the reader, the reader must admit the intertext, to allow it to come into focus, inside the text being read. And yet, for scholars like Michel Riffaterre (1978), a reader can only respond to the text because of something inherently observable about its form that may be defined, as discussed above, as its tradition(s). This gives rise to such quasi-oxymoronic entities as the 'obligatory intertext', which is found by the reader, only to be held subsequently as proof that the author put it there. Intertexts, of course, can be highly persuasive, but, like any great figure (Andromache is one), can be replaced by another (a humble swan in this case). Added to this, as J. Hillis Miller (1979) has demonstrated, is the who's-hosting-whom conundrum: does the text enfold and host the (actual) intertext, or does the text sit inside, the guest of, the (virtual) intertext?

All of which takes us back to the chicken-and-egg scenario described above. For Chambers, Baudelaire's poetic reading of the city only takes its final form when, and because, it is taken out of his hands:

'[H]is' generic invention in *Le Spleen de Paris* turned out to be less a radical transformation of lyricism, in the way that the poet himself had apparently intended, than an accidental adaptation, owing to the author's death and the posthumous intervention of his editors, of existing practices of collective flâneur writing [...] [T]hese collective practices – by definition unsystematic and uncoordinated – came to constitute in this way an authorial project, attributable to 'Charles Baudelaire'. This project I will call a poet's urban diary; and in its accidental appropriation of the noisiness of collective writing, such an intervention, I suggest, came to represent a significant early site of the writerly 'death of the author', in that phrase's Barthesian sense.

(2015: 150)[3]

Chambers's argument is that the phrase 'la forme d'une ville' in the poem 'Le Cygne' (which is homphonous with *le signe*, or sign, in French) expresses in miniature the prose poems that he calls Baudelaire's urban diary. In the framework of such a reading, this urban form pertains 'not to the buildings and material layout of the city but to the question of the poetic form appropriate to city life' (Chambers 2015: 150). The prose poems of *Le Spleen de Paris*, Chambers notes, constitute 'a writerly form – an *écriture* – devoted to the representation of the noisiness of time and change as an atmospherics of the city' (2015: 150–51). This is true, but the prose poems will also be a form of remembering Paris. Paris is a fertile ground for remembering other places in 'Le Cygne'; it is also present to the reader and named as such. It is doubly present, as we have seen, for Andromache becomes a metaphor for Paris (and *vice versa*), while Paris is still in view. In the prose poems, Paris will be held so close to the reader's gaze that any clear focus – and readability of the specific city – is impossible, and the bricks and mortar must remain decontextualized.[4] The focus is a notch closer than in 'Le Cygne' because the rubble in that poem nonetheless takes the form of the modern Carrousel. In the prose poems, Paris is not named. The bricks and mortar of the prose poems do not represent Paris; rather, they present it. This is not to say that the prose poems do not engage in representation, since they are full of abstractions that are meaningful to the reader in a way that bricks and mortar cannot be. These metaphors at work in the prose poems are part of a poetic process (indeed, they are the poetic part) of remembering Paris, which is otherwise presented but not named. As such, it is the collective (memory) work that Chambers describes above that renders the city nameable. This ultimately (and in part posthumously) takes the form of the work's title – *Le Spleen de Paris*. Always present to the poems, but equally always absent

INTRODUCTION: REMEMBERING IN PARIS AND PARIS AS REMEMBERING

from them, Paris's relationship to the prose poems is one of contiguity, that is, not metaphorical but metonymic. Metonymy will be seen to be crucial to textual remembrance in this volume.

Intertextuality is also metonymic, since the text of which one thinks, upon which one stumbles, as one moves through another is both absent (it is not that text) and present (it is here in the text). The city is similarly intertextual: forever renewed, its present form speaks, palimpsestuously, to memories of form lost. In other words, Paris presents itself *and* represents itself, and at the same time renders itself Other. Remembering and dismembering go hand in hand when one reads the city. Chambers himself speaks of remembering in his reading of 'Le Cygne':

> These different ways of referring to the same patch of ground rehearse the changes it undergoes in passing through time, while the inevitability of such passing is played out at the start, in the switch from the present tense of the exclamation: 'Andromaque, je pense à vous!' to the immediately following past tense of an explanatory narrative: 'Ce petit fleuve [...] / A fécondé soudain me mémoire fertile [...]' No sooner has the triumphant, time-denying exclamation occurred than it has already become part of a remembered past: the past that stretches back to the 'vieux Paris' (and indeed to Andromache).
>
> (2015: 153)

What we want to emphasize here, in this volume on remembering Paris, is this interplay of present and past, and their respective fertilities. Here, Chambers emphasizes the passing of the present into the past, but it is equally possible to reverse the polarity, as seen above, and to suggest that the present thinking of Andromache, which produces the poem, comes into the present from the fertile ground of the past. Memory work here reverses, however fleetingly, entropy (this resistance Chambers names negentropy). Not so much a losing battle in some reductive or unimaginative process, but the very opposite; namely, as an act of repurposing memory as a creative act.

Chambers's negative spin lies in his focus on 'Le Cygne', and its 'endlessly backward-looking forward movement', within the context of Baudelaire's oeuvre and thus as part of a textual body striving to take shape (2015: 153). For our present purposes, we are often working downstream, using Baudelaire as an intertext. In such instances, we are interested *inter alia* in the ways in which something about another textual body that we are rereading calls out to us as a *chantier* – this is our *je-pense-à-vous* moment – and makes us think of Baudelaire. Thus, our emphasis is on the way that Baudelaire's oeuvre moves forwards, and not in spite but because of its inherent tendency to look backwards. We use the term *re*read advisedly here, since we, like Chambers, see in this form of textual remembering the construction of the writerly text as theorized by Roland Barthes. For Barthes, only rereading the same text could prevent the reader from reading the same story everywhere. Of course, construction of the writerly text through an active engagement on the reader's part saves the text as much as it saves the reader. As Barthes writes,

> [r]ereading, an operation contrary to the commercial and ideological habits of our society, which would have us 'throw away' the story once it has been consumed ('devoured'), so that we can then move on to another story, buy another book, and which is tolerated only in certain marginal categories of readers (children, old people, and professors), rereading is here suggested at the outset, for it alone saves the text from repetition (those who fail to reread are obliged to read the same story everywhere).
>
> (1974: 15–16)

Rereading, or returning to the same text (and thus heading back), does more than salvage for posterity; this is a salvation that translates the text into future incarnations of itself. Mapped onto the ongoing development of Paris's cityscape, this is a rather more positive interpretation than the telescopic chain of grieving otherwise described in 'Le Cygne'.

The rereadings of text that we hope to include in, and inspire with, this volume tap into the positivity of reading Baudelaire everywhere and carrying his, and other, texts into the future. The Baudelairean intertext will be a particularly Parisian form of construction site: references to the poet's work will thus see swans as signs, making Paris appear, and to appear with legitimacy, sometimes in places where it might ordinarily be considered to be trespassing.[5] This may be considered the final (and ongoing) phase in Baudelaire's Parisian project. It sees that his poems appear intertextually in and through the works of others, which has the result of representing Paris in these works that might otherwise have little or nothing to do with Paris. The first phase, in the lyric poems, saw Paris present and named (and thus overtly) in the poems while simultaneously present metaphorically (or covertly).[6] The second phase took up the disappearance of form inherent in urban formations and produced, in the prose poems, a poetic tension of presence–absence that saw Paris too closely presented to be visible to the naked eye but always already readable thanks to the collection's overarching title (which is generally considered to have been one compiled by his editors after Baudelaire's death). The last phase, which will concern us most in this volume, sees Paris remembered in texts where it is otherwise overtly absent. In this case, remembering the city requires active work on the part of the reader, who incorporates Paris in the construction of the writerly text.

Remembering Paris in Perec and Prévert

As is hopefully emerging from this discussion, remembering is being used in this volume quite broadly as a critical strategy, either for exploring the ways in which various texts perform Parisianness and its intersection with the past, or for uncovering intertextual or other covert references to Paris in texts that may otherwise, and typically, not be considered Parisian. In this respect, Baudelaire can be seen to offer a model, even for those chapters in this volume that do not engage specifically with his poetry. Baudelaire remembers Paris even as he contemplates it in real time, representing it through metaphor while simultaneously presenting it to his readers in all its mundanity. Furthermore, his poetics never loses sight of Paris, even when its ostensible object is an unnamed city or, in some cases, nothing apparently to do with urban life. Rather than simply a poetics of Paris therefore, what we are interested in here is a Parisian poetics, and more specifically a Parisian poetics of remembrance.

In order to anticipate the kinds of analysis that we have in mind, we should like to consider two texts that, while having a clear but general connection to Paris, benefit from a Parisian(izing) lens. Specifically, since both texts are famously and explicitly about remembrance, we wish to show the ways in which memory makes Parisian connections, even when it is not necessarily Paris that generates memory. The texts are Georges Perec's *Je me souviens* (*I remember*), which was first published in 1978, and Jacques Prévert's poem 'Barbara', whose famous opening line is 'Rappelle-toi Barbara' ('Remember Barbara'). As an opening remark, we note that these two French verbs that correspond to the English 'remember' both function, albeit in different ways, with a conjoint object pronoun. The verb *se rappeler* literally means 'to recall to oneself', and the role of the pronoun *se* is clear: it is indirect in value and indicates the way that the object is called *back to* the remembering subject. *Se souvenir*, on the other hand, is more complicated, as the pronoun looks the same but, strictly speaking, has no grammatical value. It can be considered simply to be there, appended as part of the verb. In English, too, remembering functions not only to recall to mind things from the past but also our past selves (think of Baudelaire in 'La Voix'), those selves who were present to those things on those previous occasions. In French, this is the idea of re-membering self that is inherently present in the verb *per se*. And to re-member oneself is to put oneself back together, but it also necessarily highlights the difference that we present to ourselves, as we move forward in time even as our actions and the things to which we are present sail into the past. In other words, re-membering also attests to the dis-membering of our identity. In Baudelaire's prose poems, Paris overarched this self-alterity paratextually; in these twentieth-century texts of remembrance, Paris is present intertextually as a force of autodifferentiation.

Paris is also home to memories as memoirs. Natalie Barney, champion of the Sapphic tradition in Paris, wrote *Souvenirs indiscrets* (*Indiscreet Memories*), published in 1960, in which we are witness to a transparency or honesty in memory writing that owes a significant debt to the city that nurtured the life that made the memories possible, and which facilitated their release. Can we infer from Barney's memoir a similar debt in Georges Perec's *Je me souviens?* Chris Andrews (2020) includes it among a number of texts that 'are adaptations, or substantially inspired by previous works', which 'invite the reader to write a continuation' (in the case of *Je me souviens*, in the form of five and a half blank pages included for that specific purpose at the end of the book); and that 'do not impose tight constraints on the reader-and-writer who takes up that invitation'.[7] If we pass these thoughts under the Baudelairean lens that we have discussed, we can suggest that *Je me souviens* recalls the engagement with previous works on which 'Le Cygne' is predicated; that it constitutes a series of 'thinking of you' moments that reflect, even respond to, Baudelaire's own continuation of Andromache's grief and that although the constraints – to think of Baudelaire, of Paris – are not heavy-handed or necessary, they are nonetheless present. We might read Perec's *Je me souviens* and think of moments in our own lives that have nothing to do with Paris. Perec's remembrance, on the other hand, is certainly strongly coloured by that city. As Andrews notes,

> [t]he things evoked in *I Remember* are common only to a generation of French people, and more specifically Parisians. [...] The opacity that results from the programmed obsolescence of these evocations contributes to the text's promptive power. The best way to gauge the effect that the book must have had on Perec's Parisian contemporaries is to fill the blank pages at the end, recovering memories of one's own.
>
> (2020)

Andrews notes that various French writers, typically fellow Oulipians, have answered Perec's call by writing works in a similar vein.[8] The paradox in *Je me souviens*, on which Andrews picks up, is that the call to remember is based not merely on shared memories but also, and more importantly, on memories that we do not have in common, *even with ourselves*. In a post-script to the book, Perec notes that he is conscious of reconstructing the past, which includes remembering things that were not as he describes (1978: 119). His own past is a stranger as much to him as it is to others.[9]

Paris's overt presence in Perec's book also goes beyond the strict confines of its own index. The term 'Paris' sends the reader to only six of the book's 480 memories. Other terms in the index stand for the city, including 'Restaurants' and, that most famous of Parisian metonyms, the 'Métro'. Others escape any classification as Paris. We might think of memory 225, which is of 'Boris Vian', who died in 1959 in a cinema in Paris while attending the premier of a film adapted from one of his own novels (Perec 1978: 61). Among his many claims to fame, and beyond the fact of his own death in a cinema in the city, Vian was a Parisian icon. There are also a number of memories that test the city's own limits. These are the ones pertaining to the outer areas of metropolitan Paris, especially the edge of the 16th*arrondissement*, where the city meets the Bois de Boulogne. Notably, this urban threshold (the inner city, or Paris *intra muros*, is ringed by a freeway known as the *boulevard périphérique*, which traces the contours of the old city walls) is used reflexively, to stage the liminal edge of *Je me souviens* as text: the very first memory (Perec 1978: 13) takes the reader to la porte Saint-Cloud, one of the gates between city and suburban *banlieue* (again, in the 16th). Thus, to open *Je me souviens* is to enter Paris.

An interesting anecdote about *Je me souviens* is included by Brian Glavey in an article entitled 'Friending Joe Brainard'. The debt owed by Perec to Brainard's *I Remember*, which Andrews (2020) notes is of 'capital importance', is expressly acknowledged at the front of *Je me souviens*: 'Le titre, la forme et, dans une certaine mesure, l'esprit de ces textes s'inspirent des *I remember* de Joe Brainard [The title, form and, to a certain extent, the spirit of these texts draw their inspiration from Joe Brainard's *I Remember*]' (Perec 1978: 11).[10] According to Glavey, this debt, and this remembrance of Brainard, gets swept into the past after the publication of Perec's book. Noting a reference to a certain 'Joe Barnard' in an English-language interview with Perec in 1979, Glavey writes: 'This error in Perec's interview suggests that the cover of Brainard's book, which reads "I Remember Joe Brainard", makes an elegiac promise that may or may not be fulfilled' (2018: 325–26).[11] Along with the memories that Perec (re)constructs, Brainard's influence is both remembered and forgotten, his work both remembered and dismembered, or at least repurposed. Glavey argues that Perec's work appears designed for a collective writing project that extends beyond the author's personal history; indeed, the personal aspect of these memories seems specifically designed to be rendered public. Perec's Parisianization of Brainard's personal memory project turns it into an intertext and moves it into a backward-looking, forward-moving chain, which demands a communal textual future and strongly recalls Baudelaire's own repurposing of ancient memory as a metaphor for Parisian poetics. In this way, Perec's *Je me souviens* is not only Parisian because it recalls, and reworks, memories of Paris past but also because of its reflexive positioning of itself between Brainard's personal memories gone (the role given to Andromache by Baudelaire) and those of readers still to come (the famous 'others' that end 'Le Cygne'). Whether Brainard, like the objects of his memories, is remembered or forgotten, he is here, in Perec's text, the object of a Baudelairean 'I think of you'.

For Nadja Monnet, urban space, including, one might assume, of the kind created in *Je me souviens*, is space for doubt:

'Space is a doubt', Perec wrote. Space does not exist *per se*. It is constantly constructed, by practices and plans of action (from walking to urbanization projects), or by discourse and figurative or symbolic representations (the imaginary). It is conceived, interpreted and imagined at the same time as it is inhabited, lived or endured.

(2009: 4–5)[12]

We might add 'remembered' to Monnet's list of descriptors, as the kind of writerly remembering that we are proposing here is full of such doubt. As we have seen, it is a space of destruction and construction; it looks forwards (towards future formations) and backwards (to myth, including myths of creation); and it is both personal (as in Brainard's memories) and communal (in the form of communities of creative writing). It also instils, and stems from, doubt about the very identity of the specific urban space itself that is its object: remembering Paris means creating Paris as well as investigating its ways of being other than itself.[13]

Jacques Prévert's 'Barbara', one of the most famous poems of his collection *Paroles*, opens with a doubt that echoes Glavey's discussion of remembering Joe Brainard. The poem's first line addresses the Barbara of the title, appealing to her to remember: 'Rappelle-toi Barbara [Remember Barbara]' (Prévert 1949: 206 [1970: 101]). That Barbara is the direct addressee of the imperative is always assumed, as the various recordings of the poem make clear. And yet, there is no comma between 'rappelle-toi' and 'Barbara', which one might expect were Barbara in vocative case.[14] It is possible, however unlikely (given the absence of punctuation in many of the poems of *Paroles*), that an anonymous addressee is being asked to remember Barbara, just as, for Glavey, the cover of Brainard's book *I Remember* appears to declare 'I remember Joe Brainard'. Lawrence Ferlinghetti, who translated *Paroles* into English, notes that, given the fact that the poems were written around the period of the Second World War, *paroles* means 'both "words" and "passwords"' (1970: 9). It also has a linguistic sense that privileges acts of speech, in this case addressed to the unknown Barbara, over the strict conventions of written language and, especially, literary forms. As Ferlinghetti remarks, 'Prévert remains a great "see-er" if not a great seer. He writes as one talks while walking' (1970: 11). Whether this ostensible privileging of presentation over representation means that what is seen excludes what is perceived or whether it simply overshadows it, however, is unclear.

There is a certain sleight of hand in Prévert's will to simplicity, as suggested by allusions *inter alios* to Baudelaire. The following lines are a good example, referencing as they do the famous, and more complex, chiasmus of Baudelaire's 'À une passante':

> Toi que je ne connaissais pas
> Toi qui ne me connaissais pas
> [You whom I didn't know
> You who didn't know me]
>
> (Prévert 1949: 206 [1970: 101])

> Car j'ignore où tu fuis, tu ne sais où je vais
> Ô toi que j'eusse aimée, ô toi qui le savais!
> [Neither one knowing where the other goes
> O you I might have loved, as well you know!]
>
> (Baudelaire 1998: 188 [189])[15]

For Chambers, these lines from 'À une passante' point to the 'severe limits placed on human knowledge' and to both dis- and re-orientation as the speaker's attention turns from the street before him to 'another dimension of things altogether' (2015: 107). Our contention here is that the doubt as to Barbara's identity (Prévert's speaker knows only her name and that she was, at least at the point in time being remembered, loved by an unknown third party) extends equally to muddy the apparent specificity of the speaker's location. Brest is the city remembered, both the Brest of that day in the past, and the Brest of today, after the rain of a lovers' meeting has been replaced by a rain of iron and steel and blood; of this city, however, nothing remains. As the final line makes clear, Brest is a place 'Dont il ne reste rien [Of which there's nothing left]' (Prévert 1949: 207 [1970: 103]). To this extent therefore, Brest is absent to the poem as much as it is (its) present as place of remembrance and remembered place. The Baudelairean intertext suggests that this can be read as a Parisian memory, in this case an act of remembrance experienced *in* Paris and *of* another city whose destruction as a result of war itself echoes the destruction of Haussmann's *chantiers*. The location of the chiasmus – where Barbara's and the speaker's paths cross – is given as rue de Siam. Rue de Siam is one of Brest's major streets (today it is home to a light rail corridor); it is also the name of a street in Paris's 16th *arrondissement*. What we have here is the crossing of two streets, of two women passing by and of two poems. This intersection, which is as polysemous as it is anonymous (Barbara's name is the only known), dis-/re-locates what we are dubbing here a Parisian poetics of remembrance and in so doing attests to the capacity for Baudelaire's own lines of flight, his lovers and their beloved passers-by, to travel onwards in both time and space.

Ferlinghetti explains that some of the longer poems of *Paroles* were cut from his final selection because, in some cases, their word play made them untranslatable and, in others, because they contained 'outdated topical allusions impossible to explain' (1970: 11). This seems a pity, as memory work is the stuff of poetry. 'Barbara' makes this clear. It is, via the palimpsests of street names whose referents are now ghosts of their former selves, what makes the city readable as text. It is also the very definition of a speech act such as the calling out of the name Barbara by an unknown man to a woman passing by, which fixes for an instant a known event in a street otherwise made unintelligible by incessant rain. (In Baudelaire's moment of passing by, the street screams out a deluge of urban noise with much the same, deafening effect on the speaker.) This prosaic event is made poetic, however, not by the inherent amorousness of the encounter, but instead by the belatedness of the remembrance (the moment of speech is distanced not only in time but also in space, much as the artist's garret, where Beauty is made, is removed from the encounter with the model who is but beautiful). If Prévert's *Paroles* can afford, in Ferlinghetti's view, to shed a few poems whose focus is on places or events now long lost from view, Perec's *Je me souviens* appears to have been specifically designed to put readers in touch with their belatedness. It is as though, for Perec especially, to remember is to fix up, to re-fix more than it is to fix at a point in time. Certainly, for both Perec and Prévert, it is also to transform the urban mundane into poetry and, importantly, to prime it for onward translation.

Remembering in Paris and Paris as remembering

From the outset, it should be made clear that saying anything original or new about Paris or to offer a view of it that is in any way comprehensive would be a challenge to any specialist in the field. This statement immediately raises the question of what field we are talking about when we choose to discuss Paris, for any number of academic disciplines and modes of analysis might logically have it in their sights. Paris has become an archetype in so many ways and, indeed, the capital of so many fields of inquiry, eras and areas, including, to name but a few, Modernity (Harvey 2003), the Nineteenth Century (Benjamin 1999) and even the World (Higonnet 2002). More recently, an excellent volume describes it as something approaching the capital of alienation and expatriation (Orlando and Pears 2019). Academics have kept on revisiting Paris. This was a challenging thought to us, but there was also some encouragement to be drawn from it.

This particular book was born of the ways in which a group of university lecturers sought to answer the question of how best to offer a course on Paris to a cohort of undergraduate students in Australia. The staff and students were from different disciplinary areas at the university in question, the University of Newcastle. So, the course was designed to be interdisciplinary. The teaching of the course had to

INTRODUCTION: REMEMBERING IN PARIS AND PARIS AS REMEMBERING

be insightful in order to catch the interest of the students; it had to be didactic in order for them to take some key messages away and, linked to this second aim, it had to have some broader coherence so that it would not appear to be (what in a way it was, which is to say) a loose assemblage of modules on the broad area of Paris. The idea of a book that might emerge from the course flowed naturally from the latter's design, as the possibility of a textbook seemed a good way of getting the course to cohere. But, this also intensified our initial difficulties because a book on Paris would need to do rather more than present a number of chapters in a didactic way. It struck us, the course coordinators and now editors, that meeting this challenge head-on, which meant embracing interdisciplinarity, might be the best way of creating a book with broader appeal. A good example is David Musgrave's chapter. David is an Australian poet, novelist and publisher as well as a literary scholar. In Chapter 9 below, he traces the connections between the French and Australian traditions of Symbolist poetry. While Musgrave's French focus is Mallarmé rather than Baudelaire, importantly his interdisciplinary approach leads him to discover Paris in Australia, and thus 'French studies' in 'English studies' (in various forms of poetic remembrance, including translation, parody and pastiche).

One of the most influential comments for us was one made by Clive Scott in his essay in *The Cambridge Companion to Baudelaire*. In his discussion of translation in that volume, Scott claims to sense, albeit inchoately, Baudelaire's influence in the most unanticipated places. In Theodore Wratislaw's poem 'At the Empire', for example, Scott sees what appears to him to be 'a "translation" of line 88 of "Le Voyage"'; and yet, with no proof for this intuition, he wonders whether it is possible to talk in non-committal terms of 'allusions or citations'. 'If the truth be told,' he writes, 'I do not know exactly what the linguo-literary status of these lines is' (2006: 196). What interests us here is the way in which Scott's expertise in the fields of translation and poetry, as well as 'French studies' more broadly, led him to a problem that was all the more intriguing because he could not even circumscribe it in academic terms. This is, of course, another conundrum, a classic academic one in this case: the more one learns, the more one realizes what one does not know. For the purposes of the present volume, Scott returns to the question of translating Baudelaire. The approach that he adopts here casts translation as a form of remembering, or revisiting, Baudelaire's verse poetry with a particular view to gauging how that form may be considered to reflect the Haussmannization of Paris. It is 'the aptitude of translation', he writes, 'to re-set, to give new directions to, the conflicting cognitive impulses released by a source text, and here, specifically, by Baudelaire's urban poems'. While Scott's ambitions are clearly more properly textual than intertextual, translation's unmuting of the text can be seen to recall, in the sense of calling for them to be heard more clearly, aspects of the source text that can all too easily go unheard: 'It is translation's task to give voice to what is mute or muted in the

15

source text, to draw out undeveloped expressive impulses'.[16] Importantly, where intertextual approaches such as that offered by Rolls in this volume (in Chapter 7 below) trace the origins of the muted voice inside the host, or source, text's louder ones to another text, translation hears and renders audible, multiple origins in the one source. This is a particularly interesting form of autodifferentiation, one that is highly compatible with Baudelaire's ever-unsettled Paris.

With this in mind, we were struck by the possibility of deploying our respective fields of study (and our 'we' is collective and refers to all the contributors to this volume, who are associated with the following disciplines: Classics, Creative Writing, English, Film studies, French and Philosophy) in ways that might be logical (a film about Paris for a philosopher or film specialist) but that might equally be unexpected (a classicist on Paris, a specialist of twentieth-century French novels on nineteenth-century poetry, a specialist of Australian poetry on French symbolism, and so on). The more we thought about this, the more the idea of moving beyond our respective comfort zones struck us as Parisian, or at least urban. Ross Chambers notes in his study of what he dubs 'loiterature' that the experience of returning to Australia after many years of living in the United States afforded him an experience that he already knew intellectually as a scholar of Baudelaire: when walking in the streets of Brisbane or Sydney, he writes, he felt 'haunted' because the city was simultaneously unfamiliar in the way that it now presented itself to him and familiar insofar as he remembered the places that used to be where his feet now took him (Chambers 1999: 217). This uncanny doubling of presentation and representation is itself familiar to those of us, like Chambers and Scott, who know Baudelaire well. It is also something familiar to us all: as human beings, we all read the world around us via the sensations of the objects and places to which we are present, which we filter through understandings based on prior experiences, which we continuously recall and present to ourselves again, or *re*present. For those of us involved in the lectures and tutorials that were the first avatars of this book, much of our teaching revolved around explaining these concepts to our students, and using Baudelaire appeared to us an ideal way of doing this. This aspect has come directly into this book in the form of chapters on Baudelaire, where we have endeavoured to discuss these concepts in ways that will present the material differently (via different comfort zones) and in a way that is of interest even to fellow scholars with a good (and likely better) knowledge of Baudelaire. It has also come through indirectly, and this brings us back to Scott's point, and also to Chambers. When we thought about Chambers's experiences of walking in Australian cities, we wondered whether he was reading those streets as a Baudelairean scholar, and thus (also) with ideas of Paris in mind (which suggests a double haunting, where contemporary Brisbane recalls not only Brisbane past but also Paris). The question that emerges from this is whether to discuss walking in the city is necessarily Parisian (the term that comes to mind is *la* *flânerie* rather than, say, 'strolling') because we associate it so readily with Baudelaire, or whether Baudelaire's experiences of walking through Paris were allegorical at the outset – of the human condition, of modernity, of the passage of time, and so on. (One of the authors in this volume who is arguably the least 'out of her comfort zone' in this respect is Felicity Chaplin, who is known for her work on the figure of *la Parisienne* in cinema [see Chaplin 2017]. In Chapter 4 below, she focuses specifically on the Baudelairean influences on the Paris films of Agnès Varda, looking especially at the figure of *le flâneur*.) When Baudelaire invites us to travel and breaks into English in his dislocations ('any where out of the world'), does Paris stand for the whole world, or does everywhere in the world have the potential to represent Paris? Mapped onto academic inquiry, this is the nub of Scott's question: how does Baudelaire turn up where he is not expected? How has this traveller, whose travels always brought him back to Paris, travelled into other writers' work, overseas, into the future? The book that we initially had in mind became something along the lines of 'what to do with Baudelaire?'. In this light, our aim is to make Paris readable for non-specialist readers and to enable them to use Paris as a lens for reading texts (be they poems or novels, films, cultural products or urban spaces), not all of which are necessarily self-evidently 'Parisian'.

This at least seemed to get around the issue of trying (in vain) to give exhaustive coverage (especially since Paris had now grown beyond its own geographical, historical and literary borders). Baudelaire's poetry seemed to us crucial, especially the prose poems, which came to pose explicitly a number of the questions that we were asking ourselves. As Cheryl Krueger notes in a book dedicated entirely to teaching these very poems, students and scholars alike have continued to congregate around and over these works because they 'challenge conventional boundaries' and, as such, maintain today an 'historical and cultural resonance' (2017: xiii and xiv). In other words, Baudelaire's prose poems remain as arresting today as their subject matter, so many seemingly incongruous events, must have been at the time of their initial publication. As Krueger notes further, the reading, teaching and studying of the prose poems are exemplary of interdisciplinarity, extending beyond the study of nineteenth-century French poetry and cutting across 'French language courses, translation studies, English and comparative literature' (2017: xiv).

While Paris seemed too broad a concept to cover, our concern was that Baudelaire might equally be too narrow a focus for our purposes. Our theme emerged from Chambers's and Scott's respective thoughts on walking in the city and encountering Baudelaire in translation. These forms of remembering simultaneously rein in what we understand by Paris, that is, a poetics of autodifferentiation, and extend that city across the globe; and at the same time, they make us all into Baudelairean *flâneurs*, causing everything that we read to function as a memory of Paris. In the final chapter of the book, all of the themes mentioned in this introduction come to a head with Daniel Finch-Race and Valentina Gosetti's exploration of the complex interconnections between poetic form and remembrance. In a 'loiterly move of decentralizing resistance', Finch-Race and Gosetti embrace the move to #FeminizeYourCanon beyond a traditional view of nineteenth-century literature governed by men.[17] Whereas elsewhere in this volume contributors have remembered Paris via artistic modes and historical periods beyond poetry and the nineteenth century, this final chapter focuses on Paris as it is poeticized by Louise Colet and Anaïs Ségalas, notably through close formal analysis of the alexandrine and its capacity to cause the reader to remember. Finch-Race and Gosetti argue that Colet and Ségalas embed the physical geography of mutating Paris in their verse in ways that re-contextualize poetry by their male contemporaries, such as Baudelaire. On this basis, we can take the opportunity to reread the telescopic chain of metaphors at work in 'Le Cygne' as an alternative pantheon, in which so many 'great men' are replaced – in what would become the very heart of the male-dominated nineteenth-century canon – by Andromache, a black woman and a swan.

Insofar as it has allowed us to refocus our viewing lens and to see anew, remembering Paris has proven a source of pleasure for us, in the most blissful sense of the term. We hope that readers will find something in these pages that strikes a similar chord, that evokes a memory and that inspires future thoughts.

NOTES

1. Further on Corrozet, see Johnson, Chapter 2.
2. See Johnson, Chapter 3.
3. Attempting to do justice to Ross Chambers is almost as hard as doing justice to Baudelaire, hence the length of this quote. For a volume in honour of Chambers's critical work, including of Baudelaire, see Gosetti and Rolls (2020).
4. See Rolls, Chapter 1.
5. See Rolls, Chapter 7. For a reading of Edgar Wright's 2007 film *Hot Fuzz*, with its numerous references to swans, through the lens of Baudelaire's 'Le Cygne', see Rolls (2020).
6. More than similes, the metaphors used in 'Le Cygne' are of the kind that typically require the absence of the object to which they refer (in this case, Paris). In this way, Paris adopts the position as absent in relation to the metaphor that stands in its place, while at the same time remaining overtly present in the text.
7. The references here are to reflections sent to the authors by Oulipo scholar Chris Andrews. We wish to thank Chris here for his generosity in sharing his thoughts on this (only apparently simple) text.
8. These include Harry Mathews, Jacques Jouet, Jacques Bens, Hervé Le Tellier, Anne Garréta, Valérie Beaudouin and Eduardo Berti as well as writers not associated with Oulipo, like Nicolas Pagès, Christian de Montrichard, Christophe Quillen, Lydia Flem, Mathieu Lindon and Martin Kohan (Andrews 2020).

9. It is difficult not to be reminded here of Julia Kristeva's study of self-alterity, *Étrangers à nous-mêmes* (1988), which has been translated into English by Leon S. Roudiez as *Strangers to Ourselves*.

10. The translation here is ours.

11. While this is clearly important, the force of Glavey's point is weakened slightly by the presence of a forward slash on the front cover of the book (the copy that we inspected, at least), which gives 'I Remember / Joe Brainard'.

12. This, and all other secondary material originally written in French, is translated by us.

13. In reference to Perec's *W ou le souvenir d'enfance* (*W or The Memory of Childhood*), the first line of which is a paradoxical admission that the author has no childhood memories, Eric Hendrycks notes how the past becomes mythical, illusory and, literally, fabulous; in fact, 'the entire text is contaminated by the lexical field of doubt' (2011: 119).

14. Evgeniya Kozhevnikova notes that the poem contains 'two main hooks', one of which is 'the repeating of an appeal to the protagonist "Rappelle-toi, Barbara" (Remember, Barbara)' (2018: 9). Given that Kozhevnikova's concern is with transforming the poem into a musical composition, it is logical that she should hear, and thence visualize, this comma that is absent from the original text.

15. There is a double movement in this reference to Baudelaire that is in itself Baudelairean: while Prévert appears to debase Baudelaire's chiasmus, making it more prosaic (which is one aspect of the poetic project that is *Paroles*, much as it would be, in the realm of the contemporary novel, for Raymond Queneau, a Parisian author and contemporary of Prévert), by incorporating it in 'Barbara', he makes a significant, and unmissable, gesture towards poetry and thus elevates the mundane encounter that is his poem's subject.

16. These quotations are taken with his permission from Scott's abstract for his chapter in the present volume (sent by email to the authors on 10 October 2020).

17. This description of Finch-Race and Gosetti's loiterliness is taken, with their permission, from an email that they sent to the editors on 15 December 2020.

REFERENCES

Andrews, Chris (2020), email to authors, 9 September.

Barney, Natalie Clifford ([1960] 1992), *Souvenirs indiscrets, in A Perilous Advantage: The Best of Natalie Clifford Barney* (ed. and trans. A. Livia), Vermont: New Victoria Publishers, pp. 3–60.

Barthes, Roland (1974), *S/Z* (trans. R. Miller), New York: Hill and Wang.

Baudelaire, Charles (1998), *The Flowers of Evil* (trans. J. McGowan), Oxford World's Classics, Oxford: Oxford University Press.

Benjamin, Walter (1999), *The Arcades Project* (trans. H. Eiland and K. McLaughlin), Cambridge, MA and London: The Belknap Press of Harvard University Press.

Chambers, Ross (2015), *An Atmospherics of the City: Baudelaire and the Poetics of Noise*, New York: Fordham University Press.

Chaplin, Felicity (2017), *La Parisienne in Cinema: Between Art and Life*, Manchester: Manchester University Press.

De Pourcq, Maarten (2012), 'Classical reception studies: Reconceptualizing the study of the classical tradition', *The International Journal of the Humanities*, 9:4, pp. 219–25.

Felman, Shoshana (1977), 'Turning the screw of interpretation', *Yale French Studies*, 55–56, pp. 94–207.

Glavey, Brian (2018), 'Friending Joe Brainard', *Criticism*, 60:3, pp. 315–40.

Gosetti, Valentina and Rolls, Alistair (eds) (2020), *Still Loitering: Australian Essays in Honour of Ross Chambers*, Oxford: Peter Lang.

Hardwick, Lorna (2003), *Reception Studies*, Oxford: Oxford University Press.

Harvey, David (2003), *Paris, Capital of Modernity*, New York and London: Routledge.

Hendrycks, Eric (2011), 'Perec ou la mémoire trouée', *Meridian Critic*, 17:1, pp. 117–26.

Higonnet, Patrice (2002), *Paris: Capital of the World* (trans. A. Goldhammer), Cambridge, MA: The Belknap Press of Harvard University Press.

Hodges, Elizabeth (2008), 'Representing place in Corrozet's *Antiquitez De Paris*', *French Studies*, 62:2, pp. 135–49.

Kozhevnikova, Evgeniya (2018), 'Improvisation as a way of creating composition: setting the poem 'Barbara' by Jacques Prévert into Music', https://www.researchgate.net/publication/331396832ImprovisationasaWayofCreatingCompositionSettingthePoemBarbarabyJacquesPrevertintoMusic. Accessed 9 November 2020.

Kristeva, Julia (1988), *Étrangers à nous-mêmes*, Paris: Fayard.

Krueger, Cheryl (ed.) (2017), *Approaches to Teaching Baudelaire's Prose Poems*, New York: Modern Language Association of America.

Lloyd, Rosemary (2008), *Charles Baudelaire*, London: Reaktion.

Miller, J. Hillis (1979), 'The critic as host', in H. Bloom, P. de Man, J. Derrida, G. H. Hartman and J. H. Miller, *Deconstruction and Criticism*, New York: Seabury (Continuum), pp. 217–53.

Monnet, Nadja (2009), 'Qu'implique flâner au féminin en ce début de vingt et unième siècle ? Réflexions d'une ethnographe à l'œuvre sur la place de Catalogne à Barcelone', *Wagadu: A Journal of Transnational Women's & Gender Studies*, 7, pp. 1–28.

Orlando, Valérie K.and Pears, Pamela A. (eds) (2019), *Paris and the Marginalized Author: Treachery, Alienation, Queerness, and Exile*, Lanham: Lexington Books.

Perec, Georges (1978), *Je me souviens*, Paris: Hachette.

Prévert, Jacques (1949 [1993]), *Paroles*, Paris: Gallimard.

Prévert, Jacques (1970), *Selections from 'Paroles'* (trans. L. Ferlinghetti), Harmondsworth, Middlesex and Ringwod, Victoria: Penguin.

Riffaterre, Michael (1978), *Semiotics of Poetry*, Bloomington, IN: Indiana University Press.

Rolls, Alistair (2020), 'Saving Paris from Nostalgia: Jumbling the urban and seeing swans everywhere', *Australian Journal of French Studies*, 57.1, pp. 66–77.

Scott, Clive (2006), 'Translating Baudelaire', in R. Lloyd (ed.), *The Cambridge Companion to Baudelaire*, Cambridge: Cambridge University Press, pp. 193–205.

1

Charles Baudelaire's *Paris Spleen*: Re-presenting Paris

Alistair Rolls

When Jean-Michel Gouvard (2015: 140) opens his article on Charles Baudelaire's *Le Spleen de Paris* and its relationship to Paris by stating that 'contrary to what the title of the collection might lead you to believe, all the "little prose poems" are not set in Paris', it is difficult to know whether he is being ironic or not. In the framework of the present volume, which has Paris firmly centre stage and, crucially, present even when it is ostensibly absent, this appears a surprisingly literal comment to make about Baudelaire's final work. Certainly, Gouvard immediately goes some way to softening his opening gambit. He refers to other readers, for whom the prose poems are by turns 'exotic in character' (set on far-flung desert islands or in fairy-tale fantasy lands) or positioned non-specifically but recognizably 'beyond the city walls', in the *faubourgs*, areas that have since been integrated into Paris *intra-muros* and whose present-day equivalents are the suburban spaces of *la banlieue*. And yet, other references throughout the prose poems are undeniably to Paris itself. Gouvard sums up his careful, even cautious, position as follows: '[Thus,] several texts in the collection are "Parisian" not insofar as their action takes place "in Paris", which is one meaning of the adjective, but by virtue of references that are made to, and the relationship that is thereby established with, Paris' (2015: 140). One is led to wonder what motivates such a granular exploration of Paris as toponym or of the appearance of its famous landmarks in this work. Why, indeed, do any of us strive in our own ways to prove that the collection can be defined as 'Parisian'?[1] One aspect of Gouvard's summation is of particular importance for our present purposes, and it is this suggestion that 'taking place in Paris' is only one, and perhaps not the most important, meaning of 'Parisian'. In this chapter, it will be argued that this adjective pertains to a particular type of poetics, a mode of being present to, and presenting, a precise urban locale while simultaneously representing it, overlaying it with myths, memories and other varieties of absence.

In the prose poems therefore, Baudelaire establishes a framework for reading both poetry and urban space that is recognizably modern (even if, as is so often the case, it is almost impossible to find clear and commonly accepted definitions of this and other such terms) and, further, one that is exemplary of a critical form of modernity. This critical stance, this mode of reading, I shall suggest, is metonymic of modernity just as Paris is so often considered to be. One might think of David Harvey's work in the field, which argues against what he considers the common misapprehension about the modern of modernity, which is to say, that it somehow 'constitutes a radical break with the past' (2003: 1); instead, critical modernity offers a lens for remembering the past, for repatriating it, continuously and reflexively, into the present. For Harvey, there is something particularly Parisian about this. Another reason for considering the prose poems to be Parisian is rather more prosaic: it has to do with the final editing of the collection. The prose poems were first gathered together and published in 1869, that is, after the poet's death in 1867. The full title, the title by which people have since come to know them, *Les Petits Poèmes en prose: Le Spleen de Paris* (literally, *The Little Prose Poems: Paris Spleen*[2]), was chosen as part of a collaborative process. This process appears to have taken into account various titles that Baudelaire himself had had in mind.

My argument here follows Michel Covin's interpretation of the title chosen for the collection. Irrespective of the complexities of the process, and that Baudelaire himself was not alive to oversee its final stages, Covin considers the title to reflect all the complexities of the poems' relationship to the city. For him, the prose poems quite simply *are* Paris, and *vice versa* (2000: 51). Covin's belief is predicated on the nature of what he considers the 'full title' (or the conflation of various titles that have been given to the prose poems), which specifically mentions Paris. Further, the structure of the title lends itself to a chiastic analysis that brings Paris into the text paratextually, with the result that the poems are always locatable and readable as Parisian even when they make no mention of the city.[3] Structurally, the two halves of the title, which are opposed by a central colon, reflect the individual prose poems, which generally comprise two halves (one of which may often appear more 'poetic', the other more 'prosaic') separated and joined by some kind of central pivot (often an adverb of concession, say, 'however'). In this way, the two sides of the title and the two halves of the prose poems echo or cross-reference each other. In the case of the title, the first part lays out the binary opposition of the prose poems (prose *versus* poetry) as a mission statement for this new poetics. The second part, or subtitle, on the other hand, if we follow the cross-currents of Covin's chiasmus, sees Paris opposed to Spleen, which seems to confer on the city an objective signification, such as the Capital of Poetry, or poetic Ideal, while spleen takes on the role of the visceral, grounded Other.

It is important to understand here that the prose poems are very much *not* examples of 'poetic prose' or 'prosaic poetry'; instead, they stand as a non-synthetic conjoining (under considerable poetic tension) of poetry and its textual opposite, prose. Prose poetry, in other words, is an oxymoron.[4] To see Paris as an overarching frame of signification against which urban experiences happen, or from whose heights they fall, makes sense. And yet, it does not explain why this representational force itself sometimes appears, as Gouvard has shown, *inside* the prose poems. To understand this, we need to consider the possibility that Paris's role in the subtitle is to embody the oxymoronic tension of poetry *versus* prose and thus to operate both as poetry and prose throughout the collection. Covin's chiastic analysis leads him in the same direction. My aim here is to extend the logics of this reading by considering spleen also to function as an auto-antonym, or Janus word, which means one thing and the exact opposite *at the same time* (we might think of the verb 'to cleave', which means both to split one thing into two *and* to join two things together as one). I shall therefore consider the splenetic to extend to the modern urban experience that is 'reading the prose poems', for this is an experience that indiscriminately juxtaposes the stuff of everyday life (the obviously prosaic, and thus the obviously splenetic) with the motifs typical of Romantic verse poetry (Goddesses, for example).

If spleen can be seen to overarch the things and the Ideals, the stuff of existence and the Essences, of the prose poems, then we must understand Paris's role in the collection as something more than simple signifier or locale. Indeed, such an either/or understanding would lead to the kind of 'prosaic poetry' or 'poetic prose' reading of the texts noted above. Instead, Paris sits alongside spleen, matching it, locating it; it too is an oxymoron, both itself (Paris *ville lumière*, Capital of the Nineteenth Century, Capital of Modernity and all the terms by which it is recognized) and its own Other (Paris the urban experience, the places and events that we encounter in the real world of the texts). It is simultaneously the sign beneath which the prose poems sit and the setting in which they take place. This type of auto-differentiation, of failing to coincide with oneself, and its attendant auto-antonym are crucial to Baudelairean modernity. Such a Parisian space is also, for Barbara Johnson (2000), that of the 'critical difference' when it comes to reading text (or Text, to give it the capital that came when the poststructuralists wanted to differentiate the meanings created – liberated and re-fixed – by the reader from the words fixed on the page). Text's difference from itself, for Johnson, Roland Barthes and other poststructuralist and deconstructionist readers, is more important than the way in which a given text differs from other examples of text. This is equally true of Paris, which for Baudelaire in the period from the mid-1850s to the mid-1860s was being radically transformed by Baron Haussmann's urbanization project. As such, Paris was quickly becoming unrecognizable (it was not what Baudelaire remembered; it could not be Paris) while clearly still being the same place (it must be Paris, for what else could it be?). Thus, when Covin writes that Paris is a prose poem and that the prose poems are Paris, he means that both are auto-antonymic.

What is insufficiently addressed in Gouvard's commentary is precisely this balancing act. For the prose poems operate a poetics of double motion. It is not sufficient therefore to seek to privilege the poetic in them at the expense of their prosaic elements, since such a privileging of the one term over the other, which appears based on a sort of reverence for Baudelaire the 'Poet', the author of the infamous verses of *Les Fleurs du mal* rather misses the point. Certainly, it fails to take into account Baudelaire's famous letter to Arsène Houssaye, which typically stands as a preface to the prose poems:

> Mon cher ami, je vous envoie un petit ouvrage dont on ne pourrait pas dire, sans injustice, qu'il n'a ni queue ni tête, puisque tout, au contraire, y est à la fois tête et queue, alternativement et réciproquement
> [My dear friend, I send you a little work of which no one can say, without doing it an injustice, that it has neither head nor tail, since, on the contrary, everything in it is both head and tail, alternately and reciprocally.]
>
> (Baudelaire 1973: 21 [1970: ix])

It is easy to see in this statement a clue to reading and making sense of the prose poems: the head can be placed in opposition to the tail, as a transparent meaning to a textual body, a cerebral understanding to a physical experience. While there may be different degrees of each at various points throughout the work, the one depends on the other. And crucially, it will not be enough to seek to understand the events; it will remain equally as important to experience the signifiers.

Furthermore, not only does the apparent need to excuse or compensate for the prose in the little prose poems in some way mask the fundamental paradox on which they are predicated, insofar as it appears designed to emphasize the head at the expense of an embarrassing tail,[5] but it also, and importantly here, causes their Parisianness to be viewed as incidental, as a mere location among other potential (and real) locations. To understand that Paris equals the prose poems, and *vice versa*, on the other hand, is to realize that everything about them is Parisian, even when there are no references to the city and the prose poem is set on a far-flung desert island. (This is, of course, part of the challenge of the present volume, for it could well be argued that, given that Paris is not mentioned explicitly and that other great cities – London, to name but one – underwent considerable change in the course of the nineteenth century, the events of the prose poems might well *not* be set in Paris. The short answer to this argument lies in Baudelaire's facticity; the longer one – what it is about Paris that causes remembrance and what it is about various types of remembrance that speaks to Parisianness – will hopefully emerge over the course of this book.) If a prose poem about a desert island is as Parisian as one featuring, for example, the Paris Opera House, it is precisely because Paris fails to coincide with itself to the same degree that it can never escape that same self-coincidence. It is arguably for this very reason that the invitation to travel 'Anywhere out of the world', which is made to the reader in English in the original (1973: 146, 1970: 99), is necessarily an invitation that extends from, returns to and, allegorically, metonymically, never really leaves Paris.[6] The point of having Paris as not only an ever-present, but also equally ever-absent, subtitle is that the prose poems are always already Parisian, irrespective of their content.[7]

That this metonymic Parisianness, this other Paris as absence-presence and thus as metonym, should get somewhat obscured, while not being entirely erased, by Gouvard stems from his quite legitimate interest in representation.[8] Paris is indeed represented throughout the prose poems, although surprisingly infrequently (hence Gouvard's interest); it is also, by virtue of the metonym under which the texts are couched, continuously *presented*. This could, one might argue, be any urban environment (when it is not a desert island instead) because the reader cannot tell; the reader cannot tell in which city the events of any given prose poem are occurring because it is too close, too immediate. In the same way, it would be difficult for us to tell in which city we happened to be if we were teleported into its midst and had no significant landmark to use to get one's bearings, no panoramic viewing point from which to take in the city-as-a-whole. Landmarks are significant, of course, precisely because they signify; in other words, they *represent* the city. Panoramic views afford objectivity, allowing the city to be seen in its entirety, and thus to be made meaningful. A city seen from the above looks like a map; it becomes legible and evokes representations of a city that we know, that we remember, that has significance.[9] A city to which we are present may have these aspects, but it is more likely to offer up any number of those unremarkable events that constitute everyday life.[10] Buying a baguette may spark visions of Paris, whereas buying washing-up liquid may not; yet, both of these actions happen in Paris on a daily basis.

Of particular importance to my reading of the prose poems is the Haussmannization that made the Paris of the mid-nineteenth century a site of simultaneous construction and destruction. The landmarks that made Paris 'Paris' for Baudelaire were being lost (and his city consigned to memory), and new landmarks (and especially its broad new boulevards that make Paris 'Paris' for us in the twenty-first century) were taking their place. In other words, the city to which Baudelaire was present both was and was not what he could represent as such. Clearly, it is tempting to read this in a negative light, which is to say, to follow Baudelaire's trajectory downwards, which is often referred to as the Satanic aspect of his work. After all, the reflexivity of any number of the flowers of evil (we might think readily of 'L'Albatros [The Albatross]') and prose poems (Gouvard, for example, notes 'Le *Confiteor* de l'artiste [Artist's Confiteor]', 'À une heure du matin [One O'Clock in the Morning]' and 'La Chambre double [The Double Room]' [2015: 148]) makes clear the resentment that the poet felt towards an art form that had not brought him the recognition that he considered he deserved. In this light, it is difficult not to be struck by the way in which, in the prose poems, poetry is smashed onto the city streets and debased in their mire and human abjection; indeed, for Gouvard, and also for Ross Chambers, who sees in rhyme a 'salvific' (2015: 45), albeit a hard one to achieve, representation, and the valuing of the head above the tail, is the chance to catch a glimpse of Paris beneath grime of the streets (of Paris). While this aspect of the prose poems must not be forgotten, it seems equally important that attempts to salvage Baudelaire (to give him his revenge, to play on the title of Bob Van Laerhoven's novel of 2007) do not end up protesting too much and disavowing the place occupied by prose, the tail and, ultimately, the beauty of 'things' in the prose poems, in which they have equal billing from the moment of the work's inception and which is attested not only in the letter-*cum*-preface or posthumous title but also in the texts themselves.

It is for this reason that the prose poems have two halves, one of which often looks poetic, while the other is predominantly prosaic. 'La Chambre double [The Double Room]' is a good example: its spirituality and voluptuousness, which speak of odalisques and Romantic poetry, give way brutally to the horrors of a 'taudis [filthy hole]' (Baudelaire 1973: 30 [1970: 6]) once a knock on the door is sounded. The knock on the door functions as the pivot between the two aspects of the double room, but it is not just a 'however', for it does not speak simply of a break in logic; it is also an 'on the other hand' because these are two sides of the same coin, of the one room. By presenting this doubleness, it also represents it, making it a poem about doubleness. Even this is easy to forget, since doubleness is itself all too easily read as a metaphor, for example, for an addiction to opium. The problem with such a metaphorical reading is of course that it singles out one referent for overvaluation – 'la fiole de laudanum [the vial of opium]' (1973: 30 [1970: 6]) – rather than seeing in it, as doubtless would Johnson (1987), a *figure of* overvaluation, and thus just one out of many possible metaphors. To see double-ness as both a sign and an experience of Paris is, instead, to read it as a metonym, which cannot be so easily shaken off as the metaphor, which requires distance from its referent. Metonymy, as Linda Williams (2008) has famously demonstrated, is predicated on contiguity: it represents something that is neither absent, nor pres-ent, but always, and always *partially*, both.

Once one has realized that one side of a prose poem, or one aspect of a room, is necessarily contiguous to another side, one begins to see the prosaic elements in the (predominantly) poetic half, and *vice versa*: the first words of 'La Chambre double' are, after all, 'Une chambre qui ressemble à une rêverie [A room that is like a dream]', which express not a state of poetry but an aspiration on the part of a mundane object (a room) to poetry (the ethereal state of the dream), and the room is 'crépusculaire [crepuscular]', its colours 'bleuâtre et [...] rosâtre [bluish shot with rose]' (1973: 28 [1970: 5]). To be double is to be neither one thing nor the other, but continuously in movement between the two. This is a poetics of not only movement, rather than of space therefore, but also countermovement: when the principal movement is from the Heavens streetwards, there will always be tiny countermovements (in the form, say, of little flowers pointing from the mud to the skies). This plays out in the title, too. Gouvard spells *Le spleen de Paris* with a lower-case 's' on spleen; Covin for his part capitalizes it in *Spleen parisien*. With his preference, Gouvard flouts the usual conventions of French title case.[11] Typically, his title would be *Le Spleen de Paris* with a capital letter on the noun following an initial definite article. His spleen, in other words, is being demonstrably, and paradoxically, pulled streetwards at the beginning of a study that otherwise privileges (examples and the mechanics of) representation.

This constant cross-current of movement and countermovement may be couched in terms of urban noise, which is how Chambers understands Baudelaire's poetics.[12] Consider, for example, the definition that Chambers gives of 'Baudelairean allegory':

> [A] perception that the everyday real is capable at any moment of revealing an atmospheric stratum whose function – like that of the messenger from the beyond that is a daytime spectre, be it a statue, a writhing swan, a misshapen or dislocated human or other fetish-like figure – is to convey an intimation of lived time as a manifestation of supernaturalist evil.
>
> (2015: 97)

Allegory here is construed as a form of struggle against earth-bound constraints and a pathetic aspiration to poeticization; it is noisy because it is against not only the laws of physics but also poetic tradition. Far from salvific here, then, such supernaturalist intentionality speaks of pain. In the prose poems, as we have seen, Baudelaire also operates an inversion of allegory, historicizing and making actual Infinity itself. And while the beauty in this can come across as supercilious (in the case, for example, of Venus's non-communication with the motley fool), it is not without a hint of Beauty.[13] If nothing else, even as it strikes a paradox, foreshadowing the very hopelessness of salvation through allegory, it functions as a *value* (in the Sartrean sense of *une valeur*) driving us onwards (in vain, but at times in an illusion of meaningfulness) through our life in the modern metropolis.

Time, for Baudelaire, is what makes us human and what steals our poetry away from us; yet, the aspiration towards the infinite, towards Timelessness is nonetheless also present in our small moments of poetry making. Chambers, like Gouvard, tends to privilege the evil aspect of human history because he too is framing Baudelaire's poetics against the backdrop of nineteenth-century Paris and the chaos of the era. Chambers is also, however, and this time unlike Gouvard, focused primarily on the Satanic pull of the real at play in those of the verse poems of *Les Fleurs du mal*, such as 'Le Cygne [The Swan]' or 'À une passante [To a Woman Passing By]', which are almost identical thematically to the prose poems.[14]

My preference here is to go slightly against the grain and to reiterate the salvific aspect of the double movement of the prose poems. Their noise, I should argue, is not just the vocalization of Poetry's crash-landing on the streets of the real world; it is also the sound of potentiality, of aspiration, of the way, in short, that the prosaic elements of the prose poems mean that the latter are (also, nonetheless) poems. Indeed, the shift across the poems of one predominant movement towards another predominantly opposite one usually passes, as we have seen, through a central pivot. This pivot stands as a fleeting moment of clarity (a 'shock' to give it its usual Baudelairean, and often negative, term) in a relentless focalization: the prose poems work towards this mid-point by focusing in, but no sooner have they reached it than they resume their course, focusing out this time (Covin 2000: 106–08). The discussion above of infinity may remind us how difficult it is for us to conceive of endlessness; our attempts to imagine it may bring us near, but when we think we have it clear in our mind, it tends to fade from view. The prose poems embody this failure to grasp, but there is also something heroic in the endeavour, something that looks very much like what Jean-Paul Sartre would, in the twentieth century, term *qui perd gagne* (literally, he who loses wins, sometimes translated as 'loser wins'). In all the drudgery, pointlessness and entropic decline of human existence, the only heroism there is consists in our continuing to live. We live against the clock, against the odds, and in so doing, we create little moments of poetry (what Chambers describes as 'negentropy'), which require a certain objectivity, a certain frame of reference in order to emerge from the daily routine of which they are (also and necessarily) a part.[15]

Chambers devotes much of his study of what he dubs Baudelaire's poetics of noise to an understanding of disalienation, which he defines as a particular state of self-awareness, and especially the awareness of one's own lack of knowledge. He often maps this notion of reflexive ignorance onto the idea of readability:

> In offering *two* figurations of a world governed by time – as a place where (in verse) the noise of history allegorically bespeaks an evil transcending power, and as a place (in prose) where, ironically, the noise of daily process simply *exists*, in its own

limitless readability – he prepares for his readers an unstable and therefore uncertain and divided position of reading, in relation to the time-governed world of the city, that mirrors the unresolvable situation of knowing that one doesn't know – the experience of interpretability that cannot conclude – that I am calling disalienation.

(Chambers 2015: 60)

Interestingly, Chambers's limitless readability of the historically situated, urban experience is one side of the room; the other side of it is its ostensible opposite, which is to say, unreadability. This double-sidedness allows Chambers, doubtless in a conscious re-enactment of Baudelaire's own famous declaration of the right to self-contradiction, to write as follows:

In the prose poems in question [...] the effect of the act of ironic unreadability that produces disalienation is an effect of the act of reading itself, the textual irony placing the reader in a position of unbearable thirst strikingly comparable with the suffering of the swan [of the verse poem of the same name from *Les Fleurs du mal*], since it is a thirst for there to be, discoverable within the text, a site of authoritative and reliable meaning that proves to be cruelly lacking.

(2015: 128)

It is, of course, only an apparent paradox to see Baudelaire's Paris as both infinitely readable and fundamentally unreadable, and it is just such an apparent paradox that will lead, some 100 years later, to another great event in the history of reading – Roland Barthes's famous death of the author.

Unreadability here may be understood as the status of text when there is no overarching system within which it can be said to have one transparent meaning. Metaphors, for example, only signify if we can see beyond the text in which they operate. In the same way, urban events can only be seen to mean 'Paris' if we have a landmark with which to associate them or an elevated position from which to see them in their broader context.[16] In 'Le Fou et la Vénus [Venus and the Motley Fool]' (1973: 33–34 [1970: 10]) therefore, when the goddess Venus appears on the street, she is necessarily deprived of Meaning with a capital M by virtue of the impossibility of her being there (as an Essence fixed, like any existent, in time and space); she is, in other words, reduced to the same status (of unreadability) as any other object in the street. And yet, by the same token, the fact that all objects are equally objectively meaningless makes them all equally worthy of our attention. This, which we may think of as a poetics of neutrality, causes us to overvalue (to focus especially on) all kinds of things because we have to look at something. In so doing, we poeticize the prosaic and ascribe subjective meaning to the objectively meaningless. Hence, the infinite readability of the unreadable: while we encounter objects in the streets (of Paris), we are reading them just as in Barthes's scenario, the reader will replace the author as the arbiter of meaning. The death of Meaning (with the upper-case initial of, say, Poetry) does not destroy the possibility of making sense (of text, of our surroundings); on the contrary, it encourages and enables the generation of multiple meanings (with the lower-case initial of prose). As mentioned above, this is what Johnson means when she states that a text's critical difference is 'not its uniqueness, its special identity', but that instead it is its 'way of differing *from itself*' (2000: 175). To understand that *Oliver Twist* is not *David Copperfield* relies simply on comparing two sequences of words whose unique sets of meaning we can digest unthinkingly in an act of pleasurable but passive reading; to understand that *Oliver Twist* is not just a sequence of words, on the other hand, but a living text is to engage in an act of critical (active and blissful) reading. Similarly, to say that Paris is not Rome is a relatively uninteresting statement, since there are any number of indicators that make it so *objectively*. Once inside the streets, however, without an overarching system of representation, it is we who give Paris its meaning; we are responsible for reading the ways in which Paris is present to us and how it escapes coincidence with those things that we might have once been told that it means.

Herein lies the importance of Covin's capitalization of the Splenetic. To see spleen as purely visceral activity, or experience in the absence of Meaning, is to deny our ability to read critically. In addition, the splenetic contains within itself the poeticization of the experiential, including the way in which a miniscule sail shimmers on an horizon in 'Le *Confiteor* de l'Artiste', for example, or an old piece of furniture takes on the shape of an odalisque in 'La Chambre double' (1973: 25 [1970: 3] and 1973: 28 [1970: 5], respectively). As such, there is a part of pleasure in the otherwise predominantly painful Baudelairean experience of the modern city, with its loss of meanings past and headlong flight into meaninglessness. The pleasure of the text, too, I should argue is auto-antonymic in Barthes's poststructuralist schema. At face value, the pleasure (*le plaisir*) of reading is associated with the passive digestion of transparently meaningful text. Mapped onto the urban, this is the objective view of the city, which allows us to see the New Louvre or the Hôtel de Ville and know the space as Paris. Bliss, on the other hand, or *jouissance*, is associated with the loss that we experience as readers when we abandon ourselves to the text, creating new meanings for it and for ourselves alike. Loss, in this case, is akin to the urban experience of walking without direction, aimlessly, because we have no map to guide us, no defined course to give purpose to our actions. The pleasure-giving text Barthes calls the readerly (*le texte lisible*): it is easy to read because its meaning is clear. The pleasure that it gives leaves us, and it, unchanged. The blissful text he calls the writerly (*le texte scriptible*): it is read actively, created by us and thus made different from itself by our intervention, which at the same time requires that we invest ourselves and thus that we also change.[17] Just as the author dies that we may live as readers, we too must die a little (submit ourselves to *la petite mort*) in such an orgasmic scenario. These two textual experiences are inevitably interwoven, however, for one cannot make sense of a text that has no structure; it has to have some degree of meaning in order for us to reread it, to make it mean something else, something less immediately transparent. And, of course, each time we read a text we fix its meaning, for the time of that one reading, in the knowledge that we have actualized only one of an infinite number of possible lines of flight. To perform a reading is therefore to cause a text to be (historically, actually) readable while knowing it to be (infinitely, virtually) unreadable.[18]

Reading as an urban experience has a figure in Baudelaire's work, and in the prose poems, this figure walks alongside the reader, functioning as the poet-as-narrator, or poet in the text. I am referring here to the *flâneur*. Derived from *la flânerie*, which means strolling in French, the term *flâneur* conjures up images of idle, aimless wandering through the streets of Paris. Such an image, of course, can be readily equated with the urban development of Baron Haussmann, which was opening up the city and connecting its major iconic buildings with broad avenues and, at the same time, tearing down the slum dwellings of the working-class population, who in their turn were forced outwards. From the perspective of the oxymora (of prose poetry, of reading pleasure, of Paris) under discussion here, however, considerations of the *flâneur* as a voyeur whose engagement in the activities of the street is confined to observing are inadequate. In the prose poems, to walk in the streets is to be present: in the midst of his reminiscence, the *flâneur* participates. Arguably, strolling for the simple pleasure of looking on was already itself something of a memory by the mid-nineteenth century; and perversely, the introduction of streets that facilitated promenading played a role in its disappearance.

Walking in Paris's inner-city areas was not a new phenomenon in Baudelaire's day; in fact, the gentrification of the city centre, by which we mean here the use of its streets as a leisure activity by the idle middle classes, had already started by the end of the eighteenth century. It had been facilitated by a number of social and industrial advances, including in sewerage and the casting of iron that had allowed the construction of covered, glazed galleries. These galleries, which are known in French simply as *les passages*, were effectively the first shopping arcades. By the middle of the nineteenth century, some 150 *passages* existed in Paris.[19] As a result, people were able to walk further afield and, increasingly, in relative safety.[20] Their heyday, which was well and truly over by the first decades of the twentieth century, was in fact brought to an end by Haussmannization. For dandies like Baudelaire, the remembrance of the Paris of the *passages* (as famously studied by Walter Benjamin in his *Arcades Project* and used as a source of inspiration by the Surrealists[21]) was still too keen to be likened to a nostalgia for the past; indeed, he mourned the loss of Paris at the very moment that it was turning into the metropolis that we know today. To walk its streets was therefore for Baudelaire less a leisure activity than an occupation, less a trip down memory lane than a confrontation with the brutal effects of entropy.

As Covin suggests (2000: *passim*), the *flâneur* as lens of critical modernity was a hybrid of *le voyeur*, the objective onlooker who took in the activities of the world from a distance (from a café window, for example), and *le badaud* (or gawker), who walked unthinkingly with the crowd, jostled along by its activity. The resultant figure is not simply a mobile *voyeur* or a visually aware gawker; rather, like the prose poems themselves, it is a paradoxical coming together of these opposed activities. Insofar as he is active *and* passive, walking *and* observing, the *flâneur* embodies the prose poems (which, as we have seen, are patently not poetic prose or prosaic poetry), and *vice versa*, and thus modern Paris itself. The bringing together under tension of objectivity and subjectivity is crucial to an understanding of modernity and the transformation of urban space as a poetics.

Art had until relatively recently been synonymous with objective representation. If one had an encounter with a beautiful woman passing by (which is the subject of Baudelaire's verse poem 'À une passante', to give just one example), to elevate this muse to the status of Beauty would require two types of distance from the source of inspiration: first, belatedness as the artist took time to compose the verse or the painting; second, physical distance in the form of the studio or garret in which the artwork was produced. A beautiful woman is an existent, whereas Beauty, with its capital initial letter, is an essence. The former can only aspire to the latter, or, to put it another way, it is only by virtue of the latter that the former can have meaning. For how can someone be considered beautiful if an objective benchmark is not available?[22] One might also think usefully of Honoré Daumier's famous lithographic image of Nadar 'elevating photography to Art', which was published in *Le Boulevard* on 25 May 1863.[23] In that image, the famous photographer Nadar (Gaspard-Félix Tournachon, 1820–1910) is shown photographing Paris from an objective position, floating high above it in a hot air balloon. While the objectivity afforded by hot air balloon flight had existed since the experiments of the Montgolfier brothers in the late eighteenth century, photography was a relatively new procedure. In the lithograph, the idea of objectivity, and thus of artistry, is accentuated. The problem posed by photography as an art form of course was that it required neither physical distance nor belatedness; instead, one could represent *objectively* a subject to which one was physically present.

Something similar was also happening in the more traditional mode of the visual arts that was painting. Throughout the 1860s, a new style of painting was being developed by such now famous artists as Édouard Manet, Claude Monet and Pierre-Auguste Renoir. It came to prominence, in a way not unreminiscent of Baudelaire's own trajectory as a poet, by being systematically rejected by the establishment, in this case in the form of the *Salon de Paris*. Not until the mid-1870s, and thus in the years immediately following the publication of the prose poems, did Impressionism gain some traction with the viewing public. Furthermore, the art works themselves seemed to detractors and supporters alike slightly sketchy, or out of focus; so in this sense too, parallels could be drawn to the prose poems. In terms of reducing the distance between art and the presence of its subject, what is striking about the works of the Impressionists is that they were produced in the open air, and thus directly in front of the artistic subject, a technique that was made possible by the development of paints that could be transported in tubes. For their part, the prose poems give the impression of being experienced in real time: readers are present to events, experiencing them as if they too are in the street, in Paris – hence the importance of Venus being physically present as well as being represented as an abstract form, a symbol of Art, of Poetry (Baudelaire 1973: 33–34, 1970: 10).

Ultimately, however 'modern' and shocking it appeared in the 1860s, Baudelaire's poetics of modernity has an undeniably human dimension about it. (This is of course partly why it shocked: Art was not designed to present reality, but precisely to elevate the real to another, higher plane.) The cataclysmic shock of reality that accompanies the prose poems – the impossible fact of seeing Venus in the street – as well, as Chambers (2015) describes, as the 'Tableaux Parisiens' poems of *Les Fleurs du mal* is after all only a metaphor for the way in which, as adults, we understand the world around us. With the passing of time, we are unable to experience the world without ascribing meaning to it; that is to say, we represent to ourselves everything to which we are present. This double experience is typically considered to be amplified by the modern city. As Chambers (1999: 217) notes, when we walk through the city as an adult, we inhabit two urban spaces simultaneously: we see the streets in which we are walking, but we also understand these present streets by comparing them with the same streets as we remember them in the past. This experience Chambers calls a 'haunting'. While the shock for us may not always be as electrifying as it was for Baudelaire, for whom this disconnection is made genuinely traumatic by Haussmannization, it leads us to be nostalgic for a lost past, in comparison to which the present can only appear somewhat lacking as time (the ultimate Evil for Baudelaire) leads us ineluctably from the memories of our past into the unknown of the future. We might think of events that regularly fail to live up to our expectations, such as Christmas, which for Lauren Rosewarne (2017: 93) is a doubly nostalgic period, both as 'a season occurring annually throughout the life course' and as a festive period predicated on nostalgic songs, films and family recollections (as such, it is set up to fail as an event lived in the present but forever harking back to Christmases past, which of course never existed as we remember them). Christmas is often described as something for children because when children experience it they are present to it, and this for the simple reason that they have nothing against which to compare it. It is only as they become older, when they have memories of Christmases past with which to compare the event to which they are now present, that a disconnection occurs. They can now represent Christmas, which is to say that it now means something to them, and because their memories of Christmas past have taken on the veneer of a mythology, the present experience must suffer in the comparison. As adults, we can represent almost everything to which we are present, since, even if we have not lived the precise experience before, we can at least understand it by comparing it to other cognate events. For a child, there is only presentation;[24] for adults, however hard we try to 'be present', by which we mean not to think of the past or the future, the world is always experienced doubly.

This double experience, this haunting, is an absence-presence. More than anything else, this is the key to Baudelaire's poetics of modernity. The modern is not merely a movement away from the past, for it is experienced as a continuous recollection of it. And of course, the more we try to make sense of it, to understand the present by representing it, the greater the feeling of disconnection (from the origins of this meaning-making) we feel. We construct mythologies, which only accentuate the paradisiacal nature of that past away from which we are continuously moving. As I have suggested, to live our lives against this backdrop of meaninglessness is the condition of human heroism for existentialist thinkers like Sartre. For Baudelaire, it is truly shocking. As we read Baudelaire's prose poems, we must take into account the evil of time and of the simultaneous, and fundamental, disconnection and continuous reconnection of the present and the past, and at the same time, we should try to see the beauty in them. Although the adult worldview that the prose poems offer us must remain a metaphor, Paris is a metonym and as such cannot so easily be put aside. Despite the fact that Paris always fails to coincide entirely with the meanings that we ascribe to it, it remains, in all its stark urban reality, forever Paris, and wherever Beauty is debased on the streets, the streets present us with their infinite wealth of beauty.

NOTES

1. The ramifications of this single-mindedness, or perhaps, as we shall see, this 'double vision', can include seeing Paris and the traces of the prose poems everywhere. See, for example, my own analysis of Albert Camus's *L'Étranger* (*The Outsider*), which reads Meursault's

murder of the Arab through the lens of the knocking on the door that is the mid-point of 'La Chambre double [The Double Room]' (Rolls 2011).

2. The English title *Paris Spleen* refers to Louise Varèse's American English translation of 1947. This version of the prose poems will be referenced throughout this chapter. The French text cited is the edition published by Gallimard in its *Poésie* series in 1973 with a critical introduction by Robert Kopp. Otherwise, all translations of texts originally written in French are my own.

3. For ease of reference, I am using a mix of the title of the poems as they are currently published by Gallimard, which is *Petits Poëmes en prose* (with the unusual diaeresis on the first 'e') with *Le Spleen de Paris* following as a subtitle, or rather as a second title in brackets as opposed to a subtitle following a colon, and that chosen by New Directions, which privileges the subtitle, *Paris Spleen*, to the exclusion of any reference to the prose poems. Covin, for his part, notes (2000: 51) that Baudelaire himself hesitated a great deal over the title to give to the prose poems, but that he had in mind two titles containing a direct reference to Paris: *Le Rôdeur parisien* (literally, the Parisian stroller) and *Le Spleen parisien*. The 'full title' that Covin uses as the basis for his analysis is *Les Petits Poëmes en prose: Spleen parisien*.

4. I consider myself one such critic. See, for example, Rolls (2012).

5. Curiously, in his prize-winning novel *De Wraak van Baudelaire* (*Baudelaire's Revenge*, 2007), Belgian author Bob Van Laerhoven gives Baudelaire an avenging twin sister who, in addition to her diminutive stature, is endowed with a tail, which she uses to great effect. Whether the revenge of the title is hers, her brother's or that of their daughter is left unclear. What is striking in the novel is the increasing pride with which the Baudelairean tail is wielded in order to redress an imbalance – not only in power, in legacy, of course, but also in narrative.

6. One might also think here of Louis-Ferdinand Céline's famous *Voyage au bout de la nuit* (*[Journey to the End of the Night]*, 1932), which is often considered to be a purely imaginary journey, one that circumnavigates the world from the confines of a café on Paris's Place Clichy.

7. In her study of popular bohemia in nineteenth-century Paris, Mary Gluck draws a distinction between the 'popular' flânerie of the 1840s and what she dubs the 'avant-garde' variety of the 1850s. She notes that for the flâneur of the 1840s, Paris 'was synonymous with modernity', making it impossible for him to exist anywhere else in the world; his homologue of the 1850s, on the other hand, perceived himself as 'a man of the world [...] at home in all parts of the globe' (2005: 103). The poet, or poetic subject, of the prose poems, insofar as he is what we might consider a critical, or self-conscious, flâneur, appears to fuse these two attitudes, such that his space presents itself simultaneously as Paris *and* any other place on the globe.

8. Gouvard is not only interested in literal representations. As he notes, certain discourses are also equally representative of Paris, irrespective of their origins: 'Discourse [in this case,

that of the bourgeoisie of the Second Empire], for Baudelaire, is just as much part of the city's cultural capital, of its imaginary, as topological and sociological referents, even if it is those that we are tempted to think of first when seeking to determine the characteristic elements of Parisian representation' (2015: 144).

9. I am indebted here to the anonymous reviewer of this chapter who observed *inter alia* that Victor Hugo's *Notre-Dame de Paris* contains a chapter entitled 'Paris, à vol d'oiseau'. In that text, Paris's monuments recall Greek temples and even English jockeys' hats (1904–1924: 108). This can be considered for our current purposes a model of representation.

10. This dual presentation and representation can be mapped onto Katharina Niemeyer's understanding of nostalgia as a desire to recover the past in the present, which she expresses by conjoining the two terms with a hyphen: 'what is past comes along with the present, *via* re-presentation, a present that contracts parts of the past in its actualis-ation [...] and can also include imaginations of the future' (2014: 3). In the Baudelairean schema, we might talk of the conjoining, in representation, of historical time and time-lessness.

11. It is because of these rules that Evil does not have an initial capital letter in the 'original' title of *Les Fleurs du mal*. Baudelaire's preference, which is sometimes reflected in scholars' references to the text, was for *Les Fleurs du Mal*.

12. It should be pointed out that Chambers's studies of Baudelaire are as complex and nuanced as they are brilliant. It is not easy to pin down all of what he understands by noise and atmospherics, nor indeed what appear to be otherwise transparent terms, like irony for example, which in his work are put to many and varied uses. By referring to noise here, I am mobilizing the term to my own (more mundane, less ethereal) ends and am in a small way paying tribute to one of the great scholars of French studies. Ross Chambers died in 2017 as this book was beginning to take shape.

13. Moments like these explain in part what Baudelaire sometimes describes as *le merveilleux*, or the marvellous.

14. It seems clear, however, that Gouvard sees the poetry, and Baudelaire the poet, in parts of the prose poems, but this perhaps in spite of them. For him, what poetry there is in the prose poems seems to stand as so many echoes to the 'true poetry' of *Les Fleurs du mal*. Such an argument, founded on nostalgia, might easily be translated onto the type of alle-gorical reading that I am suggesting here: poetry would, accordingly, represent Paris lost, Paris as mythology, perhaps even Paris as primal scene.

15. The human condition is driven in the Sartrean schema of the years immediately follow-ing the Second World War by a value that is logically untenable, which is referred to as the being-for-itself-in-itself. The paradox of this entity lies in the fact that it is simul-taneously self-founding *and* free, a status that is only available to (an equally impossi-ble) divinity. As noted above, while this impossible ambition condemns humans to the meaninglessness of freedom, it is what underlies our various aspirations. In Baudelaire's poetics, as in the works of the Surrealists from the 1920s onwards, this impossibility,

however fleetingly, however fatally, is nonetheless realized in the form of an earth-shattering shock.

16. Equally, in the Sartrean schema, an objective view of any human life can only be given in death, at which point the sum total of one's actions forms a narrative; in hindsight, in other words, our actions become defined by their own end-point. While we are alive, our very freedom to act (differently) strips our ability to be transparently or metaphysically meaningful, even while our desire to mean drives our actions.

17. Roland Barthes develops these approaches to text in *S/Z* (1970).

18. In *Le Plaisir du texte* (1973), Barthes's use of the ambiguous genitive of 'the pleasure of the text' (which captures both the pleasure that it affords the reader and the pleasure that the reader gives to it) renders *le plaisir* a catch-all concept and seemingly makes of it an auto-antonym. That is, textual pleasure is derived from actively *making* sense out of, and against, a text's ostensible meaning (this is a fixing in time of one of the near-infinite possibilities of a text that, for Barthes, is foundationally plural) as well as simply enjoying a text *for what it is* (this is a denial of textual plurality, almost a reading in *bad faith*, to borrow a term from Sartrean Existentialism).

19. For an excellent history of Paris's *passages*, see Patrice de Moncan (2001).

20. The development of the arcades not only protected Parisians from the rain and mud, but it also brought with it public amenities, which enabled people, for example, to relieve themselves without resorting to using the bushes (various bushy areas had previously become quite unsanitary).

21. We may think particularly of Louis Aragon's *Le Paysan de Paris* (*Paris Peasant*, 1926).

22. In the same way, something can only be said to measure one metre or to weigh one kilogramme because these units have been set in stone (or, rather, forged in metal). This system of measuring was formalized by the Treaty of the Metre, which was signed in Paris on 20 May 1875.

23. In French, the caption reads 'Nadar élevant la Photographie à la hauteur de l'Art'. Note the capital letters on the abstract ideas.

24. Covin notes that Baudelaire considered children to see everything for the first time, as if they were drunk (2000: 65).

REFERENCES

Barthes, Roland (1970), *S/Z*, Paris: Éditions du Seuil.

Barthes, Roland (1973), *Le Plaisir du texte*, Paris: Éditions du Seuil.

Baudelaire, Charles (1970), *Paris Spleen 1869* (trans. L.Varèse), New York: New Directions.

Baudelaire, Charles (1973), *Petits Poëmes en prose (Le Spleen de Paris)*, Paris: Gallimard.

Chambers, Ross (1999), *Loiterature*, Lincoln and London: University of Nebraska Press.

Chambers, Ross (2015), *An Atmospherics of the City: Baudelaire and the Poetics of Noise*, New York: Fordham University Press.

Covin, Michel (2000), *L'Homme de la rue: Essai sur la poétique baudelairienne*, Paris: L'Harmattan.

Gluck, Mary (2005), *Popular Bohemia: Modernism and Urban Culture in Nineteenth-Century Paris*, Cambridge, MA: Harvard University Press.

Gouvard, Jean-Michel (2015), '*Le spleen de Paris*, un Paris pour collectionneur?', *L'Esprit Créateur*, 55: 3, pp. 140–51.

Harvey, David (2003), *Paris, Capital of Modernity*, New York and London: Routledge.

Hugo, Victor (1904–24), *Notre-Dame de Paris*, in *Œuvres complètes de Victor Hugo*, vol. 2, Paris: Paul Meurice, Gustave Simon.

Johnson, Barbara (1987), 'Disfiguring poetic language', in *A World of Difference*, Baltimore: Johns Hopkins University Press, pp. 100–15.

Johnson, Barbara (2000), 'The critical difference', in D.Knight (ed.), *Critical Essays on Roland Barthes*, New York: G. K. Hall, pp. 174–82.

Moncan, Patrice de (2001), *Les Passages couverts de Paris*, Paris: Les Éditions du Mécène.

Niemeyer, Katharina (ed.) (2014), *Media and Nostalgia: Yearning for the Past, Present and Future*, Houndmills: Palgrave Macmillan.

Rolls, Alistair (2011), 'Camus's Algerian in Paris: A prose poetic reading of L'Étranger', *Sophia: An International Journal for Philosophical Theology and Cross-Cultural Philosophy of Religion*, 50: 4, pp. 527–41.

Rolls, Alistair (2012), 'Baudelaire's Paris: A new, urban (prose) poetics', *Mascara Literary Review*, 12 July, http://mascarareview.com/alistair-rolls-baudelaires-paris-a-new-urban-prose-poetics/. Accessed 31 January 2018.

Rosewarne, Lauren (2017), *Analyzing Christmas in Film: Santa to the Supernatural*, Lanhan, MD: Lexington.

Van Laerhoven, Bob (2007), *De Wraak van Baudelaire, Antwerp: Houtekiet. [Baudelaire's Revenge* (trans. B. Doyle), New York and London: Pegasus Crime, 2014.]

Williams, Linda (2008), *Screening Sex*, Durham and London: Duke University Press.

2

Baudelaire and the Classical Tradition: Virgil, Ovid and Sappho in Paris

Marguerite Johnson

Baudelaire wanted to be read like a classical poet.
> (Walter Benjamin 2006b: 118, emphasis added)

Your country?
I do not know in what latitude it lies.
> (Charles Baudelaire, 'The Stranger' 1970 [1869: 1])

This chapter considers select poems from *Les Fleurs du mal* (*The Flowers of Evil*) from the perspective of the Classical Tradition (see Silk et al. 2017), namely, Baudelaire's engagement with Paris as a city built on top of a Gallic Rome, or a Roman Gaul, which lies literally under his feet, as well as his poetic intertextuality, which draws on both Latin and Greek literature, particularly, Virgil, Ovid and Sappho. It considers the theory of the Classical Tradition, understood as the various cultural debts to the ancient Mediterranean and the multifarious effects of such on, for example, art, literature, philosophy, architecture and politics. It also aligns the Classical Tradition with theories of nostalgia to address Baudelaire's longing for a former Paris, expressed in evocations of the ancient poets. In this sense, the voices of Latin and Greek predecessors seem to be particularly appropriate for poems on a city lost and mourned. Much of this chapter ruminates on the 'Sappho' poems from *Les Fleurs du mal* in order to extend the theme of Baudelaire and the Classical Tradition. Such ruminations also consider these poems as thematically engaged with Parisian prostitution as a form of a poetry of nostalgia. This approach is designed to push the boundaries of nostalgia in order to see if Baudelaire may be exploring the body of the prostitute as a signifier of a traditional or originary Paris, which was perceived as being threatened by zealous hygiene reform and urban renewal.

Baudelaire's Paris: Crumbling city

Walter Benjamin's unfinished masterpiece, *Passagen-Werk* (*The Arcades Project*) is immersed in Paris: its forgotten arcades, its dirty and dreamy-nightmarish streets, its squalid beauty, its Baudelairean topography. As the intellectual, artistic and spiritual reincarnation of Baudelaire, Benjamin is the critic-as-*flâneur* and – perhaps more urgently – the *flâneur*-as-critic, who traverses Paris, decrying 'modernity's alienation as a collective state of no longer being *heimisch* or at *home*' (Hanssen 2006: 2). Like Baudelaire, Benjamin also decries the obscenity of the modern city and connects with his hero in observing the ragpickers, the new 'benefactors' of industrialization and capitalism, who

> worked for middlemen and constituted a sort of cottage industry located in the streets. The ragpicker fascinated his [Baudelaire's] epoch. The eyes of the first investigators of pauperism were fixed on him with the mute question: Where does the limit of human misery lie?
>
> (Benjamin 2006b: 54)

Benjamin (2006: 53) cites stanzas two and three of 'Le Vin des chiffonniers [The Ragpicker's Wine]', which denotes the eponymous ragpicker as 'hochant [shaking]' at *l.*5 and as a man 'Buttant, et se cognant aux murs comme un poète [[who] Staggers against the walls, as poets do]' at *l.*6.

In the introduction to this volume of essays, we comment on the poetics of alienation begun in *Les Fleurs du mal* and cite 'Le Cygne [The Swan]' as a sign of the dispossessed and the estranged inhabitants of Haussmann's new city of the Second Empire who – like the ragpickers – find themselves, in Baudelaire's vision, treading water amid massive change and dislocation. We discuss the swan as a part of a chain of mourning, but Benjamin – who also associates the creature with Andromache, as we do – leads us further:

> The condition of Paris is fragile; it is surrounded by symbols of fragility – living creatures (the black woman and the swan) and historical figures (Andromache, 'widow of Hector and wife of Helenus'). What they share are mourning for what was and lack of hope for what is to come. In the final analysis, this decrepitude constitutes the closest link between modernity and antiquity.
>
> (2006: 111)

Benjamin understands Baudelaire's use of antiquity as a metaphor for his despair at the rise of Haussmann's city, which he contrasts with that of the dedicatee of 'Le Cygne', Victor Hugo,[1] who is quietly adamant of the antiquity that has always lain beneath modernity, and always will. Baudelaire seems more alienated, whereas Hugo seems more optimistic. Either way, both artists see antiquity as informing Paris, both the old and the new. Baudelaire seems to emerge more as the artist of nostalgia than Hugo, particularly if we accept Svetlana Boym's understanding of the term as 'a longing for a home that no longer exists or has never existed', 'a sentiment of loss or displacement', but also 'a romance with one's own fantasy' (2007: 7). Andreas Huyssen's more emphatically melancholic understanding of 'nostalgia's primary meaning' as 'the irreversibility of time: something in the past is no longer accessible' (2006: 7) is also applicable to Baudelaire, particularly with its emphasis on the fragile, liminal and turbulent modes of temporality,[2] which both trouble us and remind us of our own mortality.

Baudelaire's Paris: Second Troy

Latin poetry inspired Baudelaire, who also directly experienced the materiality of the culture that produced it in the midst of his city, as archaeology began to unearth the 'Roman city' of Paris (see Busson 2003). Baudelaire was not, however, the first to allegorize Paris as Troy, a tradition based on Roman Paris because of the Trojan roots of the Roman people. Gilles Corrozet (1510–68), Parisian author, poet, printer and bookseller, traced the origins of the city back to Troy in his 1532 'history' of the city, *La Fleur des antiquitez de Paris* (*The Flower of Antiquity of Paris*). Corrozet includes the legendary genealogy that traces the (then) King of France, François I, to Paris, son of Priam, and thus the royal lineage and its seat of power to the royal family of Troy. Priscilla Parkhurst Ferguson comments on the inventive genealogy, noting that it 'incidentally, make[s] good on his dedication of the work to the "Nobles, bourgeois, of Greek or Trojan origin"' (1994: 26).[3] Part history, part folklore, part travelogue or city guidebook, *La Fleur des antiquitez de Paris*, provides, in the words of Elizabeth Hodges, a 'history of place' and a 'place in history' (2008: 137, 142). In this way, Corrozet literarily (and literally) lays the path for the *flâneur*, including Baudelaire – and all *flâneurs*. *La Fleur des antiquitez de Paris* is a literary ancestor of *Les Fleurs du mal*, with the poetic offspring – a changeling of the uncanniest kind – shedding tears at the loss of Corrozet's medieval hybrid that is the city of Troy-Rome-Paris/Paris-Rome-Troy, as he walks the urbanity of Haussmann.

In the modernity of Paris, with swathes of the medieval city being torn down, while antiquities are being dug up, Corrozet's guidebook becomes the marker of urban and cultural memory. In this sense, *La Fleur des antiquitez de Paris* functions as memory and nostalgia in their most potent forms, combining ancient and medieval with the mythical and legendary Latin poetry that brought them together. Like Corrozet, the intellectual facilitator of the *flâneur*, Baudelaire sees the city through the lenses of both 'now' and 'then', with a 'then' that stretches back to Classical antiquity but is, as Alistair Rolls writes in his chapter on *Le Spleen de Paris* (*Paris Spleen*) in this volume (Chapter 1 above), the temporal 'absent-present', which also corresponds to Benjamin's 'now-time' or 'here-and-now' (*Jetztzeit*). For those seeking to nurture this 'absent-present', they must employ imagination and write or paint or sing the city of their dreams back to life. To do so, a conjoined imperative is to see the modern Paris as a city of ruins.

Baudelaire, Virgil and Ovid

Huyssen situates nostalgia firmly within a Classical autochthony, unearthing its etymology accordingly – 'The word is made up of the Greek *nostos* = home and *algos* = pain' (2007: 7) – and placing its physicality and pathology among ruins. Sifting through Baudelaire's ruins, and negotiating a Classical Tradition, one finds that his interest was principally in Roman rather than Greek antiquity.[4] As a city, both physically and psychologically, Rome captured Baudelaire's imagination and Benjamin notes that it was the 'paramount' ancient city for the poet (2006: 118). This is evident in 'Le Cygne', in which Baudelaire employs Greek mythology but via Virgil's employment of the same in the *Aeneid* (see, for example, Nelson 1961; Hampton 1982; Verdicchio 2015). Therefore, when Baudelaire begins with the reference to Andromache –

> Andromaque, je pense à vous! Ce petit fleuve,
> Pauvre et triste miroir où jadis resplendit
> L'immense majesté de vos douleurs de veuve,
> Ce Simoïs menteur qui par vos pleurs grandit,
> [Andromache, I think of you! – this meagre stream,
> This melancholy mirror where had once shone forth
> The giant majesty of all your widowhood,
> This fraudulent Simois, fed by bitter tears,]
>
> (1993 [1857: 172–73])

– he is echoing *Aeneid* 3.294–319. Virgil's description of Andromache, narrated by Aeneas as he recounts an unexpected reunion with her, foreshadows Baudelaire's careful imitation, including Virgil's inclusion of 'falsus [false]' at *l.*302 to describe Simois, a river on the Trojan plain, which he echoes in 'menteur [fraudulent]'. Baudelaire's allusions to the *Aeneid* underscore his theme of dispossession and alienation, which is facilitated by the intertextual episode of Aeneas not only meeting Andromache at Buthrotum, where he sees a simulacrum of Troy, but also his recounting of the story as a refugee. Aeneas tells Andromache's story at Carthage, where he and his men have arrived, homeless and consumed by memories of Troy, their destroyed homeland, of which Andromache acts as the metonymic signifier (see Bettini 1997). Of course, Virgil accesses his story primarily through the *Iliad*, but for Baudelaire, it is the Roman version of the story, accessed through Virgil, which interests him. This preference for the Latin version, rather than the Greek, is partly because Virgil tells of the aftermath of Troy and the dispossession of its people, whereas extant Homeric poems do not.

Baudelaire relates his nostalgia through comparison with that of Andromache (and, by extension, Aeneas), which is conveyed in stanza two, in which his own memory is prompted by the Trojan princess. He claims that the thought of Andromache

> A fécondé soudain ma mémoire fertile,
> Comme je traversais le nouveau Carrousel.
> Le vieux Paris n'est plus (la forme d'une ville
> Change plus vite, hélas ! que le cœur d'un mortel);
> [Has quickened suddenly my fertile memory
> As I was walking through the modern Carrousel.
> The old Paris is gone (the form a city takes
> More quickly shifts, alas, than does the mortal heartt);]

(1993 [1857: 174–75])

Andromache's pain is not only aligned with that of the poet's but, poignantly, also with that of the swan, the hapless creature of a 'mythe étrange et fatal [sad and fatal myth]'. But, Baudelaire, master of multi-intertextuality, is not exactly forthcoming as to which 'mythe étrange et fatal' he means. The conceit is, of course, that he is alluding to multiple myths, possibly evoked by memories of the myths of his school days in a Latin classroom, parsing the stories of Virgil and Ovid. The first story that comes to mind is that of Leda and the Swan. This myth explains the rape of the mortal woman, Leda, by the lustful Zeus (Rome's Jupiter). It relates to Andromache and the Trojan War because the offspring of the rape, Helen, who hatches from an egg, is destined to instigate the destruction of Ilium. Virgil also tells of another swan, however. At *Aeneid* 10.185–92, he recalls the Greek myth of Cycnus who, inconsolable at the death of his cousin, Phaethon (struck down by Jupiter for flying too close to the sun), turns into a swan out of grief.[5] The second Cycnus, killed by Achilles during the Trojan War, only to be transformed into a swan, is also mentioned by Virgil in the 'Catalogue of Heroes' at *Aeneid* 7.647–817. Like the myth of Leda, the story of this second Cycnus also returns the reader to Andromache's narrative.

But Baudelaire also mentions Ovid, namely in the image of the Parisian swan stretching its neck towards the sky, which concludes the poem:

Vers le ciel quelquefois, comme l'homme d'Ovide,
Vers le ciel ironique et cruellement bleu,
Sur son cou convulsif tendant sa tête avide
Comme s'il adressait des reproches à Dieu !
[Stretching the hungry head on his convulsive neck,
Sometimes towards the sky, like the man in Ovid's book –
Towards the ironic sky, the sky of cruel blue,
As if he were a soul contesting with God!]

(1993 [1857: 174–75])

The primary allusion is to *Metamorphoses* 1.84–86, in which Ovid – in a most (anachronistically) Baudelairean manner – evokes the wonderment that is the human being and its potential for greatness. Unlike the animals that come before humans, the new invention of the Creator God looks upwards towards the sky and the stars.[6] The reference to Ovid also returns the reader back to the 'mythe étrange et fatal' of the swan, which Baudelaire ensures by the conjunction 'comme [like]', comparing the swan to the nameless 'homme d'Ovide [the man in Ovid's book]'. Accordingly, the first Cycnus reappears in Ovid's *Metamorphoses* 2.369–74, which is based on *Aeneid* 10.185–92. The story of the second Cycnus is in *Metamorphoses* 12.46–145. Both Ovidian versions reinforce the link Baudelaire seeks to make between these myths of the swan and Andromache in 'Le Cygne': her sorrow matches the heartbroken Cycnus, who cries the river Eridanus to the brim with his tears over the loss of Phaethon in Book Two (and is transformed into a swan), while the death of the second Cycnus (also transformed into a swan), who is laid low by Achilles in Book Twelve, speaks yet again to the deaths of the Trojans, which is a sorrow Andromache knows only too well. The power and ingenuity of Baudelaire's engagement with the Classical Tradition in 'Le Cygne' are arguably one of the best examples of the combination of his employment of Classical intertextuality and nostalgia. As Beryl Schlossman (2005: 180) writes, '[i]n this poem, Baudelaire uses a set of analogies connecting ancient Rome to Paris in the 1850s to explore the interrelated themes of the city, political exile and the suffering of loss'.

Baudelaire and Sappho: I

While 'Baudelaire's antiquity is Roman antiquity' (Benjamin 2006b: 119), the suite of poems entitled 'Les Fleurs du mal' in the collection of the same name references the Archaic Greek poet, Sappho, whose extant lyrics are almost entirely composed of fragments.[7] The first in the series, 'Lesbos', specifies the poet, and while the two that follow – 'Femmes damnées: Delphine et Hippolyte [Condemned Women: Delphine and Hippolyta]' and 'Femmes damnées [Condemned Women]' – do not name Sappho, the inclusion of the Classical names, Delphine and Hippolyta in the second poem, and the repetition of part of its title in the third, 'Femmes damnées', bind the collection into a tight, Classically inspired triptych. Benjamin is particularly enthused about Baudelaire's use of the Greek names Delphine and Hippolyta in the cycle 'Les Fleurs du mal'. Although Baudelaire names Sappho and knows her legacy (and may even be intimately familiar with her poetry), it is likely that he came to her through the work of Ovid, expressly 'Heroides XV', which is an epistle in verse from Sappho to Phaon ('Roman antiquity' once more). The three 'Sappho' or 'Lesbian' poems may initially appear to have little if anything to do with Baudelaire's Paris. Scholars do not discuss them as explicitly Parisian poems, choosing instead to focus on issues of gender and sexuality, and/or on matters of censorship. However, the poems may be viewed as integral to the cityscape of Baudelaire if they are recast both as evocations of the urban woman – preferably the prostitute of the brothels and streets of Paris – and as examples of Classical intertextuality.

Benjamin sees Baudelaire as the poet and the allegorist, both of which are inextricably embedded in the identity of Baudelaire as the *flâneur*. To extend a reading of 'Lesbos' as a poem about the Parisian prostitute is to reinforce all three of Benjamin's epithets for the poet, especially Baudelaire as allegorist. Baudelaire explores the woman/prostitute not only as erotic object but also as literary artefact in the form of allegory-as-metonym for poetry *per se*. As Baudelaire writes in the first aphorism of *Journaux Intimes* (*Intimate Journals*): 'L'amour, c'est le goût de la prostitution. [...] Qu'est-ce que l'art? Prostitution [Love is the taste of prostitution. [...] What is Art? Prostitution]' (2014 [1897: 7]). This can be related to ideas – perhaps aphoristic ideas – of the Baudelairean Sappho through the traditional associations between Sappho, love and art. If Baudelaire indeed sees love as (the taste of) prostitution, and art as prostitution, then Sappho may well embody, poetically speaking, not only an allegory of love, an allegory of poetry or art, but also an allegory of prostitution. Reading the collection 'Les Fleurs du mal' intratextually, it is possible that Baudelaire establishes a poetic travelogue in the opening poem in order to guide his readers. Herein, 'La Destruction [Destruction]', in which he refers to the 'le Démon [Fiend]' at *l*.1, is once again feeding his ennui, calling him to wrestle with shameful needs, which may take the form of a woman; but a woman who is born of his love of art and is made manifest in the form of the prostitute:

Parfois il prend, sachant mon grand amour de l'Art,
La forme de la plus séduisante des femmes,

Et, sous de spécieux prétextes de cafard,
Accoutume ma lèvre à des philtres infâmes.
[Knowing my love of Art, he may select
A woman form – most perfect, most corrupt –
And under sanctimonious pretext
Bring to my lips the potion of her lust.]

(1993 [1857: 228–29])

The second poem, 'Une martyre [A Martyr]', shows the extreme expression of ennui in the vignette of a lover-client who beheads a woman at the height of his lust. Subtitled 'Dessin d'un maître inconnu [Drawing by an Unknown Master]',[8] the rendition of woman-into-art is the principal theme and, again, foreshadows Sappho as the ultimate woman-into-art/art-into-woman. 'Une martyre' also looks to Sappho through its inextricable link between sex and death, as Sappho, like the woman prior to her death, is also consumed by ennui and ultimately dies. Indeed, Baudelaire directly associates Sappho with martyrdom in stanza six of 'Lesbos':

Tu tires ton pardon de l'éternel martyre,
Infligé sans relâche aux cœurs ambitieux,
Qu'attire loin de nous le radieux sourire
Entrevu vaguement au bord des autres cieux!
Tu tires ton pardon de l'éternel martyre!
[You're pardoned by eternal martyrdom
Lived constantly in those with hungering hearts
Who glimpse that radiant smile beyond our grasp
That beckons from the brink of other skies!
You're pardoned by eternal martyrdom!]

(1993 [1857: 234–35])

Furthermore, the two poems are entwined by the theme of death: the woman in 'Une martyre' is murdered by her client-lover and rendered literally into art in the form of a painting, while Sappho leaps off the Leucadian cliff because of her unrequited love for the ferryman, Phaon. This fate of Sappho, which may seem odd for a lover of women to choose, became popular in antiquity a few hundred years after her actual death (the cause of which remains unknown) and is part of the apocryphal Sappho tradition (for more on the fictional lives of Sappho, see below). The suicide story is best known from Ovid's 'Heroides XV', which was popular in France during the nineteenth century and would have been familiar to Baudelaire.[9]

'Lesbos', as mentioned above, is the first poem in 'Les Fleurs du mal', and, as its title suggests, it is situated on the Greek isle of Lesbos, the home of Sappho:

> Mère des jeux latins et des voluptés grecques,
> Lesbos, où les baisers, languissants ou joyeux,
> Chauds comme les soleils, frais comme les pastèques,
> Font l'ornement des nuits et des jours glorieux,
> Mère des jeux latins et des voluptés grecques,
> Lesbos, où les baisers sont comme les cascades
> Qui se jettent sans peur dans les gouffres sans fonds,
> Et courent, sanglotant et gloussant par saccades,
> Orageux et secrets, fourmillants et profonds;
> Lesbos, où les baisers sont comme les cascades !
> [Mother of Roman games and Greek delights,
> Lesbos, where kisses languorous or glad,
> As hot as suns, or watermelon-fresh,
> Make festivals of days and glorious nights;
> Mother of Roman games and Greek delights,
> Lesbos, where love is like the wild cascades
> That throw themselves into the deepest gulfs,
> And twist and run with gurglings and with sobs,
> Stormy and secret, swarming underground;
> Lesbos, where love is like the wild cascades.]

(1993 [1857: 232–35])

Baudelaire evokes a Lesbos that is far from historical and certainly far from any Lesbos Sappho would recognize. His Lesbos is a riot of sensuality and unbridled sexual expression, a place where love is redolent with storms and secrets that swarm underground and, in stanza four, a land of nights both languid and warm. Lesbos appears more akin to a Parisian brothel – or, more precisely, 'the deluxe brothel' of 'suave eroticism'[10] described by art historian, Hollis Clayson (2003: 35) – than an idyllic island. Accordingly, Baudelaire challenges the reader to contemplate the fluidity of the allegories at play here.

Further explorations of the poem point to the two references to 'Phrynes' in stanza three; the following line opens and closes it:

> Lesbos, où les Phrynés l'une l'autre s'attirent
> [Lesbos, where Phrynes seek each other out]

(1993 [1857: 234–35])

The figure of Phryne in the plural – there are multiple Phrynes! – is the name of one of the most famous *hetaerae* (elite or expensive prostitute) of ancient Greece (*fl.* fourth century BC). Her name became synonymous with prostitution and immorality because of her profession and also a trial that saw her prosecuted for impiety. To Parisians of the nineteenth century, she was best known as a result of the painting by Jean-Léon Gérôme, *Phryne devant l'Areopage* (*Phryne Before the Areopagus*), completed in 1861, four years after the first edition of *Les Fleurs du mal*.[11] And, of course, the extension of the woman's body as art, the woman-prostitute as art is evident in artists' use of prostitutes as models, a reality that began in antiquity, when Phyrne herself posed for her client-lover Praxiteles, who cast her as his *Aphrodite of Knidos*.[12]

In her study of 'Lesbos', Judith Ryan links the allegory of Phryne to that of Lesbos:

> In 'Lesbos', Phryne is metonymic for courtesans in general. According to classical tradition, the island of Lesbos was a training school for young prostitutes, who were also educated in various other arts, notably poetry. Sappho, a star pupil who became a leader of the group, received her poetic training there. Pierre Larousse's nineteenth-century encyclopedia tells that the island fell into disrepute because the women concentrated there in large number were believed to engage in shameful sexual practices.
>
> (1993: 1130)

The Classical Tradition that Ryan references took a particularly strong hold in Paris in the nineteenth century. In 1847, for example, 'Sappho et les Lesbiennes [Sappho and the Lesbians]', an article by Emile Deschanel, was published in *Revue des Deux Mondes* (*Review of the Two Worlds*); it posited that Sappho was both a poet and a prostitute. Deschanel's work came at a time when the French were waging an ownership war over Sappho and her biography. Writers such as Philoxène Boyer and Arsène Houssaye experimented quite cavalierly with Sappho and her 'relaxed' *heterosexuality* – she was not a saint, but she was no lesbian[13] – a somewhat risqué but ultimately quaint pastiche, typical of the French neoclassicism that provoked Baudelaire's ire. Of course, the Classical Tradition, as cited by Ryan, is just that – a tradition. Phryne was not from Lesbos, although she was a *hetaera*, and Sappho was from Lesbos, but was not a *hetaera*. It is the Classical Tradition – the inheritance and adaptation of ancient writing and people by later writers, artists and historians – that creates the misleading biographies and confusion about historical individuals like Sappho. Baudelaire's 'Lesbos' is merely one in hundreds if not thousands of rewrites from antiquity to the present day. However, there is a special caveat for Sappho in terms of a Classical Tradition, namely, the fact is that it was the ancients themselves, only a hundred or so years after her death, who began the lies that problematized her identity. In Sappho's case, therefore, it would be fair to say that the ancients themselves meddled in her historical legacy long before the French unleashed their quills.[14]

Baudelaire and Sappho: II

Discourse on prostitution began to merge with discourse on lesbianism before the time of Baudelaire's poetry. Alexandre Parent-Duchâtelet's influential medico-social study, *La Prostitution à Paris au XIXe siècle* (1840, *Prostitution in Paris in the Nineteenth Century*), for example, presented 'Parisian lesbianism as a nefarious by-product of prostitution, which herded debased women into the promiscuity of prisons and brothels [...] [and] provided a vivid and influential portrait of lesbian mores, including the frightening image of older lesbians initiating young acolytes' (Choquette 2001: 150).[15] The connection – without the moral and hygiene concerns of Parent-Duchâtelet – was particularly topical as a motif in both literature and art during the age of Baudelaire, including the celebrated painting *Le Sommeil* (*The Sleepers*) by Gustave Courbet (1866), thought to have been inspired by his poem 'Femmes Damnées: Delphine et Hippolyte' (discussed below).[16] As noted by Karen Humphreys,

> [i]n the works by Hugo, Sue, and Balzac, the prostitute-protagonists are noble characters, which redeems them; in each case, however, their redemption is scripted by the hand of a humanitarian author who inscribes the heroine as subversive to the social order but who ultimately reinforces patriarchal hegemony by confining her, excluding her, or by masterminding her death.
>
> (2006: 179–80)

The connection between prostitution and lesbianism continued unabated in varied works, including the visitor's guide to the best prostitutes in the city, *The Pretty Women of Paris* (1883), which revealed that it was not uncommon among the women who worked in the commercial sex industry and one may suggest that such relations were also undertaken privately and/or for clients. *The Pretty Women of Paris* featured, among many, one Juliette Grandville who was advertised as 'often Sappho by day and Messalina by night' ([1883] 1996: 71), which indicated her ability to please both sexes (simultaneously and separately). The memoirs of Céleste Mogador published in the 1850s (1854–58) further reinforce the connections made herein, the author having been both a prostitute and lover of women (she married Lionel de Moreton, count of Chabrillan, in 1854).

Leslie Choquette's discussion of Céleste raises some interesting issues in relation to Sappho and, in turn, to Baudelaire's poem:

> [S]he [Céleste] also portrayed a world in which abused prostitutes turned to each other for emotional and sexual solace. Her firsthand experience of prison and brothel confirmed that lesbian liaisons were common there, some of them between young girls and middle-aged women. More importantly, she made clear that such relationships were not confined to institutions, but spilled out onto the city streets. Independent streetwalkers and courtesans, who multiplied as the century progressed, brought same-sex intimacy to their residential neighborhood, the Bréda quarter. Here they shared apartments, regardless of the police ruling, and even patronized their own restaurants, the prostitutes' tables d'hôte. These tables d'hôte, which were run by older procuresses, sometimes catered to women who announced their sexual preference through cropped curly hair and a boyish appearance. Beyond the Bréda quarter, lesbianism was also visible among the women of the theater world, the singers, dancers, and actresses who were often indistinguishable from courtesans.
>
> (2001: 150)

The Parisian tradition that aligned sex work and lesbianism, partly underscored by a not-so-unimportant degree of reality, provides a significant background to Baudelaire's line: 'Lesbos, où les Phrynés l'une l'autre s'attirent'. The line, reinforced by employment of the enveloped stanza, transfers the account of Céleste into literary or poetic mode, articulating the expression of love or affection between prostitutes through allusion to a Sapphic past. The transfer of this same reading – from this interpretation of Baudelaire's Phryne/Phrynes to Baudelaire's Sappho – strongly suggests that he saw her as both poet and prostitute, Phaon as both her lover and her client, and her love of other women as the comfort described in Céleste's memoirs. Indeed, as love is prostitution and art is prostitution, according to Baudelaire ('L'amour, c'est le goût de la prostitution. [...] Qu'est-ce que l'art? Prostitution'), Sappho as prostitute-lover-poet is the ultimate allegory (perhaps closely followed by her companion in 'Une martyre', who is a prostitute, a woman of love and, definitively, a painting).

In 'Femmes damnées: Delphine et Hippolyte', Baudelaire continues the allegory or conceit of evoking the image of the prostitute/lesbian. The two lovers, one older and masculine (Delphine; in Parent-Duchâtelet's list of names of superior prostitutes),[17] the other, Hippolyta (most likely a reference to the category of street walkers called the 'amazons'), younger and feminine, are immediately presented as luxuriating in a brothel-esque setting:

À la pâle clarté des lampes languissantes,
Sur de profonds coussins tout imprégnés d'odeur

Hippolyte rêvait aux caresses puissantes
Qui levaient le rideau de sa jeune candeur.
[Within the dwindling glow of light from languid lamps,
Sunk in the softest cushions soaked with heady scent,
Hippolyta lay dreaming of the thrilling touch
That spread apart the veil of her young innocence.]

(1993 [1857: 238–39])

These opening lines echo those of 'Une martyre' with its elaborate décor of the prostitute's boudoir and, along with the evocation of touch and smell (particularly perfume) and the image of women's caresses, which recall stanzas four and five of 'Lesbos', they create an intimate scene of the lesbians of the brothels. When Delphine harshly chides her doubtful and vulnerable younger lover at stanza eighteen –

Va, si tu veux, chercher un fiancé stupide;
Cours offrir un cœur vierge à ses cruels baisers;
Et, pleine de remords et d'horreur, et livide,
Tu me rapporteras tes seins stigmatisés...
[Go, if you will, and find some brutish fiancé;
Go give a virgin heart to tortuous embrace;
And, livid, with your fill of horror and remorse,
Come running back to me with scars across your breasts [...]]

(1993 [1857: 242–43])

– the reader recalls Baudelaire's Sappho from the previous poem, whose rejection of her lesbian life for the embrace of Phaon resulted in abandonment and suicide (an unhappy end to a love story that worked out better for Céleste Mogador, whose life echoes Sappho's in some ways, for even she once attempted to take her own life).[18] Additionally, the lines that speak of Hippolyta's sexual seduction by the older Delphine collide with clichés such as the one reinforced by Parent-Duchâtelet of, to requote Choquette, 'the frightening image of older lesbians initiating young acolytes' (2001: 150). Interestingly, such accusations were also part of the apocryphal biography of Sappho, which would have been familiar to Baudelaire. As the first two poems entice the reader into a complex and entangled world of antiquity, modernity, lesbianism and prostitution, underpinned by the heady and luxurious settings of both the Lesbos of antiquity and the brothels of Paris, which become conjoined as the Lesbos-brothel, the equation of the ancient Sappho (poet/lesbian/prostitute) as symbol of Lesbos itself prompts the equation of the modern prostitute as symbol of Paris.

Baudelaire moves from the lesbian brothel workers into the outdoors in the third and final poem in the Sappho or Lesbian cycle, 'Femmes Damnées'. The outdoor setting of street and park as sexual sites is as quickly and evocatively presented as the brothel interior of the previous poem. Baudelaire observes: women shivering with cold (*l*.4); some slowly walking as they ply their trade (*l*.9); others dwelling 'Qui dans le creux muet des vieux antres païens [Deep in a cave where ancient pagans meet]' (*l*.14);[19] some wearing 'les scapularies [the monkish cloaks]', presumably for warmth (*l*.17); and some with a little fetish item ('fouet [whip]') (*l*.18). Also described are the host of characters who make up the carnivalesque brothel that is the city: 'Ô vierges, ô démons, ô monstres, ô martyres [O maidens, demons, monsters – martyrs all]' (*l*.21). Baudelaire's soul has known these characters and their world, which he describes as 'enfer [hell]' (*l*.25).

Baudelaire's bodies: Woman-as-Paris

The connection between the prostitute-lesbian-as-Paris is perhaps most strongly evoked in the 'Épilogue' of *Le Spleen de Paris*, *ll*.13–15, which turns Paris ('capitale infâme [infamous city]') into both a brothel or archetypal whore and a jail or archetypal criminal ('Courtisanes / Et bandits [Courtesans/And bandits]'):

> Je t'aime, ô capitale infâme ! Courtisanes
> Et bandits, tels souvent vous offrez des plaisirs
> Que ne comprennent pas les vulgaires profanes.
> [Infamous City, I adore you! Courtesans
> And bandits, you offer me such joys
> The common herd can never understand.]

(1970 [1869: 108])

The woman's body as nation, land or city is common, and in Paris, the example of Marianne as the revolutionary symbol of France – of its liberty, fraternity and equality – represented a particularly potent icon, having emerged sometime during the revolution of 1789. Extending such ideas, the reader may see in Baudelaire's oeuvre not only the prominence of lesbians, prostitution and lesbian-prostitutes as occupying a prominent physical space in nineteenth-century Paris and accordingly its literature but also as embodying the city itself; hence the exclamation: 'Je t'aime, ô capitale infâme! Courtisanes'. As Benjamin writes, '[i]t is the unique provision of Baudelaire's poetry that the image of woman and death intermingle in a third image, that of Paris' (Benjamin 2006b: 41).

In terms of body theory and the relation between humans and urban space, Elizabeth Grosz (1995) coins the term 'bodies-cities', which is a useful concept with which to conclude this chapter. At the centre of her work, Grosz interprets the city as partly physical as well as partly imagined, which is a tenant applicable to Baudelaire's representation of the city, and the city as seen by Baudelaire. Like the demolition of the varied accommodations that served as brothels throughout the city under Haussmann and the pathologizing of the prostitutes and lesbians as contagion by Parent-Duchâtelet,[20] the lesbian-prostitute as the ultimate Baudelairian woman stands in for the city of Paris like the swan – their intense fragility exploited by modernity in the form of medical/science sociology and industrialization in the form of city rejuvenation and capitalism.

The image and reality of Paris as a diseased city, a diseased entity, underlined Haussmann's rejuvenation project. As Haussmann initiated plans to alleviate disease through schemes such as the sewerage restructure, prostitutes were required to undergo medical assessments at places such as the Dépôt, where working women were examined by the sanitary police.[21] In this sense, both programmes were predicated on an understanding of an intimate connection or relationship between the human body and the 'body' of Paris that, as Matthew Gandy comments in relation to Haussmann and his sewers, 'drew on a series of organic analogies to compare the new city with a healthy human body' (1999: 24). In contrast, the city that Baudelaire once walked as *flâneur* becomes one of distrust amid the new lightness, openness, visibility and surveillance as both the professional sanitizers and urban designers demarcate what is normal and what is pathological. As Barbara Hooper writes, Haussmann's new regulations of urban renewal extended to the female body:

> This rationalization and regularization of the city is repeated in the nineteenth-century struggle to control the female body. Ridding the city of pathological spaces by controlling the streets comes to mean, in language that is frequently stunning in its explicitness, a ridding of the city of the disorderly, pathological, sexually dangerous female, paradigmatically the prostitute but potentially any body marked female and her replacement with a planned or controlled body that functions in accord with hegemonic needs. As Paris is conceptualized as a diseased body, a 'she' [...] so the female body is conceptualized as a medicalized, pathologized city, a geography to be conquered and operated on by the authority and science of male minds.
>
> (1998: 240)

The process marked the end of Baudelaire's inspiration. As Rolls writes in Chapter 7 below: 'for Sartre, Baudelaire's obsession with dissolution and death at a time when the French were predominantly forward-looking, inventing the future, saw him "living against his time" [...] Baudelaire hated progress, Sartre concludes, because it privileged long-term projects, which the poet simply could not bring to fruition'.

The shock of the new for Baudelaire is perhaps nowhere more dramatically and sadly evoked than in his addendum to his second poem in the lesbian cycle; for therein, the last five stanzas of 'Femmes damnées: Delphine et Hippolyte' were added just prior to the publication of the definitive collection in 1857 in order to assuage legal proceedings for obscenity (Pichois 1: 1126–27). These awkward, insincere and troubling lines that condemn the women and their desires include sentiments that echo the values of the architects of the new city with its squeaky-clean morality:

> Jamais un rayon frais n'éclaira vos cavernes;
> Par les fentes des murs des miasmes fiévreux
> Filtrent en s'enflammant ainsi que des lanternes
> Et pénètrent vos corps de leurs parfums affreux.
> L'âpre stérilité de votre jouissance
> Altère votre soif et roidit votre peau,
> Et le vent furibond de la concupiscence
> Fait claquer votre chair ainsi qu'un vieux drapeau.
> [Never a freshening ray will shine within your caves;
> Through cracks along the wall will filter deadly mists
> That cast a lantern's glow of pale and dismal flame
> And penetrate your bodies with perfumes of death.
> The harsh sterility of all your acts of lust
> Will bring a dreadful thirst and stiffen out your skin,
> And your concupiscence become a furious wind
> To snap your feeble flesh like an old, weathered flag.]

> (1993 [1857: 244–45])

The bodies of these women are swept clean as far as the poet's conscience and morality are concerned, although, as Baudelaire censors his own artistic output, his cleansing of the miasma from the bodies of the city's women seems half-hearted or, more poignantly, more ironically cynical in its shallowness (albeit with an element of weariness). In this sense, if one extends the allegories of Baudelaire's poem to suggest that in sanitizing the prostitutes and their penchant for lesbian intimacy in the new world order of Haussmann, the inspiration and its manifestation that mark the art of the *flâneur* are rendered flaccid, the work cauterized. Socially designated deviance, and the dark, threatening environments that ensure it, must resist hegemonic borders, and the body of the woman-as-city must remain static – as must the city as physical entity – in order for poetry to be composed.

NOTES

1. Baudelaire dedicates 'Le Cygne' to Victor Hugo, who, Benjamin observes, was 'one of the few men whose work, it seemed to Baudelaire, produced a new antiquity' (2006: 112). Benjamin's insight into the difference between the two artists' understanding of pre-Second Empire Paris, Haussmann's Paris, and the ideal of antiquity is informed by the words of Charles Péguy, which, he suggests 'reveal where the difference between Hugo's and Baudelaire's conceptions of classical antiquity lies' (2006: 112). Benjamin quotes Péguy accordingly: 'One thing is certain: when Hugo saw a beggar by the road, he saw him the way he is, really saw him the way he really is, […] saw him, the ancient beggar, the ancient supplicant, on the ancient road. When he saw the marble inlay of one of our fireplaces or the cemented bricks on one of our modern fireplaces, he saw them as what they are – namely, the stones from the hearth, the stones from the ancient hearth. When he saw the door of a house and the threshold, which is usually a squared stone, he recognized in this squared stone the antique line, the line of the sacred threshold that it is' (2006: 112–13).

2. See Willis (2019) on concepts of 'temporal turbulence'.

3. An expanded edition with the extended title was published in 1550: *Les Antiquitez, histoires, croniques et singularitez de la grande & excellente cité de Paris, ville capitale & chef du Royaume de France* (*The Antiquities, Histories, Chronicles, and Singularities of the Great and Excellent City of Paris, Capital City and Head of the Kingdom of France*).

4. Baudelaire excelled in Latin and also received awards in Classical Greek from the Lycée Louis-le-Grand (Henry 1974: 87n1).

5. See also, Virgil *Eclogues* 6.62–63.

6. This looking up towards the ether recalls the divine, essential side of verse poetry. The French term *un vers*, which is homonymous and homophonous with the preposition *vers* (which means 'towards') repeated by Baudelaire in this verse, and in both instances prominently, at the head of the line, can refer to a poem or part of a poem. Its use here is also reflexive: it is an act of looking that is aware of its poetic value and an act of looking as poetry. The repetition of the word, of course, both draws attention and echoes its double meaning.

7. The exception is Poems 1; Fragments including 16, 31 and 58 are extensive.

8. Most likely, Delacroix's sketch for *The Death of Sardanopal* (*La Mort de Sardanapale*) of 1827. On the poem and a discussion of the poet-as-prostitute, see Sanyal (2006: 105–12).

9. The text of the collection known as the *Heroides* was present in France from the Early Modern European age, and was read for both pleasure and, in the schoolroom, as a Latin text.

10. Possibly a lesbian brothel, which operated in the city and usually catered for 'society' ladies.

11. Phryne was a popular subject for artists, particularly French artists, both before and after Gérôme's masterpiece; see, for example, *Phryne* by Gustave Boulanger (1850); *Phryne* by Claude-Marie Ferrier and Hugh Owen (1851); and Élias Robert's *Phryne* on the North facade of the Louvre's Cour Carrée (1855).

12. See Athenaeus, *Deipnosophistae* (*Scholars at Dinner*) 13.590. Roman miscellanist Pliny records, in *Naturalis Historia* (*Natural History*) 36.20, that a man became so enamoured with one of Praxiteles's versions of the statue that he raped it, an uncanny precursor to the suggestions of necrophilia in 'Une martyre'.
13. See Andreadis (2014: 19) for a survey of the extensive tradition of French rewritings of Sappho as a heterosexual.
14. The story of Sappho the prostitute began sometime during the Hellenistic age and was first linked to a writer by the name of Nymphodorus/Nymphis (*fl.* third century BC). On the complicated tradition, see Thorsen (2019: 36).
15. The evocation of the prostitute-lesbian was linked to a 'police ruling against apartment sharing by streetwalkers in 1843' (Choquette 2001: 150). (I have cited the English translation of the second edition of Parent-Duchâtelet, which lists the author as M. Parent Duchatelet and is without a publisher; the edition is listed as 'Sold by T. Burgess, 28 Coventry Street, Haymarket'.)
16. See also, Edgar Degas, *Two Women (Scene in a Brothel)*, c. 1879–80 or 1876–77.
17. Parent-Duchâtelet (1840: 27).
18. Céleste Mogador also wrote plays. Her one piece of fiction, the novel *La Sapho* (1858), describes the lives and hardships of the *demi-mondaines* in Paris. Her heroine, Marie Laurent, is seduced but later abandoned, and after her unsuccessful suicide attempt, she reinvents herself as La Sapho in the *demi-monde* scene of London and seeks her revenge.
19. 'The last class to be noticed does not differ very essentially from the preceding one and is termed "pierreuses", from their being generally found in remote, obscure, and out-of-the-way places, and especially in the midst of blocks of stone, building materials, &c., where they conceal their disgusting ugliness, and practise, in obscurity, every vice that it is possible to imagine' (Parent-Duchâtelet 1840: 36).
20. From gambling dens, assigned spaces in flophouses, impressive lupanars and even family homes.
21. As McMillan notes: 'Parent-Duchâtelet's study lent the weight of scientific opinion to the regulatory controls imposed on prostitution by the French state. In Paris, control was in the hands of the Prefect of Police, with whom all prostitutes were obliged to enrol: in the provinces, the municipal authorities carried on the necessary supervision. Women registered as prostitutes were subjected to periodic examinations and could be detained in prison for infringements of the regulations. When treatment for venereal disease was necessary, they should be assigned to special hospitals, such as the sinister prison hospital of Saint-Lazare in Paris' (2000: 107).

REFERENCES

Andreadis, Harriette (2014), 'The Sappho tradition', in E. L. McCalum and M. Tuhkanen (eds), *The Cambridge History of Gay and Lesbian Literature*, Cambridge: Cambridge University Press, pp. 15–33.

Anonymous ([1883] 1996), *The Pretty Women of Paris*, London: Wordsworth Classics.

Baudelaire, Charles ([1869] 1970), *Paris Spleen 1869* (trans. L. Varèse), New York: New Directions.

Baudelaire, Charles (1973), *Baudelaire: Œuvres complètes*, vol. 1 (ed. C. Pichois), Paris: Gallimard.

Baudelaire, Charles ([1857] 1993; 1857), *The Flowers of Evil* (trans. J. McGowan), Oxford: Oxford University Press.

Baudelaire, Charles ([1897] 2014), *Journaux Intimes*, Paris: Arvensa Editions.

Benjamin, Walter, (2006a), 'Paris, Capital of the Nineteenth Century' ('Paris, die Hauptstadt des XIX') (trans. H. Eiland), in M. W. Jennings (ed.), *The Writer of Modern Life: Essays on Charles Baudelaire*, Cambridge, Massachusetts: Harvard University Press, pp. 30–45.

Benjamin, Walter (2006b), 'The Paris of the Second Empire in Baudelaire' ('Das Paris des Second Empire bei Baudelaire') (trans. H. Zohn), in M. W. Jennings (ed.), *The Writer of Modern Life: Essays on Charles Baudelaire*, Cambridge, MA: Harvard University Press, pp. 46–133.

Bettini, Maurizio (1997), 'Ghosts of exile: Doubles and Nostalgia in Vergil's *parva Troia (Aeneid* 3.294ff.)', *Classical Antiquity*, 16, pp. 8–33.

Boym, Svetlana (2007), 'Nostalgia and its discontents', *The Hedgehog Review*, 9: 2, pp. 7–19.

Busson, Didier (2003), *Paris, A Roman City*, Paris: Monum Editions du Patrimoine.

Choquette, Leslie (2001), 'Homosexuals in the city: Representations of Lesbian and Gay space in nineteenth-century Paris', *Journal of Homosexuality*, 41: 3–4, pp. 149–67.

Clayson, Hollis (2003), *Painted Love: Prostitution in French Art of the Impressionist Era*, New York: Getty Publications.

Deschanel, Emile (1847), 'Etudes sur l'antiquité. Sappho et Les Lesbiennes', *Revue des Deux Mondes*, 73, pp. 336–57.

Ferguson, Priscilla Parkhurst (1994), *Paris as Revolution: Writing the Nineteenth-Century City*, Berkeley: University of California Press.

Gandy, Matthew (1999), 'The Paris sewers and the rationalization of urban space', *Transactions of the Institute of British Geographers*, 24: 1, pp. 23–44.

Grosz, Elizabeth (1995), *Space, Time, and Perversion: Essays on the Politics of Bodies*, London: Routledge.

Hampton, Timothy (1982), 'Virgil, Baudelaire and Mallarmé at the sign of the swan: Poetic translation and historical allegory', *Romanic Review*, 73: 4, pp. 438–45.

Hanssen, B. (ed.) (2006), *Walter Benjamin and the Arcades Project*, London: Continuum.

Henry, Freeman G (1974), 'Baudelaire: The Plato controversy', *Romance Notes*, 16.1: 87–90.

Hodges, Elizabeth (2008), 'Representing place in Corrozet's *Antiquitez de Paris*', *French Studies*, 62: 2, pp. 135–49.

Hooper, Barbara (1998), 'The poem of male desires: Female bodies, modernity, and "Paris", capital of the nineteenth century', in L. Sandercock (ed.), *Making the Invisible Visible: A Multicultural Planning History*, Berkeley: University of California Press, pp. 227–54.

Humphreys, Karen (2006), 'French literature', in M. H. Ditmore (ed.), *Encyclopedia of Prostitution and Sex Work*, Vols. 1 & 2, Connecticut: Greenwood Press, pp. 177–81.

Huyssen, Andreas. (2006). 'Nostalgia for ruins', *Grey Room*, 23, pp. 6–21.

McMillan, James (2000), *France and Women 1789–1914: Gender, Society and Politics*, London: Routledge.

Nelson, Lowry (1961), 'Baudelaire and virgil: A reading of "Le Cygne"', *Comparative Literature*, 13: 4, pp. 332–45.

Parent-Duchâtelet, Alexandre (1840), *Prostitution in the City of Paris from the French of M. Parent Duchatelet*. 2nd ed. https://books.google.com.au/books?id=XiJeAAAAcAAJ&printsec=frontcover&source=gbsgesummaryr&cad=0#v=onepage&q&f=false. Accessed 27 January 2021.

Ryan, Judith (1993), 'More seductive than Phryne: Baudelaire, Gérôme, Rilke, and the problem of autonomous art', *Proceedings of the Modern Language Association of America*, 108: 5, pp. 1128–41.

Sanyal, Debarati (2006), *The Violence of Modernity: Baudelaire, Irony, and the Politics of Form*, Baltimore: Johns Hopkins University Press.

Schlossman, Beryl (2005), 'Baudelaire's place in literary and cultural history', in R. Lloyd (ed.), *The Cambridge Companion to Baudelaire*, Cambridge: Cambridge University Press, pp. 175–85.

Silk, Michael, Ingo Gildenhard, and Rosemary Barrow (2017), *The Classical Tradition: Art, Literature, Thought*, London: John Wiley & Sons.

Thorsen, Thea S. (2019), 'Sappho: Transparency and obstruction', in T. S. Thorsen and S. Harrison (eds), *Roman Receptions of Sappho*, Oxford: Oxford University Press, pp. 27–43.

Verdicchio, Massimo (2015), 'Rereading Baudelaire's "Le Cygne"', *Modern Language Notes*, 130: 4, pp. 879–97.

Willis, Ika (2019), 'Temporal turbulence: Reception studies(') now', in M. Johnson (ed.), *Antipodean Antiquities: Classical Reception Down Under*, London: Bloomsbury, pp. 211–21.

3

Sappho in the Salons

Marguerite Johnson

Sappho is a figment of the modern imagination. During her recovery by early modern scholars, she was completely a French fantasy. And throughout the entire span of her modern existence, she has remained largely a projection of the French imagination.
(DeJean 1989: 1)

This chapter discusses two major figures of the Parisian Left Bank in the twentieth century: Natalie Clifford Barney and Gertrude Stein. It focuses on the homes of both women and the significance of them for the creation of sexual and artistic freedom. It underlines the stories of Barney and Stein with that of Sappho and employs the figure of the Greek poet as both lesbian icon and source of artistic inspiration. In this sense, it seeks to achieve somewhat of a blending or merging of Sappho – lesbian and poet – with Barney and Stein – lesbians and poets. As Mytilene is a source of personal and creative nourishment for Sappho, this chapter also traces the Parisian Left Bank as providing the same nurturing environment for the ex-patriot Americans. It is, in many ways, a response to my chapter on Baudelaire and Sappho (Chapter 2 above). Naturally, therefore, memory and nostalgia also feature here, but in very different ways. While Baudelaire invoked the ancient poets as a means of mentally, emotionally and creatively rescuing Paris from rejuvenation (at least in his own mind, or soul), Barney sought to bring Mytilene into her Parisian homes, reflective of some form of romantic sorcery on her part to materialize a nostalgic but false memory of a lesbian utopia on a dreamy Greek island. Stein would have none of this nonsense. Nevertheless, she is, whether she would ever admit it or not, inadvertently embracing a Sapphic enclave of her own. With Sappho as a presence throughout this chapter, emerging consistently in Barney's artistic endeavours, the analysis that follows also explores the female creative process, and some of its outputs in the case of Barney and Stein, to flesh out a picture of lesbian writing on the Left Bank.

Rescuing Baudelaire's Sappho

While Sappho as poet and as both lesbian and prostitute came to symbolize the problematic, contradictory 'woman' of Paris in a Baudelairean context, she came to a new maturation in the lesbian salons of twentieth-century Paris. What Baudelaire saw as a figure worthy of both inspiration and a strange distrust, combined with an awkward voyeuristic admiration, was remoulded and re-loved by the lesbians living in the gay diaspora on the Left Bank from around the turn of the twentieth century to approximately the 1940s.[1] Particularly for homosexuals, Paris at the turn of the twentieth century provided a space for self-expression, security and communal support. For expatriates who identified as being outside sexual and social norms, it was a city in a country where homosexuality was not a crime punishable by incarceration.[2]

Rather than walking and observing, expressing and rebelling, the lesbians of the Left Bank had no creative use for the ways of the *flâneur*. Instead, they stayed put, occupying the artistic and liberating domesticity of the studio or salon.[3] A stroll in the evenings would suffice. Paris at the dawn of the twentieth century offered freedom to 'stay-at-home' lesbians – a freedom both nurtured and protected by the landscape they inhabited and in turn inscribed in the terrain of 'Paris *rive gauche*, an undulating and uneven landscape famous for the sharp turns of its narrow, winding streets' (Benstock 1986: ix). The urban landscape as sanctuary was in marked contrast to Baudelaire's (and Benjamin's) decrying of the obscenity of the modern city of Paris, and their railing against the inequity and sheer ugliness of its industrialization and capitalism.

From 25, rue de Bois de Boulogne to 20, rue Jacob

20, rue Jacob, located in the Latin Quarter of the 6th arrondissement was the home of American feminist, novelist, poet and playwright, Natalie Clifford Barney (1876–1972).[4] From 1909 to the late-1960s, Barney hosted a salon as weekly gatherings of bohemians gravitated to her seventeenth-century pavilion to discuss literature, music and art. Barney, dubbed 'The Amazon of Letters',[5] was an enthusiastic and unabashed lover of women. She was also an admirer of Sappho, not only immersing herself in the poet's work but also reinterpreting it in plays such as *Équivoque* (*Ambiguity*).[6] Indeed, it was this play – a daring revisioning of Sappho's (pseudo)biography – that landed Barney on the Left Bank, owing to the objections of the landlord of her previous residence, 25, rue de Bois de Boulogne, in the Parisian suburb of Neuilly-sur-Seine. Performed in the garden of her home in Neuilly, *Équivoque* was apparently too close to 'nature' for her landlord's liking and it seems that their differing views on art resulted in Barney cancelling her lease (see Rodriguez 2002: 172), or being evicted (Dorf 2019: 60).[7] But, in terms of French musical (and literary) history, Barney was merely following a well-travelled path when it came to *Équivoque*, her production being one of many operatic and choreographic interpretations of Sappho's life, or her poetry, or both, produced in Paris over the centuries (see Dorf 2009).

Barney's liking for outdoor performances of Sapphic inspiration and subject matter reflected her interest in establishing an all-female poetry school along the lines of her (mistaken) understanding of Sappho as some type of Archaic Greek schoolmistress. In 1904, she had travelled to Lesbos with Renée Vivien (1877–1909), an expatriate from England (who occasionally made the Left Bank her home).[8] So entranced were the women, they were determined to, at least, bring Lesbos to France, and thus Mytilene to Paris.[9] And so they did. And to facilitate the Mytilene-to-Paris transformation, Barney worked with and within the milieu of Paris to entrench a new lesbian identity – Sapphism – both materially and literarily. To expand further, the appropriation of a specific urban space – be it in Neuilly or the Left Bank (and primarily 20, rue Jacob) – enabled Mytilene to (re)materialize and the cultural activities of its inhabitants brought Sappho to Paris metaphorically, culturally and sexually. The imagined space became real. As Joanne Winning writes, 'As has been clear since the biographical surveys of the women involved in both Anglo-American modernism and the Avant-Garde, there is a complex nexus between cultural production, lesbian sexuality, and the experience of the modern metropolis' (2006: 20).

Physical space is important to the reimagining and reanimation of Sappho at 25, rue de Bois de Boulogne and 20, rue Jacob. Sheila Crane, in her study of the houses and gardens of Barney and Elsie de Wolfe (the latter's residence, the Villa Trianon, was located in Versailles), describes 20, rue Jacob as follows:

> In the midst of the city, at 20, rue Jacob, Barney discovered a protected refuge that would [...] allow her to insert herself more directly into the contemporary literary world. Barney's dwelling stood at the far end of a cobblestone courtyard behind the four-story apartment building that fronted the street. This seventeenth-century *pavilion* was a two-story, semi-detached residence, with its own private gardens. According to Barney, the miniature Greek temple, known as the Temple de l'Amitié (Temple of Friendship), that stood in the rear garden made her particularly interested in moving there.
>
> (2007: 214)[10]

At 25, rue de Bois de Boulogne and 20, rue Jacob, Barney could realize her fantasies surrounded by a coterie of like-minded artists, writers, poets, dancers, musicians and actors. As Samuel Dorf writes, 'Barney created a space (a garden in Neuilly or at 20 rue Jacob) and a time outside of the rhythms of her nonqueer neighbors and peers, a place where one could engage in queer historical play' (2019: 65). These interpretations around Barney's creation of a new space mark her agenda as different to that of, for example, Baudelaire in his nostalgic yearning for the pre-Haussmann Paris. There is no real sense of an immediate (urban) 'haunting' as Ross Chambers (1999: 217) has defined it, meaning that as an expatriate in a queer diaspora, Barney is in a sense liberated from witnessing a Paris that is simultaneously both past and present. Barney's literary, cultural and sexual agenda sets her on a more positive trajectory of nostalgia as she embraces the city as a *tabula rasa* on which to inscribe a new Lesbos. Here, cityscape and the creation of a new home also involve the familial – the people one places in one's home – as described by Dorf: 'In lieu of a family tree of queer mothers and fathers, they sought historical sources; to commune with them, they performed them, re-enacting Greek poetry, music, dance, and drama' (2019: 55).

Équivoque, as noted above, was performed in Barney's garden in Neuilly on 25 June 1906 (although Sappho-inspired productions began around 1900). Historical photographs that record the event in the grounds at Neuilly show an extensive garden with well-established trees; an expansive, levelled lawn and ample space for simple Grecian props, such as statuary.[11] While Dorf (2019) has discussed in detail the transitory or ephemeral nature of the production, and the resultant challenges this poses to scholars,[12] the existence of a published version of the play has proved useful to literary historians. A version of *Équivoque* was included in the 1910 publication by Barney, *Actes et entr'actes*,[13] and the script reveals a plot that marks a strong rebuttal to the heterosexual Sappho of the previous century, including Baudelaire's tragic heroine in 'Lesbos'.[14] Rejecting the standard apocryphal tale that insists on a leaping Sappho, a heartbroken and beaten-down woman – a devastated heterosexual who jumps off the Leucadian cliff because of her unrequited love for the ferryman, Phaon – Barney's Sappho is enamoured with Phaon's bride and her ex-student, Timas.[15] Sappho still leaps, but at least she leaps for the right sex. Barney also extended her interest in producing a more authentic treatment of, and interaction with, Sappho – not only by returning her to a more historically accurate identity (Sappho's extant work demonstrates her female-centric vision) – but also by incorporating Sappho's own words into the play (and then diligently reproducing the corresponding fragments in an accompanying appendix [1910: 82–83]).[16]

The Sappho as manifest in works such as *Équivoque* shows both a debt to and a moving away from Baudelaire's Sappho, which prompts a consideration of the extent to which Barney's work could be said to be aligned to, or sympathetic with, Baudelaire's Sappho project. Of course, this is a discussion that has been addressed by several scholars; yet, it is worthwhile revisiting, albeit briefly, in order to consider the two Parisian poets' take on Parisian Sappho. Despite the significant presence of what one may describe as the deeply unsettling elements around sexual identity, most expressly lesbianism, in Baudelaire's Lesbos triptych in 'Les Fleurs du mal [The Flowers of Evil]' from *Les Fleurs du mal*, Barney was enamoured of the poet and these particular poems. Several anecdotes attest to Barney's love of Baudelaire, such as the one recorded by Chelsea Ray:

> The importance of the particular poem 'Delphine and Hippolyta' to Barney is under-scored by the fact that she gave her friend Elisabeth de Gramont embroidered curtains with the following verse taken from it: 'Let our closed curtains, then, remove us from the world'.
>
> (2005: 34)[17]

This anecdote speaks to Barney's appreciation that Baudelaire, in her opinion at least, captured the rapturous intimacy of, in this instance, female-to-female sensuality. Modern feminists[18] may be much harsher on the poet for his apparent insistence on the morbidity of female-to-female eroticism, underscored as it is by violence, masochism and what may well have been a genuine repellence at the body – the very essence – of woman (although in the context of his oeuvre, the 'Les Fleurs du mal' sequence is hardly extraordinary). Like Barney, Renée Vivien, once her lover, and regarded by some (and, suggestively at times, by Barney herself) as her most significant intimate companion, aligned herself with Baudelaire, finding solace and also a strangely pleasurable torment in his poetry. Indeed, Vivien's fascination with Baudelaire has gone on to become part of her legend – exemplified by the following vignette: 'She has been called everything from a feminist to a masochist, an anorexic, an alcoholic, a virgin, a devoted Roman Catholic, a pagan, a mystic, a Sappho reincarnated, Baudelaire's daughter, a symbolist, and a romantic' (Engelking 1992: 128).[19]

There are discernible Baudelairean traces in the evocation of Sappho in *Équivoque*; for example, when Sappho is about to commit suicide as a result of Timas's betrayal, she threatens to haunt the young woman on her wedding night:

> Je serai, cette nuit, l'hôte qu'on craint de voir. (1910: 66)
> [I will be, that night, the guest that you are afraid of seeing.] (trans. DeJean 1989: 285n95)

> J'occuperai ma place invisible à la table. (1910: 66)
> [I will occupy my place, invisible, at the table.] (trans. DeJean 1989: 285n95; edits by Johnson)

> Comme autrefois c'est moi qui viendrai vers ta couche,

Ce sera son baiser, mais ce sera ma bouche.
Tu me désireras à travers son désir
Et tu redonneras mon nom à ton plaisir. (Barney 1910: 67)
[Like before, I will come to your bed,
It will be his kiss, but it will be my mouth.
You will desire me through his desire
And once again you will give my name to your pleasure.] (trans. DeJean 1989: 285n95)

Far from any lines extant from the Sapphic corpus, these excerpts not only reflect the Baudelairean legacy, recalling lines 238–39 of 'Femmes damnées: Delphine et Hippolyte [Condemned Women: Delphine and Hippolyta]' (see Johnson in this volume), but also intimate familiarity with other Classical poets, particularly the Latin poet Propertius (*c.50-c.15* BCE), whose morbidity – expressed through his obsession with sex and death – is evident most powerfully in *Elegy* 4.7.93–94, in which the ghost of Propertius's lover, Cynthia, chastises him from beyond the grave:

nunc te possideant aliae: mox sola tenebo:
mecum eris, et mixtis ossibus ossa teram.
[Now, let others have you: soon I alone will hold you:
with me you will be, and I will grind bones mixed with bones.] (trans. Johnson)

While Propertius is not castigated for infidelity, but rather for inept funeral rites for his beloved, the macabre image resonates with the lines from *Équivoque*. Other intertextual allusions are to Sappho herself, and as noted above, Barney directs readers to the specific fragments in an appendix to the published version.[20] As she explains,

Les chiffres entre parenthèses se réfèrent aux fragments de Sappho utilisés et qui se trouvent à la fin de pièce. (Barney 1910: 57)
[The numbers [footnotes] correspond to Sappho's fragments that have been used here and that can be found at the end of the play.] (trans. Dilts 2019: 98)

An example of both the presentation of Sappho and the use of an original fragment is evident in the following excerpt:

Eranna: Leurs regards nuptiaux sauront t'humilier
Si tu restes […]

Sappho: Je reste […]

Gorgo: Et tu crois oublier!
Songeant au proche hymen, ton front penché se trouble.

Sappho: Je ne sais que choisir car ma pensée est double. (Barney 1910: 57)
[Eranna: Their nuptial gazes will humiliate you
If you stay […]

Sappho: I'm staying[…]

Gorgo: And you believe you can forget!
Thinking of the marriage so imminent, your inclined face is troubled.

Sappho: I do not know what to choose because my mind is double.] (trans. Dilts 2019: 98)

The last line spoken by Sappho in this excerpt is a reference to *fragment 51* in Barney's notes, which print the Greek:

οὐκ οἶδ᾽ ὅττι θέω· δύο μοι τά νοήματα (1910: 82)
[I know not what to do; I am in two minds] (trans. Johnson)

The translation in French – 'Je ne sais que choisir car; ma pensée est double' – is by Renée Vivien (the Greek fragments in the appendix are without a translation), on which Dilts comments: 'By citing Vivien's translation, Barney leads her audience to Vivien as well as to Sappho' (2019: 99). The other element of relative authenticity is Barney's inclusion of the name 'Gorgo' – a figure mentioned in Sappho's fragments (see, for example: *testimony* 20; fragment 29; *fragment* 144; *fragment* 155 in D. A. Campbell 1990). And as for 'Eranna', the source for the name is, again, Vivien's 1903 edition of Sappho (85), which is a translation of *fragment 91* that includes the name Ἰραυα (Irana) – hence Vivien's Eranna, hence Barney's Eranna.[21]

Vivien translated fifty pieces from the Sappho corpus, which were published in the volume, *Sapho: Traduction nouvelle avec le texte grec* (*Sapho: New Translation with the Greek Text*) in 1903. While the majority of translations and biographies of Sappho had been undertaken by men, Vivien and Barney became two of the best-known female translators and interpreters of the twentieth century. Vivien's translations are not, however, without their critics. Scholars such as Joan DeJean have criticized Vivien's translations for their infidelities, the merging of the voice of the original poet with her translator, and the interventions into the fragments to make them 'into full-fledged poems' (1989: 250).[22] Critics aside, both women dedicated themselves to extensive instruction in Greek and undertook painstaking translations of Sappho's difficult Aeolic dialect into French. This was part of an agenda underscored by the premise that to reanimate an authentic Sappho entailed not only experiencing her place of birth but also experiencing her poems in their original language. Of course, this (along with Barney's Sapphic performances) is characterized in part by what Eric Hobsbawm defines as an 'invented tradition' (1983: 1), namely, revitalizing a historical person and/or epoch but with selective 'truths' to accommodate a new identity (see also Jay 1988: 71).[23]

While Barney and, more emphatically, Vivien were inspired by the decadence of Baudelairean aesthetics with its overtone of the Symbolist *danse macabre* that extended to the image of the lesbian, Barney, especially, brought *jouissance* to the reception of Sappho in several significant ways. One of the most important ways was through the outdoor performances of various revisionings of Sappho's work (as mentioned above). This entailed the two women travelling from Paris to Mytilene and then back to Paris, in something akin to a female version of the hero's journey, in order to present an authentic, female-centred Sappho to twentieth-century Paris. While this was ostensibly a physical journey, both women also embarked on a metaphorical and spiritual one, resulting in their 'bringing Sappho back' to Paris on their return voyage. In this sense, they banished Baudelaire's golem-like Sappho and replaced his shapeless mass with a poet drenched in light, emanating warmth and celebrating woman's love for woman.

27, rue de Fleurus to 5, rue Christine

As Amy D. Wells observes (2017: 355), the move from 25, rue de Bois de Boulogne to 20, rue Jacob also saw a move from the focus on intimate theatre, played out at Barney's Neuilly address, to a literary salon. Barney's famous garden and its equally famous Temple de l'Amitié[24] were major attractions at her Left Bank pavilion, along with the guests and the conversation topics. She continues:

> The *Académie de femmes* lectures began in 1927, and this format dedicated each Friday afternoon to a specific woman writer, with honorees including Djuna Barnes and Gertrude Stein. It is no accident that the lecture series is called the *Académie de femmes* – it is a direct spoof on the *Académie française*, which despite its inception in 1635, did not admit women amongst its ranks until 1980.[25]

Gertrude Stein's friendship with Barney grew out of shared intellectual pursuits, sexual identity and, naturally, urban geography (with perhaps a touch of the *flâneur*), as Barney records (1992: 166 [1963]): [26]

> Our Walks
>
> Often in the evening we would walk together; greeted at the door of 5 rue Christine by Gertrude's staunch presence, the pleasant touch of hand, the well-rounded voice always ready to chuckle. Our talks and walks led us far from war paths. For generally having no axe to grind nor anyone to execute it with, we felt detached and free to wander in our quiet old quarter where, while exercising her poodle, 'Basket', we naturally fell into thought and step.

Barney's vignette of the walks, and their friendship, references Stein's second home on the Left Bank, 5, rue Christine (1938–44). Prior to that location, Stein and Alice B. Toklas had lived at 27, rue de Fleurus (Toklas moving into the space that Stein had previously shared with her brother, in 1910).

The Paris that freed Barney also freed Stein but as far as Sappho was concerned, Stein was less interested in partaking in any encomium of the sort practised by her neighbour. Stein wanted to demonstrate her own genius and to do so through the creation of literature rather than take inspiration from Sappho, whom she never mentions by name in her work. However, Sappho's desires for women may be said to be echoed in some of Stein's erotic writing. This may be extended to a consideration of Stein as a writer more akin to the ancient conceit of *mascula Sappho* than to Sappho per se.

First coined by the Latin poet, Horace (65–68 BCE) in *Epistles* 1.19.28, *mascula Sappho* is explained by Porphyrio (*c*.234–*c*.305 CE):

> 'mascula' autem 'Saffo', vel quia in poetico studio est <incluta >, in quo saepius viri, vel quia tribas diffamatur fuisse.
> ['Masculine Sappho', either because she is <famous> for achievement in poetry, in which men are usually, or because she is maligned as having been a tribad.]
> (Testimony 17; Campbell 1990: 18; trans. Johnson)

The conceit is enough to irritate modern feminists, yet it makes an interesting companion to Adele's statement in Stein's female-queer novel, *Q.E.D.*: 'I always did thank God I wasn't born a woman' (1903, 1971: 58). Of course, there are limits to an author's identification with a character, but it remains tempting to associate the often-quoted sentence to Stein's refusal to identify with any gender. As Lisa Ruddick reminds us, 'Stein tends to think of herself as variously male and female; in her erotic relationship with Alice Toklas, for example, she pictures herself alternatively as "sister" and "husband", and even as "king"' (1990: 53). While her literary characters and the character of Stein herself demonstrate a gender fluidity, when it came to Stein's thinking around genius, she privileged men.

In the case of Barney's oeuvre, Wells uses the term 'geo-*parler femme*' to denote a literary strategy employed – not only by Barney but also by 'Left Bank women writers' – 'to transform "space" into "place" – "places" adapted to women and their sexual and artistic needs' (2017: 349). Stein's *Tender Buttons* (1914, 1997) may also be analyzed within the context of Wells's 'geo-*parler femme*' in terms of both the house and the space it occupied on 5, rue Christine. At evening, walking with Barney, Stein walks a lesbian path in the lesbian enclave within the Left Bank. Their respective homes are not only salons but also homes: 20, rue Jacob was characterized by chocolate cake as much as literature, and 5, rue Christine by Toklas's hash cookies as much as Modernism. In this way, *Tender Buttons* is as much about 'A New Cup and Saucer' (11) and 'A Petticoat' (13); 'Roast Beef' (20–25), 'Mutton' (25–26), 'Breakfast' (26–28), 'Sugar' (28–29) and 'Cranberries' (29); or 'Rooms' (41–52) as it is about experimental-abstraction-poetry. It is as much a homage to Toklas and the interiority and domesticity of 5, rue Christine – as much a product of the diaspora of the Left Bank that cultivates 'geo-*parler femme*' – as it is to Stein's own experimental genius.

As Sappho composed poetry at Mytilene, on an island that became synonymous with her name, sufficiently engaged in female-centredness to define her poetry as 'geo-*parler femme*' in content, Stein's *Tender Buttons* reflects the creative potentiality of the Left Bank that enabled her to write. Taking this idea further and in conclusion to this chapter, I examine some examples from *Tender Buttons* as sapphic, if not necessarily Sapphic, in their concerns, and then consider the leftovers of Sappho's books of lyrics as a possible source of both interest to and influence for the form that Stein adopted for her own book. This last point is perhaps better interpreted as an analytical strategy on my part, rather than as a consciously literary one on Stein's.

To the contemporary feminist, the concept of feminine spaces, interests and duties has become a thing of the past, and certainly not anything to valorize. Sappho's concern with female rites, flowers, garlands, missed friends, soft cushions and the like, as with the importance Stein places on 'A New Cup and Saucer' (11), 'Roast Beef,' (20–25) and 'Rooms' (41–52), does not necessarily sit well with modern feminism and gender politics. However, within the male-dominated social structures in which both women lived and created, one may argue that the poetic embrace of the things of (traditional) femininity functions as an act of artistic (and gendered) rebellion in their work, thereby rendering it not only original but also subversive.

Sappho's subversiveness is powerfully conveyed in one of her most famous works, *fragment 16.1–20*:

> ο]ἴ μὲν ἰππήων στρότον οἰ δὲ πέσδων
> οἰ δὲ νάων φαῖσ' ἐπ[ὶ] γᾶν μέλαι[ν]αν
> ἔ]μμεναι κάλλιστον, ἔγω δὲ κῆν' ὄτ-
> τω τις ἔραται   4
>
> πά]γχυ δ' εὔμαρες σύνετον πόησαι
> π]άντι τ[ο]ῦτ', ἀ γὰρ πόλυ περσκέθοισα

κάλλος [ἀνθ]ρώπων Ἐλένα [τό]ν ἄνδρα
τὸν [πανάρ]ιστον   8

καλλ[ίποι]σ' ἔβα 'ς Τροΐαν πλέοι[σα
κωύδ[ὲ πα]ῖδος οὐδὲ φίλων το[κ]ήων
πά[μπαν] ἐμνάσθη, ἀλλά παράγαγ' αὔταν
]σαν   12

]αμπτον γάρ [
] . . . κούφως τ[   ]οησ[.]ν
. .]με νῦν Ἀνακτορί[ας ὀ]νέμναι-
σ' οὐ] παρεοίσας   16

τᾶ]ς κε βολλοίμαν ἔρατόν τε βᾶμα
κάμάρυχμα λάμπρον ἴδην προσώπω
ἢ τά Λύδων ἄρματα κάν ὅπλοισι
πεσδομ]άχεντας·   20

[Some believe a team of cavalry, others infantry,
and still others a fleet of ships, to be the most beautiful
thing on the dark earth, but I believe it is
whatever a person loves.   4

It is very easy to make this
clear to everyone: the one who by far
outshone all mankind in beauty,

Helen, abandoned her high-born husband   8
and sailed away to Troy with no thought whatever
for her child or beloved parents,
but led astray (by eros / Cypris?) […].
lightly […].   12

for (this)
reminded me
now of Anactoria, who is
no longer here;   16

I would prefer to gaze upon her
lovely walk and the glowing sparkle of her
face than all the chariots of the Lydians and their armies.]   20
(Campbell 1990: 66–67; trans. Johnson)

Here, the content comprises female concerns, which is communicated with an almost agonistic tone. Sappho challenges the social norms of her era by rejecting a social hierarchy that privileges military concerns over emotional ones. Hans Fränkel writes of this revolutionary affirmation: 'We do not desire what is in itself beautiful, but we find what we desire beautiful. This anticipates half of the dictum of the sophist Protagoras, according to which man is the measure of all things' (1975: 187). The homoerotic edge, evident in the poet's longing for Anactoria, is focalized through the reference to her gait (*l*.18) and her complexion (*ll*.18–19) only. In Sappho's small world, details matter. Details also matter in *Tender Buttons*, a fact highlighted in its subtitle: *Objects Food Rooms*.

Sappho's extant work is inorganically detailed – or, its detailedness is exaggerated – because of its largely fragmented condition. It most regularly comes to us as torn, ripped and shattered, with only small details remaining. Thus, we have:

]πεπλ[, τ]οὶ[ς] ὄρμοις Γόργοι
[robe(s) the necklaces Gorgo]
(*fragment* 29; Campbell 1990: 78–79; trans. Campbell)

πόδας δὲ
ποίκιλος μάσλης ἐκάλυπτε, Λύδι-
ον κάλον ἔργον
[and multi-coloured
footwear covered her feet, lovely
Lydian work.]
(*fragment* 39; Campbell 1990: 84; trans. Johnson)

. .] . θος· ἀ γάρ με γέννα[τ

σ].φᾶς ἐπ' ἀλικίας μέγ[αν
κ]όσμον, αἴ τις ἔχη φόβα⟨ι⟩ς[
.πορφύρῳ κατελιξαμέ[να πλόκῳ,   4

ἔμμεναι μάλα τοῦτο δ[ή·
ἀλλ' ἀ ξανθοτέραις ἔχη[
.ταὶς κόμαις δάϊδος προ[7

σ]τεφάνοισιν ἐπαρτία[ις
ἀνθέων ἐριθαλέων·
μ]ιτράναν δ' ἀρτίως κλ[10

ποικίλαν ἀπύ Σαρδίω[ν
. . .] . αονίας πόλ{ε}ις
[ ]ffor my mother

in her youth it was a great
ornament if someone had hair
bound with purple –

a very great ornament indeed
But for the one who has hair yellower
than a pinetorch

crowns
of blooming flowers
and just lately a headbinder

spangled from Sardis
]cities]
(*fragment* 98a; Campbell 1990: 122; trans. Carson 2002: 195)

And in Stein, fully-formed, we have poems such as:

A BLUE COAT.
A blue coat is guided guided away, guided and guided away, that
is the particular color that is used for that length and not any width
not even more than a shadow.
(1997: 9 [1914])

A PETTICOAT.
Alight white, a disgrace, an ink spot, a rosy charm.
(1997: 13 [1914])

RED ROSES.
Winning of all the blessings, a sample not a sample because
there is no worry.
(1997: 14 [1914])

The fragmented condition of most of Sappho's poems renders them Modernist arte-
facts, as the (surface) incoherence of Stein's Modernist poems renders them fragments.

Both need deciphering because they are 'polysemous', to use a term employed by Skinner (1996: 182) in relation to Sappho's poetry. The inaccessibility, interiority, domesticity and female-centricity of the work of both poets reflect what Cristanne Miller describes (in relation to Stein's use of language) as 'a medium to destabilize thought, particularly the kind of thinking associated with patriarchal logic and categorization' (2017: 28). We see this in *Tender Buttons* in both form and thought, and we see it in Sappho's *fragment* 16 in subject matter and personal philosophy.

The productions, poetry, translations and homes of Natalie Barney, Renée Vivien and Gertrude Stein are, as Marilyn B. Skinner writes in relation to Sappho's works, 'conspicuously non-phallic' (1996: 182). Writing without a penis, and writing about people and things without a penis, is to discover 'a distant but discernible women's country' (Kantsa 2002: 39).[27] But this 'woman's country' must first exist in nascent form as a physical entity: a Greek island or an urban space, for example. This physical entity, functioning as protean 'woman's country', will give rise to a space within a space: some unknowable female-centred community in Sappho's case, and a pavilion or salon in the case of Barney and Stein. And within this developed space, part real and part imagined, women's voices will emerge.

NOTES

1. Here, I am providing a timeframe based on the work of Benstock (1986).
2. Oscar Wilde sought refuge in Paris after his prison term, and Radclyffe Hall and Una Troubridge found themselves there after the publication of *The Well of Loneliness*. See Sherman (1996: 70); Choquette (1999: 122–32); also Hall, who casts Paris as a city of 'like to like' in *The Well of Loneliness* (1928; 2005: 226).
3. This is not to suggest that the women were reclusive – far from it; in fact, they were very sociable, albeit, usually, as generous hosts.
4. On the history of the pavilion as it relates to Barney, who rented it for over 50 years, see Dorf (2019: 47).
5. As per Remy de Gourmont (Salmonson 2015: 18), Barney also promoted the Amazon connection: in 1920, she published *Pensées d'une Amazone* (*Thoughts of an Amazon*). Romaine Brooks also painted Barney with the title, 'L'Amazone' in the same year.
6. *Équivoque* was published in 1910 in *Actes et entr'actes* (49–81).
7. "Why Miss Barney's Sapho Had to Move", *Dayton Journal*, 2nd ed., November 14, 1909, 13. The article states that Barney cancelled the lease.
8. On Vivien's various French locations, including her house in Nice, see Hawthorne (2017).
9. Initially, the plan was to establish a school in Mytilene, and Barney records their fervour in one of her memoires, *Souvenirs indiscrets* (1960; 1992: 45). Although never realized in Lesbos, Barney manifested the dream in the form of her literary salon. Vivien did, eventually, purchase a house at Mytilene.

10. See also Crane (2005). On the Temple of Friendship, Amy Wells-Lynn writes (2005: 98): 'After the street name and number, references to the Temple de l'Amitié are used simultaneously with the salon. [...] The temple interior or steps often hosted part of the salon activities such as readings, political protests, and plays or tableaux vivants. Though the history of the temple is not known for sure, Rodriguez reports that: "Many experts believe it was built during the First Empire, while the present owners say it is the sole survivor of half a dozen Freemason temples built in the fifth and sixth arrondissements during the nineteenth century." The unknown origins of the temple contribute to its credibility as a temple of Friendship, where literary and female sexual relationships could be cultivated. In *Aventures de l'esprit*, the Temple de l'Amitié, which is present both in words and image, symbolizes salon activities.'

11. In the published version in *Actes et entr'actes* (n.6 above), Barney has noted a list of props to be included in the garden setting: 'Mytilène. Dans un jardin, devant l'école de Poésie dont on aperçoit quelques colonnes. Deux trépieds. Un banc de pierre. A gauche, le temple de Cypris, vers lequel montent des marches. Petites statues de Cypris et d'Eros. A droite, on achève d'élever un petit autel [The setting is in Mytilene, outside of Sappho's School of Poetry; there are columns, a stone bench; a temple to Cypris (Aphrodite) is included (clearly raised, as there is reference to steps); included is one statue of Aphrodite, and one of Eros; and, finally a small altar]' (1910: 51; trans. Johnson).

12. For example, the problematic nature of establishing the music (Dorf 2019: 58).

13. See n.6 above.

14. See also Barney's 'Sonnet', which forms the Preface to *Cinq petits dialogues grecs* (1902: 10), an ode to (a personified) Lesbos that calls upon the island to take revenge on the ugliness of virtue. 'Sonnet' ends with a reference to Sappho, thus aligning her with Lesbos, which suggests Barney's familiarity with Baudelaire's poem.

15. A name from the *Greek Anthology* and a poem ascribed to Sappho, although most likely Hellenistic. Included in the edition of Sappho by Henry Thornton Wharton (1885: 135), with which Barney was extremely familiar.

16. There are sixteen Sapphic pieces included in the appendix.

17. Barney is also said to have had the same curtains in her bedroom; see Chalon (1992: 125); Crane (2005: 215).

18. And here I include myself.

19. The macabre nature of Vivien's embracing of the Baudelairean lesbian trope or identity is summarized by Elisa Glick (2009: 37): 'This view of the Sapphic *femme damnée* and the decadent tradition from which she emerges has, of course, had a major effect on the reception of Vivien's work. For example, because she sees decadence primarily as a masculinist and misogynistic movement, Lillian Faderman presents Vivien as a misguided and self-destructive follower of Baudelaire and [Pierre] Louÿs. Faderman argues that, because Vivien imbibes the decadent movement's figure of the "flower of evil", her poetry reiterates decadence's failings by privileging images of lesbian evil and exoticism.'

20. See n.16 above.

21. 'Eranna' may have been confused with or deliberately aligned to 'Erinna'. While a historical figure, a poet of the fourth century BCE, known only for one extensive fragment, the magisterial (and arguably homoerotic) *Distaff*, Erinna had often been associated with Sappho's circle – mistakenly. Among the most famous representations of the two poets is Pre-Raphaelite artist Simeon Solomon's 'Sappho and Erinna in a Garden at Mytilene' (1864). While it is impossible to gauge with certainty whether or not Barney was familiar with this painting, or other works that pair Sappho and Erinna, in the case of Solomon, his association with Algernon Charles Swinburne (himself fixated with Sappho), along with his own exploration of the subject of homosexuality, particularly Sapphism, may have brought him to her attention. The Sapphic fragment that includes the name 'Irana' (*fragment 91*) reads – ἀσαροτέρας οὐδάμα πΩἶρανα σέθεν τύχοισαν (Campbell 1990: 114) – marks the elision of πω Εἴρανα with πΩἶρανα; a literal translation reads: 'Irana, having never found you more annoying' (trans. Johnson), which Vivien (1903: 85) correctly translates as: 'Jamais je n'ai vu plus orgueilleux que toi, ô Èranna.' ('I have never seen anyone haughtier than you, oh Eranna;' trans. Rolls). Vivien also rightly notes: 'Erannà est proprement un adjectif qui signifie aimable' ('Eranna is probably an adjective that means lovely;' trans. Johnson). Irana is also named by Sappho in *fragment 135* (Campbell 1990: 151).

22. See also Jacqueline Fabre-Serris (2016: 78–103), who provides a salient discussion of the translations, but is inclined to read them as intellectual endeavours and female experimentation rather than traditional translations. For a similar approach, see Rebekkah Dilts, who considers the translations through the lens of French theorists such as Luce Irigaray, thereby privileging female subjectivity: 'For her [Irigaray's] part, the figure of Sappho, whomever she may have been, seems capable of intervening in the sexual politics of disparate historical moments' (2019: 102).

23. Evidenced, perhaps, in Vivien's augmented translations (to produce what Sappho 'would have said').

24. 'Many experts believe it was built during the First Empire, while the present owners say it is the sole survivor of half a dozen Freemason temples built in the fifth and sixth arrondissements during the nineteenth century' Suzanne Rodriguez (2002: 69).

25. For an excellent discussion of Barney's tribute to Gertrude Stein in the form of dedicating one of her 'Fridays' (salon gatherings) to her, as an expression of 'space-literature-space cycle', see Wells (2017: 356).

26. The prose portrait of Stein is dated 1954, although it was published in 1963 in *Traits et Portraits* (*Traits and Portraits*).

27. In reference to Vivien's poems 'While Landing at Mytilene' and 'Towards Lesvos'.

REFERENCES

Barney, N. C. (1902), *Cinq petits dialogues grecs (antithèses et parallèles)*, Paris: Éditions de la Plume.

Barney (1910), *Équivoque in Actes et entr'actes*, Paris: E. Sansot, 1910, pp. 49-81.

Barney, N. C. (1920), *Pensées d'une Amazone*, Paris: Émile-Paul frères.

Barney, N. C. ([1963] 1992), 'Gertrude Stein', in A. Livia (ed. and trans), *A Perilous Advantage: The Best of Natalie Clifford Barney*, Norwich, VT: New Victoria Publishers, pp. 165–76.

Benstock, Shari (1986), *Women of the Left Bank: Paris, 1900–1940*, Austin: University of Texas Press.

Chalon, Jean (1992), *Chère Natalie Barney: Portrait d'une séductrice*, Paris: Flammarion.

Chambers, Ross (1999), *Loiterature*, Lincoln and London: University of Nebraska Press.

Choquette, Leslie (1999), 'Paris-Lesbos: Lesbian social space in the modern city, 1870–1940', in B. Rothaus (ed.), *Proceedings of the Western Society for French History 26*, Denver: University of Colorado Press, pp. 122–32.

Crane, Sheila (2005), 'Mapping the Amazon's salon: Symbolic landscapes and topographies of identity in Natalie Clifford Barney's literary salon', in J. Carubia, L. Dowler and B. Szczygiel (eds), *Gender and Landscape: Renegotiating the Moral Landscape*, London: Routledge, pp. 145–61.

Crane, Sheila (2007), 'Elsie de Wolfe, Natalie Clifford Barney and the Lure of Versailles: Picturesque Spectres and Conservative Aesthetics of Female Homoeroticism', in R. Günther and W. Michallat (eds), *Lesbian Inscriptions in Francophone Society and Culture*, Vol. 30, Durham Modern Languages, pp. 205–36.

DeJean, Joan (1989), *Fictions of Sappho, 1546–1937*, Chicago and London: The University of Chicago Press.

Dilts, Rebekkah (2019), '(Un)veiling Sappho: Renée Vivien and Natalie Clifford Barney's radical translation projects', *Refract: An Open Access Visual Studies Journal*, 2: 1, pp. 79–110.

Dorf, Samuel N. (2009), 'Seeing Sappho in Paris: Operatic and choreographic adaptations of Sapphic Lives and Myths', *Music in Art*, XXXIV: 1–2, pp. 291–310.

Dorf (2019), *Performing Antiquity*, Oxford: Oxford University Press.

Engelking, Tama Lea (1992), 'Reneé Vivien's Sapphic Legacy: Remembering the "House of Muses"', *Atlantis*, 18: 1–2, pp. 125–41.

Fabre-Serris, Jacqueline (2016), 'Anne Dacier (1681), Renée Vivien (1903): Or What does it mean for a woman to translate Sappho?', in R. Wyles and E. Hall (eds), *Women Classical Scholars: Unsealing the Fountain from the Renaissance to Jacqueline de Romilly*, Oxford: Oxford University Press, pp. 78–103.

Fränkel, Hans Hermann (1975), *Early Greek Poetry and Philosophy* (trans. M. Hadas), Oxford: Oxford University Press.

Glick, Elisa (2009), *Materializing Queer Desire: Oscar Wilde to Andy Warhol*, Albany, NY: State University of New York Press.

Hall, Radclyffe ([1928] 2005), *The Well of Loneliness*, Hertfordshire: Wordsworth Classics.

Hawthorne, Melanie (2017), 'Two nice girls: The psychogeography of Renée Vivien and Romaine Brooks', *Dix-Neuf*, 21: 1, pp. 69–92.

Hobsbawm, Eric, and O. Terence (1983) 'Ranger', *The invention of tradition*, Cambridge: Cambridge University Press.

Jay, Karla (1988), *The Amazon and the Page: Natalie Clifford Barney and Renée Vivien*, Indianapolis: Indiana University Press.

Kantsa, Venetia (2002), '"Certain places have different energy": Spatial transformations in Eresos, Lesvos', *GLQ: A Journal of Lesbian and Gay Studies*, 8: 1, pp. 35–55.

Miller, Cristanne (2017), '(Women writing) The modernist line', *Transatlantica. Revue d'études américaines. American Studies Journal*, 1. https://journals.openedition.org/transatlantica/8065. Accessed 27 January 2021.

Rodriguez, Suzanne (2002), *Wild Heart: A Life: Natalie Clifford Barney and the Decadence of Literary Paris*, New York: HarperCollins.

Ruddick, Lisa (1990), *Reading Gertrude Stein: Body, Text, Gnosis*, Ithaca: Cornell University Press.

Salmonson, Jessica Amanda (2015), *The Encyclopedia of Amazons: Women Warriors from Antiquity to the Modern Era*, New York: Open Road Media.

Sappho (1990), *Greek Lyric: in Four Volumes. Sappho and Alcaeus*. vol. 1 (trans. D. A. Campbell), Harvard, MA: Cambridge University Press.

Sappho (2002), *If Not, Winter: Fragments of Sappho* (trans. A. Carson), New York: Vintage.

Sherman, Antoinette (1996), 'A Hermeneutic reading of Natalie Barney and Renee Vivien', *Anthós (1990–1996)*, 1: 5, pp. 57–97.

Skinner, Marilyn B. (1996), 'Woman and language in Archaic Greece, or, Why is Sappho a woman?', in E. Green (ed.), *Reading Sappho: Contemporary Approaches*, Berkeley: University of California Press, pp. 175–92.

Stein, Gertrude ([1903] 1971), Q.E.D., in L. Katz (ed.), *Fernhurst, Q.E.D., and Other Early Writings by Gertrude Stein*, New York: Liveright, pp. 51–134.

Stein, Gertrude ([1914] 1997), *Tender Buttons*, New York: Dover.

Vivien, Renée (1903), *Sapho, Traduction nouvelle avec le texte grec*, Paris: Alphonse Lemerre.

Wells, Amy D. (2017), 'Feminist geocritical activism: Natalie Barney's writing of women's spaces into women's places', in R. T. Tally (ed.), *The Routledge Handbook of Literature and Space*, London: Routledge, pp. 349–59.

Wells-Lynn, Amy (2005), 'The intertextual, sexually-coded Rue Jacob: A geocritical approach to Djuna Barnes, Natalie Barney, and Radclyffe Hall', *South Central Review*, 22: 3, pp. 78–112.

Wharton, H. T. (1885), *Sappho: memoir, text, selected renderings and a literal translation*. London: David Stott.

Winning, Joanne (2006), 'The Sapphist in the city', in L. Doan and J. Garrity (eds), *Sapphic Modernities: Sexuality, Women and National Culture*, London: Springer, pp. 17–33.

4

Memory, Modernity and the City in Agnès Varda's Paris Films

Felicity Chaplin

L'homme y passe à travers des forêts de symboles
Qui l'observent avec des regards familiers
[Man passes through a forest of symbols
Which observe him with a familiar regard][1]

(Charles Baudelaire, 'Correspondances')

Memory is not an instrument for surveying the past but its theater.

(Walter Benjamin, 'Berlin Childhood around 1900')

For me, Baudelaire is still the prince of poets – I've never stopped reading Baudelaire.

(Agnès Varda)

Memory and modernity

Walter Benjamin begins his essay 'Some Motifs in Baudelaire' with a digression on memory. He cites theses on remembering from Bergson, Proust, Freud and Valéry. What these theses have in common is the involuntary nature of memory; that is, memory linked to the senses and not the intellect; memory as 'accumulated and frequently unconscious data' (1968: 157). For Proust, 'only what has not been experienced explicitly and consciously' can become part of our memory (Benjamin 1968: 160–61); for Freud, memory is made up of the unconscious impressions of daily life which entered the psyche without first becoming conscious and for

Valéry, recollection is a process for organizing stimuli and processing shocks. To speak of remembering, then, is to speak of first times, of experiencing something past in the present. Varda's Paris films provide just such an experience. As Steven Ungar writes of *Cléo de 5 à 7*,

> [the] numerous sequences recording period details such as open-platform buses, the Gare Montparnasse before it was modernised and Citroen taxis, all of which exude a nostalgic glow as a record of Paris in June 1961. In this instance, long tracking shots overlay Cléo's brief walk with images and sounds of a Paris that no longer exists.
>
> (2008: 44)

It is, for the viewer, a Paris at once lost and found, and it is this aspect of Varda's Paris films that leads Ungar to describe them as 'archival', and Varda herself as a 'self-styled archaeologist out to unearth what the passage of time had covered' (2008: 44, 11).

What does it mean to remember? Benjamin devotes the opening half of his essay on Baudelaire to this question. With reference to Bergson, Benjamin introduces the idea of memory as the 'spontaneous afterimage' of modern life (1968: 157). Indeed, memory, for Benjamin, is a peculiarly modern product, replacing tradition as the means by which the past is retained. Unlike tradition, however, there is a randomness to memory, which makes it unreliable as a mode of transmission. Hence, memory appears on the site of the gradual erosion of tradition, and shock is the mechanism by which this erosion is brought about. The experiences of modernity, primarily those of shock and speed, leave traces which become memory. Varda's Paris films can, following Freud, be classified as just such memory traces: 'most powerful and most enduring when the incident which left them behind was one that never entered consciousness' (Benjamin 1968: 160). In order to understand this in cinematic terms, it is possible to speak of the 'apparatus' of the camera in much the same way as Freud (1926) speaks of the 'apparatus' of the psyche: the intention of the director (the shot) and the stimuli or 'shocks' which enter the frame independent of this intention. No more is this the case than with the street and café scenes in *Cléo de 5 à 7*. Varda's wide-angle shots capture not only the subject moving through space but also the very dynamics of this space itself. Predominant here is the crowd, for Benjamin the most obvious and prevalent signifier of modernity.

While the camera may not strictly speaking be the apparatus of memory, it does, according to Benjamin, extend its range because it makes possible the permanent fixing of an event in sight and sound (1968: 186). The introduction of the daguerreotype was met with ambivalence by Baudelaire. At times, he dismissed it as a preoccupation of the masses; at other times, he conceded that photography 'should be free to stake out a claim for ephemeral things' (Benjamin 1968: 186), provided that it did not impinge on the realm of the intangible and the imaginative. Photography was to provide the archive for our memory, but not the experience. This ambiguity is captured in the title of Varda's *Daguerreotypes*, which sits somewhere on the spectrum between archive and memory. Varda, in voiceover, describes the film in the following way: 'Ces daguerréotypes en couleurs, ces images à l'ancienne, ce portrait collectif et presque dagué-stéréotypé de quelques types et typesses de la rue Daguerre [...], tout cela est-il un reportage, un hommage, un essai, un regret, un reproche, une approche? [These colour daguerreotypes, these old images, this collective and almost daguerreo-stereotyped portrait of some men and women of the rue Daguerre [...], all of this, is it a report, a homage, an essay, a regret, a reproach, an approach?]'.

The influence of Baudelaire

Varda was an avid reader of Baudelaire, and his influence on her work, particularly her Paris films, cannot be underestimated. Jill Forbes (2002) includes four of Varda's films under the appellation 'Paris films': *L'Opéra-Mouffe* (1958), *Cléo de 5 à 7* (1962), *Daguerreotypes* (1975) and *Les dites Cariatides* (1984); however, the appellation can also be extended to include *Le Lion volatil* (2003), in some ways the most Baudelairean of Varda's Paris films.[2] According to Beryl Schlossmann, Baudelaire's 'interpretations of the arts and of modern life have shaped the understanding of modernity as a trajectory that leads from Baudelaire's times and places to our own, and from Paris as the capital of the nineteenth century to the modern world of the twenty-first century' (2005: 175). For Schlossman, Baudelaire's poetry 'combines aspects of the old and the new to create a Modernist poetics' (2005: 175). This aesthetic, which Schlossman calls 'transromantic' (2005: 175), is particularly evident in Varda's Paris films, which employ certain Baudelairean motifs, including the presence of the past in the present; a spontaneity or capriciousness in both subject matter and narrative; a fascination with cats (they appear in one form or another in three of the Paris films), the elderly, and the sick or infirm and the occasional appeal to the occult. For example, the tarot de Marseille appears in both *Cléo de 5 à 7* and *Le Lion volatil*, serving both a supernatural and a narrative function, linking the present with both the past and the future. The primary function of the tarot de Marseille for Varda is nonetheless aesthetic, and this is something else she has in common with Baudelaire. Magic is also referenced – albeit in a vaudevillian manner – in *Daguerreotypes* in the figure of the magician Mystag who, in the preamble to his performance, references both the ancient world and the distant future which situates the present of the film in a precarious position of flux.

The main point of convergence between Baudelaire and Varda is that their respective arts make use of symbols, or what Schlossman calls an 'aesthetics of suggestion' (2005: 176). It is, as Schlossman points out, through 'the use of simile, correspondence and allegory' that Baudelaire 'emphasises the power of images to evoke time and place' (2005: 175). The power of a correspondence lies in the buried past and how it makes itself known in the present by 'Laisse[r] parfois sortir de confuses paroles [Letting out sometimes confused utterances]' (Baudelaire 2015: 17). Like Baudelaire, the overt and obvious have no place in Varda's universe. Rather, certain things are 'suggested' which resonate either personally with the filmmaker herself, or in a more broadly cultural context with the viewer. Correspondences are symbols and are part of the symbolist agenda. For example, as Alistair Rolls points out, in Baudelaire's 'Le Cygne' the eponymous swan is, 'for evident reasons of homophony, dual as both bird and sign' (2020: 73). Varda employs a double signification most frequently at the level of the image; however, she also uses words to convey a complex message. This is most notable in the titles of her films. As Rebecca DeRoo notes, the title *Daguerreotypes* is

> a pun referencing the 'types' of people who live on the rue Daguerre and the documentary tradition of typology, that is, mid to late nineteenth and early twentieth-century photographs of what were considered different 'types' of workers. This double meaning of the film's title – referencing both a tradition of documentary photography and a specific neighborhood in Paris – telescopes Varda's ambitions for this project.
>
> (2018: 86)

As DeRoo further points out, Varda's title also 'refers to the street shopkeepers as "types and typesses." In French, "type" can convey different meanings: a person who is representative of a category or a person who is idiosyncratic and unusual. Again, she suggests the tension between the individual and the general' (2018: 108). The title *L'Opéra-Mouffe* is, as Alison Smith writes, 'a play on the phrase *opéra bouffe* (comic opera) but *bouffe* is also slang for food, a connection which the film quickly makes' (1998: 93–94). Varda films the type of boulangeries, boucheries and épiceries for which Rue Mouffetard is famous. On the visual plane, to take perhaps the most obvious example from *Cléo de 5 à 7*, Cléo's preposterous wig is a typically symbolist visual cue, at once absurdly comic and replete with meaning. It calls to mind both the title and the eponymous character of Jacques Becker's 1952 film *Casque d'Or*, played by Simone Signoret, and this reference is strengthened by the casting of Dominique Davray as Cléo's friend and confidant, Angèle (Davray played a similar role to Signoret's Marie in Becker's film). Further,

Varda's evocation of *Casque d'Or* unearths the lost Paris of the Belle Epoque, which is momentarily superimposed over the Paris of the 1960s. The era of *Casque d'Or* was also the height of French Symbolism, when Baudelaire's poetry was being revived as a model for a modern aesthetic. That both Marie in *Casque d'Or* and Cléo are in their own ways kept women or courtesans adds a further layer of meaning to Varda's film. Cléo is a courtesan not only to the wealthy playboy José (José Luis de Vilallonga) but also to the culture industry, something she attempts to rid herself of when she removes the wig in the second half of the film.

Perhaps, the most Baudelairean use of symbolism in Varda's Paris films is the lion in *Le Lion volatil*, primarily because, in this film, the lion/cat remains a symbol in line with Baudelaire's notion of a correspondence, that is, less a hermeneutic phenomenon than a sensorial one. The word *volatil* can be, in this context, translated in the chemical sense of a substance which evaporates easily. 'Paris change [Paris changes]' writes Baudelaire in 'Le Cygne [The Swan]', and it is to this kind of instability typical of modernity that this line refers. Indeed, Varda shot this film when the sculpture the Lion of Belfort (the mascot of the 14th arrondissement) had literally disappeared when it was removed temporarily for restoration. The lion is also a symbol, in the sense of correspondence, because the lion we look at becomes the cat which looks at us. The lion-cat also figures in *Les Fleurs du mal*. In the poem 'Le Chat [The Cat]', the poet entreats the cat to 'Retiens les griffes de ta patte [Retract the claws of your paws]' (Baudelaire 2015: 54). In 'Les Chats [The Cats]', the poet references the ancient world when he refers to cats as 'Des grands sphinx allongés au fond des solitudes [Grand sphinxes stretched out deep in solitude]' (2015: 101). Varda's fascination with cats extended to her using the image of a cat for the label for her production company, Ciné-Tamaris.

According to Benjamin, the correspondences 'are the data of remembrance [...] The murmur of the past may be heard in the correspondences' (1968: 182). When Baudelaire writes of the 'forêts de symboles [forests of symbols]', which watch us with knowing looks, he identifies something essential in the nature of memory: it resides not in us, but in the objects which surround us. In other words, the data of memory may be stored in the recesses of our minds, but remembering as an experience depends on whether or not we recognize the look which looks at us. In a sense, Varda's films incite remembrance, not so much of a lost Paris, but of a forgotten one. A film like *Daguerreotypes* is, in this respect, as much a film about objects as it is about people: milk cans, old clocks, perfume bottles, all contain a Paris which for Varda is both real and mythological, both personal and archaeological. As Rolls remarks of Baudelaire's 'Le Cygne', Paris is 'simultaneously presented as itself and other'; that is, one finds in this poem 'the explicit co-presence in the text of Paris past (mythical, metaphorical) and Paris present (existential, real)' (2020: 72). In Varda's Paris films, framing, *mise en scène* and editing create a Paris in which mythos and topos intersect. *Daguerreotypes*, although shot in 1975, has the feel of a much older Paris; similarly, in *L'Opéra-Mouffe*, shot in 1958, the footage has the effect of already being that present's past, particularly when set to George Delerue's nostalgic score. *Les dites Cariatides*, shot in 1984, is really set in the late nineteenth century, connecting modern Paris with the Paris of Baudelaire through direct citation of his poetry. Here, Varda invites us to remember that these statues we look at today were once looked on by the likes of Hugo, de Banville and Baudelaire himself, whose poem 'Beauté [Beauty]' Varda reads over images of the statues.

A filmmaker of neighbourhoods

Baudelaire's 'Le Cygne' stages the condition of memory as one of the reactions to the rapid changes of modernity. When, as Baudelaire writes, 'Vieux faubourgs, tout pour moi devient allégorie [Old neighbourhoods turn to allegory]' (2015: 131), they have become unrecognizable. Varda's neighbourhoods are the sites of archaeological digs. They appear to us as they once were, even at the time of filming. Like Baudelaire, Varda made her films for a reader/viewer yet to come. This does not mean that they were not capable of being appreciated in their own time, as Baudelaire's poetry was; however, their full effect would only manifest once their present had become our past. This is because Varda's Paris films, like certain of Baudelaire's poems, stage both the present and its inevitable passing as part of the condition of modernity. Forbes argues that in Varda's Paris films one finds again and again 'the idea that the city is changing and a nostalgia for its old forms' (2002: 84). In *Daguerreotypes*, there is a brief scene in which Varda lingers on two old women conversing in the street. Some of the dialogue is inaudible; however, what can clearly be heard is one of the women remarking on how her memory is fading. This points to a certain preoccupation in Varda's Paris films with the role of cinema in documenting the present as the past.

As Forbes points out, in spite of any pretence they have to narrative or fiction, Varda's Paris films are ultimately about Paris (2002: 84). This is true even of *Cléo de 5 à 7*, which, as Ungar notes, can best be 'understood as a fictional portrait of a woman set within a documentary about Paris' (2008: 20). *Daguerreotypes*, on the other hand, is a documentary which conceals a personal narrative: it was 'made while Varda herself was pregnant and it concerns the shopkeepers in the road she herself lives in' (Forbes 2002: 84). In *L'Opéra-Mouffe*, a quasi-symbolist documentary about Varda's recollections of Rue Mouffetard in the 5th arrondissement of Paris not far from where she lived, 'we see witty montages of gossiping shoppers as well as the careworn people who shop and live in the neighbourhood' (Conway

2015: 33). Varda, who was a photographer before becoming a filmmaker, 'wanted it to be in the spirit in which Cartier-Bresson sometimes does his photos' (cited in Conway 2015: 33). Varda's Paris films, according to Ungar, function primarily as 'documents of a specific time and place' (2008: 7). *Cléo*, *Daguerreotypes* and *L'Opéra-Mouffe* are 'devoted to neighbourhoods of Paris' (Ungar 2008: 7). *L'Opéra-Mouffe* in particular 'developed on the basis of a sense of place that enhanced changes in perception related to a Parisian neighbourhood' (Ungar 2008: 12). Rue Mouffetard was, however, not Varda's preferred faubourg or neighbourhood. Three of the five Paris films – *Cléo*, *Daguerreotypes* and *Le Lion volatil* – are set in and around the 14th arrondissement, where Varda had lived since 1951. Conway refers to Varda as being 'besotted' with the 14th; so much so that *Cléo* 'constitutes a classic Left Bank idyll that places Paris's 14th at the epicenter of the known World' (2015: 1). It is not surprising that she saw the forces of modernity as both inevitable and, in some ways, regrettable. Conway describes the 14th in the following way: 'cradled between the green swaths of the Luxembourg Gardens to the north and the Parc Montsouris to the south. To the west beckons Montparnasse and its nightlife, while the vast walled prison and hospital complexes bordering the neighboring 13th discourage further exploration eastward' (2015: 1). Two things in this description immediately recall Baudelaire: the prison and the hospital. In 'Le Cygne', the poem most relevant to Varda's work, the poet thinks 'Aux captifs, aux vaincus! […] à bien d'autres encor! [Of prisoners, of the vanquished! And of others as well!]' (Baudelaire 2015: 312). In the prose poem 'N'importe où Hors du Monde [Anywhere Out of the World]', Baudelaire compares life to a hospital: 'où chaque malade est possédé du désir de changer de lit. Celui-ci voudrait souffrir en face du poêle, et celui-là croit qu'il guérirait à côté de la fenêtre [where every patient is possessed with the desire to change beds; one man would like to suffer in front of the stove, and another believes that he would recover his health beside the window]' (Baudelaire 1998: 71 [72]). In the first instance, it was perhaps this line from 'Le Cygne' which Varda had in mind when in *Daguerreotypes* she refers to Madame Chardon Bleu as 'avec sa douceur de captive [with the meekness of a captive]' and films her in her favourite place, gazing out the window of her shop into the darkening street. In the second instance, Varda set the concluding scenes of *Cléo* in the grounds of the L'hôpital de la Pitié-Salpêtrière.

The camera-flâneur

According to Ungar, in *Cléo*, Varda 'undertook a narrative in which local geography was a primary concern' (2008: 87). The film employs 'a mix of measured and subjective time in the geography of Paris with an attention to spatial detail that was close to topographic' (Ungar 2008: 34). For this reason, many scholars are inclined to view Cléo herself as the embodiment of the flâneuse who maps the geography of this part of Paris. However, it is not Cléo who undertakes this mapping but Varda herself or, more importantly, Varda as camera-flâneur.

Cléo de 5 à 7 is Varda's most written-about film, both in terms of narrative and place. As Jennifer Wallace points out,

> One of the most prevalent references in writings on the film is the figure of the flâneuse. Sandy Flitterman-Lewis, Janice Mouton, Valerie Orpen, Steven Ungar and Mark Betz have all discussed Cléo as the embodiment of a New Wave flâneuse, with each writer attributing various components of flânerie to her character according to their own interpretations.
>
> (2017: 25)

Flitterman-Lewis argues that, as soon as she steps out, Cléo becomes a 'Baudelairean flâneur' (1996: 274). Janice Mouton refers to Cléo as a 'rambling, street-haunting flâneuse [...] who becomes a part of the world in which she rambles and observes' (2001: 8–9). Mark Betz includes Cléo alongside other examples of European new cinema like *Ascenseur pour l'échafaud* (1957, *Elevator to the Gallows*), *La Notte* (1961, *The Night*), *Vivre sa vie* (1962, *My Life to Live*) and *L'Eclisse* (1962, *The Eclipse*), in which the 'female protagonist's flânerie itself structures modern filmic narrative [and] her looks designate her as the agent of the visible' (2009: 98). Others have called into question the use of the term *flâneuse* to describe Cléo while maintaining that the designation is nonetheless appropriate. Jim Morrissey writes: 'Given the extent of Baudelaire's influence on our image and understanding of Paris, it is tempting to call any incidence of strolling around the city flânerie. But how reasonable is it to call Cléo [...] a flâneuse?' (2008: 100). Morrissey goes on to argue that flâneuse is appropriate for Cléo only if the gender of the term is rethought. While *flâneuse* has lost much of its nineteenth-century baggage, it still needs to be divested of the connotation of prostitution. However, the citation that Morrissey uses from Baudelaire to justify his designation of Cléo at the Dôme café as the modern equivalent of the flâneur describes not so much the flâneur as what Benjamin calls the 'man (sic) of the crowd': 'In the window of a coffee house there sits a convalescent, pleasurably absorbed in gazing at the crowd [...] rapturously breathing in all the odours and essences of life [...] Finally he hurls himself headlong into the midst of the throng' (cited in Morrissey 2008: 101). Baudelaire is here describing painter Constantin Guy, and the important word in this passage is 'throng', for it is the throng, or crowd, which precisely renders flânerie impossible.

Wallace is right to point out that in arguing for Cléo as a flâneuse, critics appeal to a historically specific figure which has only limited currency in the milieu of Paris in the 1960s. However, it is important to note that critics also tend to conflate the flâneur with Baudelaire when in fact the figure of the flâneur was already something of a historical anomaly in Baudelaire's time. In Baudelaire's modernity, the flâneur was replaced with the pedestrian or 'man of the crowd' who, unlike the flâneur, was no longer free to stroll the city and arcades. The 'man of the crowd', according to Benjamin, 'is no flâneur' (1968: 172). The crowd is not the natural habitat of the flâneur, and 'the man of the crowd' exemplifies 'what had to become of the flâneur once he was deprived of the milieu to which he belonged' (1968: 172). The crowd is inimical to the flâneur because it does not permit of the strolling necessary for flânerie. The modern city largely replaced the flâneur with the pedestrian who, according to Benjamin, 'would let himself (sic) be jostled by the crowd' (1968: 172). This is in contradistinction to the flâneur who 'demanded elbow room and was unwilling to forgo the life of a gentleman of leisure' (Benjamin 1968: 172). Cléo is not a flâneuse in the historical sense of the term. When she steps into the street, she becomes one with the crowd and is frequently borne along with it, as exemplified by Varda's long and crane shots. At other times, she is, as Morrissey points out, 'isolated in the foule (throng) that is Paris' (2008: 99).

Describing the Paris of *Cléo*, Varda uses strikingly similar words to Benjamin when he describes the Paris of Baudelaire: 'What did Paris evoke for me? A broad fear of the big city, of its dangers, and of losing oneself there alone, misunderstood and even jostled' (cited in Ungar 2008: 87). Varda uses three words here which take her out of the realm of the flâneur and into that of the 'man of the crowd': fear, danger and jostled. Being jostled is an experience unknown to the flâneur, as are fear and danger, both of which are experienced by Cléo in the Parisian streets. At one point during her excursion in the quartier, Cléo encounters, in Ungar's words, 'a bare-chested street performer who runs a long dagger through his biceps' and 'a man who swallows frogs' (2008: 70). These two instances, according to Ungar, 'embody medieval Paris whose violence Cléo is unable to bear' (2008: 70). Fear and danger are both linked to a particularly modern experience of the city: shock. Three insights of Benjamin's confirm this experience. He notes 'the close connection in Baudelaire between the figure of shock and contact with the metropolitan masses, or the amorphous crowd of passers-by, the people in the street' (1968: 165); that '(m)oving through this traffic involves the individual in a series of shocks and collisions' (1968: 175); and that '[f]ear, revulsion, and horror were the emotions which the big-city crowd aroused in those who first observed it' (1968: 174).

Baudelaire writes of 'hurrying across the boulevard [...] amidst this moving chaos in which death comes galloping at you from all sides at once' (cited in Benjamin 1968: 192). Commenting on *L'Opéra-Mouffe*, Varda describes the crowd in the streets as a 'swarm [...] so intense that one couldn't isolate the shots' (cited in Conway 2015: 33). There are two things here which indicate a modernity in which the flâneur has no real place: the intense swarming of the crowd and the incapacity to isolate moments, to consciously process each one as a singular event. Indeed, Conway describes *L'Opéra-Mouffe* as 'a portrait of the river of humanity moving along the street' (2015: 33).

The argument for Cléo as flâneuse rests on scenes in which she is shown walking the streets of Paris, browsing shop windows, going to cafés, and generally taking in the spectacle of the city and its people. As Wallace remarks, 'What many of these writers are engaging with is the historicised, 19th-century imagining of the flâneur and its more recent feminist revision, the flâneuse' and their arguments are 'grounded in the culture of the 19th century, and the term always entails some form of consumerism: the flâneuse as either a buyer or a seller of a specific commodity' (2017: 126). Wallace goes on to argue that Cléo, 'being a woman of 1962, only briefly a shopper and not a prostitute, must be seen outside the restrictive parameters of the flâneuse' (2017: 126).[3]

In a monograph from 1876 entitled *Ce qu'on voit dans les rues de Paris* [*What Happens on the Streets of Paris*], M. Victor Fournel compares the flâneur to the daguerreotype: 'C'est un daguerréotype mobile et passionné qui garde les moindres traces, et en qui se reproduisent, avec leurs reflets changeants, la marche des choses, le mouvement de la cité, la physionomie multiple de l'esprit public, des croyances, des antipathies et des admirations de la foule [He is a passionate and mobile daguerreotype who retains the slightest traces, and who has reproduced in himself, with their changing reflections, the progression of things, the movement of the city, the multiple physiognomies of the public spirit, the beliefs, the antipathies and of the awe of the crowd]' (1867: 268). Almost a century later, Susan Sontag in *On Photography* argued that the camera began as 'an extension of the eye of the middle-class flâneur', looking upon the city and its inhabitants with curiosity and detachment (1973: 42). For Sontag, the photographer 'is an armed version of the solitary walker reconnoitering, stalking, cruising the urban inferno, the voyeuristic stroller who discovers the city as a landscape of voluptuous extremes. Adept of the joys of watching, connoisseur of empathy, the flâneur finds the world "picturesque"' 1973: 42). The romanticization of the working classes in Varda's Paris films may be the result of this 'middle-class' gaze which portrays the Parisian streets of working-class neighbourhoods as 'picturesque'; however, what is more important to note here are the ideas of curiosity, detachment and empathy. Varda's camera, like the flâneur, both identifies with and distances itself from its subjects. Rather than being swept along with the crowd, as Cléo is, the camera is placed at times at a distance from, at times in close quarters to the crowd.

There was, according to Benjamin, an ambivalence in Baudelaire's relationship to the crowd: he is at once part of the crowd and apart from it; as a flâneur, he was 'made one' with the crowd, yet, he also maintained a certain critical distance from it (1968: 172). This was Varda's modus operandi in her Paris films. As Conway points out, when Varda was shooting *L'Opéra-Mouffe*, she 'borrowed a 16mm camera and took a folding chair to the rue Mouffetard, put the camera on a tripod, and stood on the chair to shoot the life of the street' (2015: 32). At other times, there is an empathy with her subject typified by lingering close-ups.

Cléo is more a pedestrian than a flâneur. She is jostled by the crowd, exposed to shocks (street performers, a shooting, etc) and only on rare occasions is she afforded the elbow room necessary for strolling. If there is a flâneur in Varda's Paris films, it is not Cléo but the camera. It is the camera which moves through the city's streets unimpeded, taking in the spectacle of modern life of which Cléo is a part, the object and not the subject of the film. As Mouton points out, 'As we see Cleo walking through the city's "sensory streets", vital and dynamic with their mix of people, newsstands and bookstalls, trees and flowers, bicycles, cars, and buses, dogs and pigeons, shops and cafes, our attention is focused on the city as much as on the woman' (2001: 3). Ungar too notes Varda's 'attentiveness to sensory detail' (2008: 29). The camera-flâneur expresses itself in three main shots: tracking shots, close-up shots and wide-angle shots. Taken together, these shots constitute the two sides of the camera-flâneur: movement/stasis and involvement/detachment. In this sense, when arguing for the camera-flâneur, it is important to consider not only what Phil Powrie identifies as Varda's 'use of tracking shots to usher in key moments' (2011: 80) but also the very movement of the camera itself. Indeed, in this respect, Powrie argues that *Cléo* be understood not as a 'flâneu-rie' film but more broadly a 'travelling' film or a film about travelling: 'Varda's cinema is a nomadic cinema; it is by a traveler, about travelers, and often uses iconic traveling shots, which are key to understanding how Varda's use of space functions' (2011: 68).

It is highly doubtful that the flâneur (unlike his or her aesthetic counterpart, the dandy) can ever be the object of the gaze or, in filmic terms, can ever belong to the *mise en scène* of modern life. Cléo may stroll the Paris streets, first as a dandy and then as a pedestrian or 'man of the crowd', but the question remains: when she is absorbed in watching the spectacle of the city streets, who is watching her? Anonymity is certainly a feature of the flâneur, and Cléo does achieve an anonymity of sorts in the second half of the film after removing her trademark blonde wig, the signifier of her desire to be seen and recognized. At one point, she even has to inform a taxi driver that she is the singer he is listening to on the radio. Nonetheless, she does not cease to be the object of a particular gaze. Even the famous café scene, which is cited as an example of a point of view shot establishing Cléo as subject, is ambiguous. Mouton describes this scene in the following way:

> One remarkable scene in *Cleo from 5 to 7* makes clear the tie between the city and the woman in her ongoing process of transformation: when Cleo enters the Montparnasse cafe le Dôme in her new role of flâneuse, she notices everything in this rich sidewalk café: posters on the bulletin board, paintings on the walls, tables, chairs, a pinball machine, a jukebox, a newspaper rack. She seats herself momentarily at a small table, positioned next to a floor-to-ceiling column covered in mirror mosaics, a mirrored surface into which, for the first time, Cleo does not look. In becoming part of the café world, she ceases to be a spectacle on display, for herself or for anyone else.
>
> (2001: 10)

The inference here is that we as viewers are receiving the data of the café through Cléo's eyes; however, rather than understanding this as a point of view shot pure and simple, it can be better grasped as an example of the camera-flâneurist 'empathy' identified by Sontag. This reading is strengthened by the fact that at the end of this shot, Cléo appears in the frame, emerging from a momentary empathic unity with the camera-flâneur to take her place once more in the *mise en scène*.

How, then, is Cléo to be understood, if not through the figure of the flâneuse? Varda's relationship to Baudelaire may hold a possible answer. Two motifs from Baudelaire's poetry may better serve as figures through which Cléo can be read: the *passante* and the *muse malade*. Benjamin's analysis of Baudelaire's 'À une passante [To a Passerby]' is prescient. He notes that in this sonnet, the crowd is nowhere directly referenced, yet 'the whole happening hinges on it' (1968: 168). It is, according to Benjamin, 'this very crowd which brings to the city dweller the figure that fascinates' (1968: 169). Cléo can be read in just this way: she is a figure which emerges momentarily from the crowd and which fascinates Varda's camera in just the same way as Mme Chardon Bleu in *Daguerreotypes*. The poem 'La Muse malade' begins with the following stanza:

> Ma pauvre muse, hélas! qu'as-tu donc ce matin?
> Tes yeux creux sont peuplés de visions nocturnes,
> Et je vois tour à tour réfléchis sur ton teint
> La folie et l'horreur [...]
> [My poor muse, alas! what's wrong with you this morning?
> Your hollow eyes are full of nocturnal visions,
> And I see turn by turn reflected in your complexion
> Madness and horror [...]] (Baudelaire 2015: 22).

The streets where Cléo walks 'teem with signs of death' (Ungar 2008: 105). Indeed, Cléo sees harbingers of death everywhere she turns: the unnamed 'death' card from Tarot de Marseille in the opening scenes with the fortune teller, which Cléo reads literally as predicting her imminent death; the ebony masks and African artefacts seen from the window of a taxi, which 'alien to her world [...], are sure signs of death' (Martin 2006: 119); the masked faces of the art students who shortly after accost the taxi; the street performers from which she flees; a funeral procession which momentarily blocks her way as she crosses the Boulevard Edgar Quinet and a crime scene in which a man has been shot, signified by a bullet hole in a shop window. Commenting on Cléo's wanderings, Varda remarked: 'I imagined a character walking in the city. I thought about the master in *Jacques le fataliste* [...] I turned him into a female singer, making her way through Paris, driven mad by a fear of cancer' (cited in Ungar 2008: 88). The film ends in the grounds of the Salpêtrière hospital where Cléo receives the news of her illness. A reading of Cléo as both *passante* and muse reinstates her as part of Varda's vast Parisian *mise en scène*: as *passante*, she belongs to the catalogue of fascinating types captured by Varda's camera; as muse she becomes the momentary inspiration for a narrative which the poet weaves around her before leaving her to her own fate.

Conclusion

Benjamin says of Baudelaire: 'His work cannot merely be categorised as historical, like anyone else's, but it intended to be so and understood itself as such' (1968: 162). The same can be said of Varda's Paris films: they are more than history, yet they are the product at the same time of a historical intention which is both document and allegory, demonstrating what Ungar calls 'the ever-increasing gap between past and present' (2008: 45). What these Paris films reveal is that Varda is above all a Baudelairean filmmaker: she is a filmmaker of correspondences who has frequent recourse to symbolism; she employs a flâneurist filming technique; she is a filmmaker of neighbourhoods and her films feature motifs of modernity often taken directly from Baudelaire. The Paris Varda constructs in these films can be described as Baudelairean in the sense that, on the one hand, they deal primarily with notions of memory and place, and on the other hand, their imagery works by way of a symbolism which creates an allegorical, romantic and at times nostalgic relationship to Paris.

NOTES

1. All translations are my own unless otherwise stated.
2. Schlossman (2005) notes Baudelairean resonances in Varda's *Jacquot de Nantes*; however, she does not explicitly mention the Paris films.
3. Cléo's status as a kept woman must be understood outside the framework of the prostitute as 'street walker'.

REFERENCES

Baudelaire, Charles (1998), *Twenty Prose Poems* (trans. M. Hamburger), San Francisco: City Lights.

Baudelaire, Charles (2015), *Les Fleurs du mal*, Paris: Editions Ligaran.

Benjamin, Walter (1968), *Illuminations* (trans. H. Zohn), New York: Schocken.

Betz, Mark (2009), *Beyond the Subtitle: Remapping European Art Cinema*, Minneapolis: University of Minnesota Press.

Conway, Kelley (2015), *Agnès Varda*, Champaign: University of Illinois Press.

DeRoo, Rebecca J. (2018), *Agnès Varda between Film, Photography, and Art*, Oakland, California: University of California Press.

Flitterman-Lewis, Sandy (1996), *To Desire Differently: Feminism and the French Cinema*, New York: Columbia University Press.

Forbes, Jill (2002), 'Gender and Space in Cléo de 5 à 7', *Studies in French Cinema*, 2: 2, pp. 83–89.

Fournel, Victor (1867), *Ce qu'on voit dans les rues de Paris*, Paris: E Dentu. Gallica, Bibliothèque numérique. https://gallica.bnf.fr/ark:/12148/bpt6k757298.texteImage. Accessed 10 October 2020.

Freud, Sigmund (1926), 'The Question of Lay Analysis', in *The Standard Edition of the Complete Psychological Works of Sigmund Freud, Volume XX (1925–1926): An Autobiographical Study, Inhibitions, Symptoms and Anxiety, The Question of Lay Analysis and Other Works* (trans. J. Strachey), London: Hogarth Press, pp. 177–258.

Martin, Florence (2006), '*Cléo de 5 à 7/Cleo from 5 to 7*', in P. Powrie (ed.), *The Cinema of France*, London: Wallflower, pp. 112–21.

Morrissey, Jim (2008), 'Paris and voyages of self-discovery in *Cléo de 5 à 7* and *Le Fabuleux Destin d'Amélie Poulain*', *Studies in French Cinema*, 8: 2, pp. 99–110.

Mouton, Janice (2001), 'From Feminine Masquerade to Flâneuse: Agnès Varda's Cléo in the City', *Cinema Journal*, 40: 2, pp. 3–16.

Powrie, Phil (2011), 'Heterotopic spaces and Nomadic gazes in Varda: From *Cléo de 5 à 7* to *Les Glaneurs et la glaneuse*', *L'Esprit Créateur*, 51: 1, pp. 68–82.

Rolls, Alistair (2020), 'Saving Paris from Nostalgia: Jumbling the urban and seeing swans everywhere', *Australian Journal of French Studies*, 57: 1, pp. 66–77.

Schlossman, Beryl (2005), 'Baudelaire's place in literary and cultural history', in R. Lloyd (ed.), *The Cambridge Companion to Baudelaire*, Cambridge: Cambridge University Press, pp. 175–85.

Smith, Alison (1998), *Agnès Varda*, Manchester: Manchester University Press.

Sontag, Susan (1973), *On Photography*, New York: Rosetta Books.

Ungar, Steven (2008), *Cléo de 5 à 7*, Basingstoke: Palgrave Macmillan.

Wallace, Jennifer (2017), 'Beyond the Flâneuse: The Uniqueness of Cléo de 5 à 7', in P. Powrie and G. Vincendeau (eds), *Paris in the Cinema: Beyond the Flâneur*, London: British Film Institute.

5

Looking (Back) at the Moon in Parisian Cinema

Alistair Rolls

In her discussion of what she dubs a 'nostalgia wave', which is to say, many films and television series of the second decade of our new millennium focusing on earlier decades of the twentieth century, and particularly the 1920s,[1] Katharina Niemeyer includes Martin Scorsese's *Hugo* (2011). This wave, Niemeyer argues (2014: 2), is symptomatic of a 'crisis of temporality', a 'twofold phenomenon' (of progress but also of crisis) that is strongly reminiscent of the double movements of nineteenth-century Parisian poetics previously discussed in this volume. She describes these two parallel but opposed phenomena as 'a reaction to fast technologies, despite using them, in desiring to slow down, and/or an escape from this crisis into a state of a wanderlust (*Fernweh*) and nostalgia (in the sense of *Heimweh*) that could be "cured", or encouraged, by media use and consumption' (2014: 2). As Dirk Gibb has demonstrated (2019: *passim*), films that capture these phenomena do not simply seek to respond allegorically to particular moments of crisis that the viewer is experiencing in the present of the viewing moment; they also stage a period in the past that is itself always already in the grip of this same twofold crisis.

In this chapter, I want to map the kind of response that Niemeyer is discussing onto other reactions to cinema's fast technologies. To this end, I will discuss two famous moments of moon gazing in French cinema. This moon gazing, I will argue, looks forwards and upwards, but to a certain extent uses this manifest gaze so as to mask another retrospective one, which for its part looks backwards, towards the past, towards slower times, perhaps, and also other genres, other traditions. I shall begin with George Méliès's *Le Voyage dans la lune*. This film stands at the beginnings of cinema, at a time when technical developments were creating all kinds of new visual possibilities. And yet, Méliès's film, which uses this new art form to explore the common theme of science fiction that is travelling to the moon, also attests to the dying art form of theatrical magic. In this way, futuristic, extra-terrestrial adventure is at the same time a vehicle for remembrance of more local events – those of Paris's theatres. This aspect of Méliès's legacy is captured neatly in Scorsese's *Hugo*, which itself uses state-of-the-art cinematography (in this case, 3D technology) to tell its story of cinema's past. *Hugo* revels simultaneously in mechanical wonders and nostalgia; indeed, in it, Méliès's cinema comes to embody a nostalgic longing for a lost era that was truly, and almost literally, magical. I shall then turn to Luis Buñuel and Salvador Dalí's *Un chien andalou*, whose own pioneering status lies in its screening of Surrealism. By working both with and against Linda Williams's famous analysis of the film's prologue, according to which the film uses metaphor and metonymy to project forwards in a reflexive act of cinematic self-generation, it will be seen that the moon gazer of the film's beginning looks backwards as well as forwards. Nostalgia in this case takes the form of the moon as intertext, and, in keeping with the Baudelairean echoes of the present volume, this intertext will be located in none other than Baudelaire's *Les Fleurs du mal*. This remembrance of the past articulated in and through an instance of looking to the future, I argue, constitutes the film's Parisianness. Taken together, these instances of looking at the moon will be shown to play their part in the history of Parisian remembering and of Paris as a site of remembrance.

George Méliès, Le Voyage dans la lune *(1902)*

In an excellent study of Scorsese's *Hugo* and revisionist historiography, Constance Balides notes how the film treats those who watch it as historians and particularly as historians of cinema. Notably, she comments on the palimpsestic folds of historical photographs (recreated by the actors, including the famous image of Georges Méliès in his kiosk in Paris's Gare Montparnasse, where he sold sweets and toys from the mid-1920s through to the early 1930s)[2] and clips from old movies. Scorsese's telescoping of cinema spectatorship has us watching a contemporary film set in an earlier period in which the young eponymous hero rediscovers his own past by watching films of an earlier period. Throughout the film, however, such scenes reveal a progressive inoculation of audiences, whose initial fear of trains hurtling towards them is replaced as a metonym for film history by astonishment and then awareness of the medium's artificiality. In its staging of this transition, Balides writes, 'the film enacts a revisionist analysis of the early cinema audience, a strategy reinforced by framing' (2016: 143). This history lesson is perhaps at its most interesting in the framework of the present volume, with its focus on presentations and representations of Paris in and as modernity, when it plays with inversions of mobility and stillness. Balides notes the way in which Hugo's leafing through a book of still images is brought to life by the magic of contemporary cinema (in a mapping, and almost a transmediation, of early cinema audiences' experience of the new medium): 'While the montage of film clips visualizes the book as moving images, it also foregrounds the transformation from still to projected moving images, a key intervention of cinema in an era that included photography, projected lantern slides, and optical toys' (2016: 147). This bringing to life of photographic stills, which includes restoring a lust for life in the ageing and jaded Méliès, is also counterbalanced, in a chiastic narrative strategy typical of Baudelairean poetics, by a making still. For, while it is clear that movement (excessive in the figure of Hugo, impeded in that of the Station Inspector, and systematized in the clockwork running of what was a state-of-the-art transport hub) is front and centre in the film, Scorsese's Méliès also embodies stillness; indeed, it is my contention here that Méliès latches onto the developing technical capacity of cinema to harness the reality present in movement (which is reflected in Scorsese's choice to film *Hugo* in 3D) in order, in his own films, to capture the dreams of the past, and the past as dream, by suspending time and animating stillness itself.[3]

This can perhaps be most clearly demonstrated by a brief analysis of one particular historical moment captured in *Hugo*. Ben Kingsley, in the role of Georges Méliès, addresses those assembled in a Parisian cinema to watch a retrospective of Méliès's films, many of which have been restored after having previously been thought lost. In this scene, the spectators in Scorsese's cinema ensure that the position held by us viewers – as we watch *Hugo* (at the cinema or on another screen) – is doubled. This is no simple play on the famous fourth wall, as we are never the direct recipients of Kingsley–Méliès's gaze, which remains instead on the audience *en abyme* (at one moment, he winks pointedly at his wife and muse, Jeanne d'Alcy, played by Helen McCrory). What, then, is the effect of our, the viewers', not being addressed directly by Kingsley–Méliès, even as Scorsese's film, which is at least in part itself a retrospective of Méliès's films, puts itself on stage, reflexively, before our very eyes? Certainly, we are placed on an almost equal footing with the other characters, who join us in watching Méliès present his films. Yet, at the same time, we are not addressed directly by them or by him, which reminds us of their double status as real fictional characters in the film, which is to say, as people *not* watching a movie. And if they are not watching a movie, it is not simply because they are bringing *Hugo* to life more effectively for us (as the character Hugo restores Méliès, who is *not* the protagonist, and his work to life) but also because Kingsley's performance is principally theatrical, that is, the stuff of the theatre rather than of the cinema. This seems to me important, for the inversion appealed to in Kingsley–Méliès's invitation to his audience, in this cinematic portrayal of an event that actually took place in Paris's Salle Pleyel in December 1929, is not only one of cinema *versus* real life; rather, when he says the magic words – 'And now, my friends, I address you all tonight as you truly are: wizards, mermaids, travellers, adventurers, magicians [...] Come and dream with me' – he invokes the very history of bringing dreams to life in the early years of silent cinema, which in his case involved any number of tricks and what Erik Barnouw has called 'nitrate magic' (1981: 85–105). The idea of the dream as an accessible alternative to the real world is an appeal *inter alia* to Surrealism (André Breton's seminal text *Nadja* was published in 1928, and Luis Buñuel and Salvador Dalí's film *Un chien andalou* was filmed in Paris and Le Havre in the same year before being released in 1929, the year of Méliès's retrospective). Just as important, however, is the reflexive aspect given in Scorsese's *mise en abyme* to retrospection itself. Even at the time of their production, Méliès's films, including his iconic *Le Voyage dans la lune* (*A Trip to the Moon*), deployed futuristic themes in order to showcase the dying art of the magician and his place on the Parisian stage.[4]

Even as I write this chapter in 2019, on the fiftieth anniversary of mankind's journey to the moon, we are conscious that in 1929, Méliès's reminiscence of his own trip to the moon brought back a journey that was always as much, if not more so, to do with nostalgia than with the development of the cinema itself. We might think of the way in which *Hugo* adds colour to Méliès's black and white films by showing (and staging, which is to say, artificially reanimating) the reality of their filming. For Balides, the 'contrast between the colored costumes and imagined film reinforced by the monochrome film strip [that Méliès examines frame by frame] makes the point that color was applied later' (2016: 143). It also, of course, shows Méliès looking backwards, from the film that he is making in black and white to the vividly coloured reality of its original performance on stage. In addition to, and rather than simply, bringing the present to life through the movement of cinema, Méliès is leveraging the medium in order to freeze for posterity the theatrical movement on stage of his actors and beautifully painted sets, whose filmic representations, tricks aside, can only ever be a pale imitation, or better still a faded memory, of their original selves.

As Rémi Fournier Lanzoni points out, Méliès's rather cumbersome camera was almost always used in a static position, which meant that his films fixed his theatrical performances not only in time but also in the sense that their viewers were afforded a more limited range of 'views' than those available to traditional theatre-goers (2002: 34).[5] This is the paradox of making still(s): while participating in the future of the cinema, Méliès was dreaming of art forms of the past and, effectively, consigning himself, not only as a magician but also as a cinematographer, to history. As Barnouw notes in relation to Méliès's films, 'it can be seen on close examination that the camera was stopped at crucial points to accomplish the transformations and other illusions. In other words, an on-camera magician no longer needed to be a magician'; in this way therefore, '[m]agicians, by helping to create this form, had helped to make their own skills excess baggage' (1981: 88).

Before I turn to what is arguably French cinema's most iconic image of the moon, that of Luis Buñuel's *Un chien andalou*, I shall comment briefly on the portrayal of the moon in Méliès's *Le Voyage dans la lune* and its reprise in *Hugo*. First, in Méliès's film, the moon is anthropomorphized in the classic form of 'the man in the moon' and the rocket, in a move that brings together the two chains of images from the prologue to *Un chien andalou*, lands right in the man in the moon's eye, partially blinding what has heretofore been the object of men's gaze. The personification of the moon is quickly followed by a realization, on the viewer's part, that the inhabitants of the moon themselves strongly resemble the human explorers; indeed, not only are they humanoid in form but also their courtroom, and the acrobatic movements that they display inside it, is a replica of the room in which the astronomers meet at the beginning of the film and in which they too display great agitation in their movements. The message seems clear: Méliès's lunar landscape is a human one, its conquest a sign of mankind's achievement rather than a celebration of the moon's symbolism or poetic value. The slogan of Méliès's production company is itself suggestive of this: '*Le monde à portée de la main* (The world is within reach)' (Lanzoni 2002: 34). Interestingly, this slogan is something of a mirror image of Baudelaire's 'any where out of the world': rather than anywhere being Paris, Méliès's studio in Paris could become anywhere, and it could do so without moving. Excessive theatrical movement, including a trip to the moon itself, becomes, as suggested above, a statement of non-movement, of difference within sameness and *vice versa*. *Le Voyage dans la lune* is also, Lanzoni notes (2002: 35), inspired by French science fiction literature of the nineteenth century. In this way, it is backward-looking. One only has to look at the illustrations of Jules Verne's novel of 1865, *De la Terre à la lune, trajet direct en 97 heures 20 minutes* (*From the Earth to the Moon*), to recognize the origins of Méliès's spacecraft (which is basically a large artillery shell) and the rudiments of his plot.[6]

In *Hugo*, Méliès's image of the moon is further removed from the idea of extra-terrestrial travel. In Scorsese's film, the famous image of the partially enucleated man in the moon is discovered by Hugo Cabret (Asa Butterfield), while the latter strives to recover memories of his father. The journey is therefore one into the past, and its scientific mechanics, although impressive, even magical, are also antiquated. The image is drawn by a small automaton, which Hugo is able to set in motion. In saccadic bursts of furious movement, the automaton sketches Méliès's classic image, thereby setting in motion, in parallel, the film's search for another important man of the past, which is to say, the rediscovery of Méliès himself. In this way, the small-scale embodiment of science fiction sends Hugo and viewer alike into the history of the genre on screen. This movement is paralleled, chiastically, by the film's other automaton, in the form of the Station Inspector (Sacha Baron Cohen), who is only able to move, following injuries to his leg sustained during the First World War, thanks to a mechanical leg brace, which transforms him in part into a mechanical man. The technical advances of medicine enable him to move; they also, however, limit his movement, recalling his disability and its cause in the past. In *Hugo*, therefore, Paris, and its cinematic history, is reduced in scale – everything plays out in and around Gare Montparnasse, and all narrative momentum, all futuristic technology, appears fundamentally designed to discover the past.[7]

Luis Buñuel, Un chien andalou *(1929)*

In her seminal analysis of Buñuel's film, Linda Williams writes that the 'famous metaphor of moon and eye that concludes the prologue to *Un Chien andalou* is perhaps the most often cited example of filmic Surrealism – to the extent that audiences usually remember it and forget the rest of the film' (1981: 63).[8] In this way, this metaphor has become not only a metonym for *Un chien andalou*, not to mention for French surrealist film more broadly, but also, in an ostensibly perverse twist of fate, something of a fetish, screening the film in its entirety with the para-doxical, double action of the Freudian screen memory. Following a discussion, precisely, of filmic metaphor and metonymy and the various paradigmatic and syntactic chains that comprise the film, Williams proposes a brilliant reading of the latent meaning of the prologue in light of the remainder of the film or what we might consider its diegesis proper. This retrospective illumination of the film's beginning by its end is couched, in Freudian terms, as 'secondary revision' (1981: 100).[9] Thus, the beginning of the film drives its main body, and the prologue's own meaning is entirely self-founding at the time of its projection onto the screen. Only with the benefit of hindsight can its metaphors of cutting be understood to repre-sent castration in the Freudian sense. This is typical of Williams's focus throughout the essay, which interprets the elements in *Un chien andalou*'s various chains in light of what follows them. When she notes that the 'image of a woman's eye cut open by a razor has been isolated as a still in countless posters, film histories, and anthologies, to become the very emblem of surreality in film', she is not surprised by this emphasis on the eye at the expense of the moon; indeed, 'the bizarre simi-larity between the eye cut by a razor and the moon cut by a horizontal sliver of cloud [...] is so striking in this episode' for Williams precisely because the meta-phor appears to be the wrong way round (1981: 63). Whereas Williams explains the metaphorical importance of the moon through the cutting of the eye and, in turn, the latent meaning of the cutting of the eye through the symbolic images of the female genitals that comprise the subsequent diegesis, my aim here is not to read against Williams's analysis but, instead, to follow its trail, its metaphoric and metonymic chains, in the opposite direction. My purpose, in other words, is to consider other allegorical and intertextual chains that may shine new light on Buñuel and Dalí's moon.[10]

The key to Williams's reading of the prologue (1981: 63–69) lies in the way in which the film uses the contiguity of images to suggest narrative continuity. Thus, following nine shots of a man looking first down, then outwards (from a balcony) and then upwards, interspersed with shots of a razor being sharpened on a strop, the same razor being used to nick a fingernail and of a moon shining in the night sky, we see a woman's face in close-up; a man is holding her left eye open with his fingers. Following another view of the moon, this time cut by a passing cloud, a final shot shows a razor being drawn across an eyeball. The narrative that emerges is of a man preparing a razor to cut the woman's eye, an action that is prompted in some way by the vision of the cloud passing before the moon. Williams notes (1981: 68) that this understanding of the sequence fails to take into account the fact that the man who is holding the woman's eye open is wearing a tie, whereas the other man, who otherwise dominates the screen time of the prologue, is not. Furthermore, the extreme close-up of the eyeball being cut by the razor, when viewed in isolation, can clearly be seen to be that of an animal. Indeed, if we take what may be considered a contrarian, or perverse, position one step further, we can also suggest that the shots of the moon are potentially unrelated. There is a moon in a sky and a man gazing up from a balcony at night, but only the contiguity of the shots leads us to believe that this moon is being seen by this man. The moon being cut by a cloud only stands as a metaphor (first for the cutting of an eye, but subsequently, as Williams will show in her reading of the remainder of the film, for castration) after its interweaving – as a metonym – into one continuous narrative sequence.[11]

In addition to noting how the narrative of the prologue includes shots that are ostensibly out of place within that narrative, Williams describes how Buñuel reverses the standard sequence of filmic metaphor (1981: 70). Typically, the tenor is set first (what the metaphor will be of) before being replaced by a shot of an image that functions as the vehicle for the metaphor. Williams is struck by the fact that the shot of the moon precedes the cutting of the eye. In her analysis, the prologue is fundamentally about the figure of castration that is the cutting of the eye, which is therefore the tenor, or action; the vehicle is the moon (the moon and cloud stand as a metaphor for the cutting of the eye). That the vehicle, or décor, precedes the tenor, or what she considers the 'hierarchically more significant' element of the film's action, makes the sequence (and even reduces it to) 'a self-reflecting comment on the very process of making metaphors' (1981: 71).

Broadly, Williams performs two critical manoeuvres on the basis of this reading: first, she points out the artificiality of the narrative continuity, reminding us that we viewers play something of an editorial role, joining together in narrative logic shots that are otherwise only (albeit suggestively and deliberately) juxtaposed; second, she adopts the position of the viewer who reads the prologue as one continuous narrative by choosing nonetheless to privilege the cutting of the eye as the dominant event, on which she then predicates her reading of the remainder of the film (as a story of a castration complex, which itself both relies on and retrospectively conditions this reading of the prologue). Thus, while noting the way that the narrative is cut by the individual shots, its logic always already ruptured, she bases her reading on the continuity of these same shots; indeed, hers is a hermeneutics of continuity through contiguity. As noted above, I do not wish to contradict this reading, which is thoroughly convincing; instead, I wish simply to highlight the double-edged blade that the razor, and the image of cutting, presents. Arguably, it is Williams's obsessive focus on castration metaphors that blinds her to the potential significance of those images that are less dramatically emphasized in the framework of the diegesis, or textually, and that signify more clearly beyond its borders, which is to say, intertextually, or allegorically. To focus on what appear to be the less significant elements of the prologue, narratively speaking, is not only to look beyond the framework of the text, but it is also, and at the same time, to adhere to a more typical narrative sequence in terms of the filmic construction of metaphor. In such a reading, the moon and its cutting precede the eye and its cutting *because* the moon is the tenor and the eye the vehicle. In other words, it is possible to read the prologue against the grain of Williams's exemplary and seminal reading, and, in so doing, to view it in step with Buñuel's narrative sequence and to argue that the cutting of the eye stands as a metaphor for the moon.

Clearly, insofar as powerful images of gazing are combined with (what have proven to be even more memorable) images of the gaze cut, the prologue presents a double story of alternate (and very nearly simultaneous) cutting and conjoining. Williams, it seems to me, is quite right to move beyond meta-cinematic interpretation into the realm of the psychoanalytic, as the metonymy that works in lock-step with the metaphors at play strongly recalls the double, and paradoxical, mechanics of that other screen that is the screen memory in Freud's account of fetishism. So, while the cutting of the eye in *Un chien andalou* reflects the trick played on us viewers, it also stages the double-edged nature of disavowal. That is to say, it severs and removes the source of truth from the fetish objects onto which the desire of the fetishist is displaced, but it also, and *at the same time*, conjoins the fetish object and the truth at its source, for it continues to symbolize the truth even as it partially represses it. In this sense, we might usefully capture the paradoxical double agency of the fetish as staged in Buñuel's prologue by talking not so much of a cutting as of a cleaving, which term functions auto-antonymically to describe both the act of dividing (in this case, the chain of images) in two and that of conjoining two (sets of images) as one.

Surely, one might suggest, a fetishistic reading of the prologue is precisely what Williams provides. And yet, this does not seem to me quite what she does. In fact, Williams reads the prologue as an extended (disjointed and conjoined) metaphor for castration, which then conditions the remainder of the film in terms of a fetishistic gaze. In other words, the cutting of the eye serves as the source of the trauma on which the diegesis proper's fetishism is founded. What escapes this analysis is the very metaphorical and metonymic nature of the prologue, which speaks symbolically, that is, it *speaks of* castration at one remove. The prologue itself, in other words, gazes at castration. It is my contention here that this gaze of the prologue, especially since it is always already cut and conjoined, and thus conditioned by disavowal, is that of a fetishist who has already been exposed – prediegetically, and thus in this case prior to the prologue itself – to a traumatic revelation of truth. In this way, the film does not only, as Williams argues,[12] intend forwards, its narrative emerging from the interplay of its constituent filmic elements as they unfurl on screen, but it also looks backwards. If the tenor of the moon is restored, the film can be read precisely as nostalgia for the (illusion of the) past.

It should be noted that the potential for desire to be more than simply self-generating and prospective is already present in the Lacanian revisions of Freudian psychoanalysis on which Williams draws. As she notes, the 'notion of the image in the Surrealists' discourse on film derives from two contradictory impulses', which are, 'on the one hand, a nostalgia for the unity of a prelinguistic Imaginary [...] and, on the other hand, the confrontation of the misrecognition of this Imaginary with the knowledge of difference obtained from the Symbolic' (1981: 41). In terms of the present chapter, it is important to retain here this retrospective, 'nostalgic' impulse, which is sacrificed in Williams's reading of *Un chien andalou* in favour of a desire that is unidirectional. As a result, when Williams reads in the cutting of the eye 'an intentional specular trap sprung on the spectator' (1981: 41), she overlooks, not unreasonably in the framework of her argument, the possibility that the principal viewer of the prologue, the man wielding the razor (and thus ostensibly the cutter, not the cut), is himself a victim of the same trap.[13] One of the figures of his desire is the moon. However deeply cut this figure is, first by cloud and then by the shock factor of filmic metaphor, it is still graphically present. It is worth speculating whether it is itself the object of desire or at least an intertextual trace or memory of a lost object. We may recall Claire Johnston's explanation of the object of desire, according to which it is 'the memory trace of a previous gratification which can never be obtained but will always be the lost object forever reincarnating itself in a series of objects' (Johnston cited in Williams 1981: 38).

As the cinema history lessons of *Hugo* attest, Méliès's moon has demonstrated the power to endure beyond its own demise. Even as his journey to the moon simultaneously celebrated the future of the cinema, and magic yet to come, and lamented the passing of the theatrical tradition of magic, Méliès conjured an image of the moon that was, even then, paradoxically metaphorical: one of its eyes is punctured by a bullet-like rocket ship, while the other looks on, with the result that it is blinded, but only partially. That moon's gaze was therefore nostalgic as well as prospective and reflexive (back to Earth, back at the viewer and inwards, reflecting on Méliès's curiously static journey of cinema itself) and expansive (to the Heavens, beyond the reach of poets and cinematographers). Allegorically, of course, such a moon was also powerfully metonymic of a French brand of cinema, and, as *Hugo* captures, of Paris as capital of cinematic (and theatrical) magic. By reflecting back on this intertextual moon, Buñuel, who plays the moon gazer and first fetishist in his own movie, is able to experiment and innovate (as a Surrealist and a non-French practitioner) while cleaving his film to the history of French cinema.

We might say that *Un chien andalou* aligns itself with Méliès's *Le Voyage dans la lune* via Scorsese's exhortation for audiences to 'come and dream [with me]'. Just as Méliès's appeal to dreamers is a nostalgic call for them to remember the 'real' magic of the stage and to see that magic, via the tricks of a new sleight of hand, on the screen, it is also a desire to look again to reconstruct the dream (in films made, and lost, in the past and then restored for future nostalgics). This is a cinema about dreams, on which Buñuel's film can build; indeed, because of Méliès's foundational call to dream, *Un chien andalou* can allow itself to be that dream. As Williams writes:

> If Breton and Desnos devised schemes to disturb the fictional signified of non-Surrealist films by calling attention to the imaginary nature of the medium, in the Surrealist films and screenplays this was not necessary. In these works the signified of the fiction is not emphasized. What happens instead is a very peculiar and paradoxical phenomenon: the Surrealist goal with respect to the cinematic signifier is to approximate as closely as possible the dreamer's belief in the reality of the signifier, a signifier that the dreamer *thinks* is perceived but is really only imagined. If the film is to inspire belief in the signifier, it must provide images that are easily perceived, that are clear and straightforward *as* images even (or especially) if their content is bizarre in the extreme.
>
> (1981: 48, original emphasis)

And yet, of course, if *Un chien andalou* is (just) a dream, it is also (nonetheless) the recollection of a dream already dreamt. Buñuel's moon may well be quickly cast aside, but it is also present, among figures of desire, including the desire for, and as, death. It also symbolizes the persistent trace of Méliès's journey to the moon and the adventure of cinema's exploration of its own death. While, as has been seen, Méliès's cinema was born of tricks, including, of course, innovative cutting techniques, Surrealist cinema was not without its own special effects, a prime example of which is 'the famous eye-slicing' sequence (Williams 1981: 49). The latter are dubbed profilmic effects by Christian Metz in reference to the fact that they are produced prior to filming; by contrast, the kinds of procedures pioneered by Méliès, which cause the image to be distorted, are called cinematographic effects (Williams 1981: 49). If Méliès's cinematic journey to the moon can be considered, like Baudelaire's invitations to journey far-afield, a fetishistic response to the death of a certain Parisian tradition (in this case, of magic), then it is not impossible to see *Le Voyage dans la lune* as a *prefilmic* effect.

And yet, the intertext that constitutes the prediegetic space, on which the fetishism of *Un chien andalou* can be deemed to be founded, also includes moons beyond those of Méliès's cinema, including those of what is considered elsewhere in this volume something of an Urtext of Parisian nostalgia. The moon features twice in Baudelaire's *Les Fleurs du mal* – in 'Tristesses de la lune' (known in English *inter alia* as 'The Melancholy Moon' and 'Sorrows of the Moon') and 'La Lune offensée' (variously, the insulted or affronted moon). It is with the first of these poems that I shall conclude the present chapter.

The presence of Charles Baudelaire's poetry often seems inescapable in French texts of nostalgia. Clive Scott has noted that he often reads poetry (in French or English) by other poets only to hear Baudelaire. 'I do not know', he writes, 'exactly what the linguo-literary status of these lines is', whether they might for instance be translations, allusions or citations; perhaps, he concludes, it is none of these: 'I might easily be falling prey to a self-deceiving ear' (2006: 195–96). Scott's particular interest lies in the translation of poetry, including of Baudelaire. In light of the way that the translation of poetry, and the creation of poetry in translation, can betray other sources of influence, I should like to reproduce here the first stanza of Baudelaire's 'Tristesses de la lune', followed first by James McGowan's English translation from the Oxford World's Classics volume of *The Flowers of Evil*, which may be considered a reasonably faithful rendering of the French, and then by Walter Martin's version, which recreates the poem quite differently:

> Ce soir, la lune rêve avec plus de paresse;
> Ainsi qu'une beauté, sur de nombreux coussins,
> Qui d'une main distraite et légère caresse
> Avant de s'endormir le contour de ses seins,
> 'Tristesses de la lune', Charles Baudelaire (Baudelaire 1998: 132)

[The moon tonight dreams vacantly, as if
She were a beauty cushioned at her rest
Who strokes with wandering hand her lifting
Nipples, and the contour of her breasts;]
'Sorrows of the Moon', James McGowan (Baudelaire 1998: 133)

[How pensively the Moon slides by tonight,
An odalisque reclining on her couch
Of cloud, one unselfconscious cloudy white
Hand, slipping down her breast for one last touch.]
'The Melancholy Moon', Walter Martin (Baudelaire 1997: 173)

Readers of Baudelaire's lines who are familiar with *Un chien andalou* will recognize the juxtaposition of moon, beautiful woman and the caressing of breasts. As has been seen, the first two elements appear, in this order (moon first, then woman), in Buñuel's prologue; the third element, the caressing of breasts appears in the main section of the film that follows, which Williams reads as a screen memory of the prologue. Interestingly, Martin's translation appears to go one step further in facilitating the pairing of Baudelaire and Buñuel's moons; this he does by explicitly providing the source of Baudelaire's metaphor, which is not named in the body of the original text.[14] Thus, the cushions and caressing hand are translated as the 'couch of cloud' and 'cloudy white', respectively. In the case of the caress, Baudelaire's metaphor appears to hinge on the conjoining of the hand and breast, the former giving the lightness of vapour and the latter a plumpness redolent of a cloud. Both McGowan and Martin produce a justifiable translation of the poem's cloud metaphor, one choosing to leave the tenor metaphorical (and thus, in this case, absent) and the other focusing on it and making it clearly visible.

What of course also happens is that we readers primed to read Baudelaire everywhere, including in Buñuel's *Un chien andalou*, find ourselves in a position akin to Scott's, albeit with the tables turned. Now, Baudelaire is a source of other intertexts, in this case exposing a hypotext that is, chronologically speaking, a hypertext. Indeed, it is difficult not to *see* Buñuel's slicing clouds in Martin's translation of Baudelaire's dreaming moon, which now 'slides by', whereas in the original French the sole movement comes with the distracted caressing that follows. In other words, whatever the 'linguo-literary status' of Martin's lines, they appear to hear Baudelaire and see Buñuel in an instance of singular-plural poetic-cinematic text. And given the emphasis that they give to the mechanics of poetic metaphor,[15] which is precisely what Williams sees at work in *Un chien andalou* (although her focus is the specific medium of film, which requires the co-presence of tenor and vehicle), it is tempting to read in the nexus of these two texts, and these two metaphors, an identical hesitation. In both texts, the question of *what is metaphorical of what* arises.[16] This is perhaps an instance of what Barbara Johnson has called 'metaphorical equivalence'.[17]

In conclusion, I argue that the appearance of the cloud before the eye in Buñuel's prologue betrays a Baudelairean hypotext. This film, which appears to project itself forwards, and indeed to be a film about projection forwards, or the self-genera-tion of filmic text, is also an act of recuperating the past. In nostalgic terms, one might suggest that the status of this text is one of mimesis. As Niemeyer argues, the recovery of the past in the present 'can only be re-enacted, repeated, reconstructed, reshown, rethought and restored by an artificial act, by *mimesis*' (2014: 3, original emphasis). Buñuel's focus on the cutting of a woman's eye, which works against the metaphorical emphasis on the moon and effectively disavows the latter in the film, prompts the reader of Baudelaire to question what 'Tristesses de la lune' can be considered to be about. Although the sequencing of images in the poem places the moon before the beauty caressing her breasts, which sees tenor logically precede the vehicle, the relative weight of imagery in this opening stanza suggests that it is a likening of a woman to the moon rather more than it is of the moon to a woman. Arguably then, the mechanics of metaphor and the peritextual privileging of the moon (in the poem's title) are counterbalanced by the woman's dominance of the textual body. Furthermore, both nouns (*la lune* and *une beauté*) are feminine in French, which enables the reader to catch a glimpse of the moon behind the woman in the subject pronoun *elle* that follows in the remaining stanzas.

This same glimpse can also be caught in the eye of Buñuel's moon gazer; indeed, when Baudelaire's nostalgia is translated onto *Un chien andalou*, the look in the man's eyes, as he prepares his razor, is highly suggestive of someone lost in thought.[18] To moon gaze is to dream first and to caress second. In the context of a French cinema of invention and the moving forward of the medium, this is one more image of someone whose dreams are of the past. Put simply, Buñuel's moon gazer is a man remembering, and this long before he is remembered as a symbol of oblivion.

NOTES

1. A phenomenon that Gibb (2019) calls variously the '1920s revisited' and the 'twen-ty-first-century revival'.
2. This photograph is reproduced in Barnouw's study (1981: 104).
3. To this extent therefore, I agree partially with Rémi Fournier Lanzoni's assessment that Méliès was the 'antithesis of the Lumière cinema', which is referenced in *Hugo*'s history lessons *en abyme* and had a strong focus on presenting reality. For Lanzoni, it is Méliès's focus on fantasy, trickery and elaborate props that makes him 'the first genuine artist of motion pictures' (2002: 32). My caveat would be that these fantasies are always already

and, at the same time, grounded in reality; indeed, the tricks and theatre of Méliès's film fantasies were laboriously constructed by hand and thus constituted a celebration of magic that was, to this extent at least, real. His fantasy could certainly not be accused of the commodity fetishism that distances a product from the source and labour of its production.

4. In *Le Voyage dans la lune*, the astronomers who gather for a lecture on the moon, at which the plan to travel there in a vessel fired from a giant artillery piece is unveiled, initially all sport long robes adorned with stars and moons and long pointed hats. Those who decide to embark on the journey, amid a scene of great agitation, remove these ceremonial robes in favour of everyday coats and hats. This appears to be a nod to the step into a future in which the art and mystery of the magician will be replaced by the world of human endeavour through technology. It seems that Méliès, who plays the leader of the astronomer-explorers, is quite conscious of his role in the demise, and nostalgic remembrance, of theatrical magic shows.

5. Rather appropriately, the camera used by Méliès was one of R.W. Paul's models, which were known as Theatrographs, with an emphasis on theatre, as opposed to Thomas Edison's Kinetoscope, whose name celebrates the moving image.

6. Interestingly, Verne's explorers are Americans. Méliès's reprise of the story includes a change of flag: the French tricolore is in evidence in the film; its three vertical stripes are recognizable even in the black and white version.

7. There is also a fetishistic function here: technology enables us to bear the present. An obvious example is the Station Inspector's mechanical leg, which is an ever-present souvenir of past trauma as well as a means of movement, of freedom, albeit of a limited, or partial, kind. The cinema itself also plays this role: although nostalgic, or perhaps because of this nostalgic edge, it affords spectators the possibility to flee the present and to travel, briefly and in full consciousness of the artifice, to the moon.

8. Michel Marie includes Buñuel among the filmmakers of modern cinema who sought to emphasize the free form of 'aesthetic interactions' at the expense of 'all rigorous narrative constraints'; furthermore, Marie cites *Un chien andalou* as an example of a period of French cinema 'rich in experimental research' (2003: 134 and 135, respectively). The film's title is typically given in English, as by Williams, as *Un Chien andalou* (An Andalusian Dog). In this chapter, I use French title case, according to which the noun that follows the indefinite article has a lower-case initial letter.

9. For Williams, the main body of the film functions fetishistically – or as a staging, or performance, of a fetish, at least – to replay and reiterate the opening sequence; indeed, she uses it to explain the beginning. It is, of course, a central paradox of the film that the main body is a narrative of disavowal, designed to replace the beginning, but that it ends up playing the part of a sort of extended coda to a primal scene that, ultimately, disavows it.

10. Dalí's role in the film is generally considered to be confined to the composition of the screenplay.

11. As will be seen at the end of this chapter, when the Baudelairean intertext that I wish to advance here is revealed, the moon and the woman are linked grammatically: both are feminine in French. The moon, too, has traditionally been associated with seeing (a kind of celestial eye). In this way, both the moon and the woman's eye reference the cinema in quite a reflexive way.

12. Williams reiterates this point throughout her essay, writing at one point that: '*Un Chien andalou* is a film composed entirely of visual formations of (sexual) desires and fears. But these desires and fears are not anchored in a character; they are figures generated by film text itself – a text whose dynamics are modeled upon the rhetorical figures of unconscious thought'. Later, she notes that 'none of the events of the prologue can be read as the illusion of past events, but only as configurations arising out of the act of writing, out of the desire expressed by the figure itself' (1981: 51–52 and 72, respectively).

13. Ironically, Williams may be said to be sprung in her own trap. As we have seen, the major part of the diegesis of *Un chien andalou*, that part that follows the prologue, consists, for Williams, in a sustained attempt to deny the meaning of castration in the form of various fetishistic scenarios. By focusing on the metaphors of castration, she ultimately closes her eyes to the seat of the trauma, the primal event that generates the castration anxiety on which the film *in its entirety* is predicated and in the absence of which its image chains appear to be self-generating.

14. Again, in the second stanza, Baudelaire's vague 'visions blanches [white visions]' become 'white clouds' in Martin's translation (Baudelaire 1997: 172–73).

15. It seems a deliberate strategy on Martin's part to 'translate' the metaphor by making explicit in English what is implicit in French. His translation of the poems for Carcanet's Poetry Pléiade collection is generally considered domesticating insofar as he often appears to give the verses a contemporary American setting. Doing a degree of the metaphorical work for the reader, while doubtless compensating elsewhere in the new English-language versions of what very much remain works of poetry (with careful rhyme schemes and so on), may indeed be justifiable from a perspective of translation ethics.

16. If the moon is a metaphor for a beautiful woman, then the poet may well be remembering Johnston's moment of 'previous gratification'; in contrast, if the beautiful woman is a metaphor for the moon, the object of desire must remain tantalizingly out of reach. In the second scenario, the moon represents desire as an aspiration for an impossible, essential (and, in this case, celestial) body and such caresses as there are must remain metaphorical in the sense of a vehicle standing in place of an absent tenor. That another metaphor, and another mode of metaphor (according to which the tenor and vehicle remain co-present), is possible is what makes this poem such a rich interrogation of desire.

17. Barbara Johnson uses this term in her comparison of the verse and prose versions of Baudelaire's 'Invitation au voyage'. Of course, as Johnson notes, using language that echoes Williams's own discussion of metaphor, the comparisons in a poem are not, ultimately, what makes it work *artistically*. That quality depends on something 'incomparable', and

'[t]he economy of the work of art is thus organized around a signifying surplus that transcends the mere exchange between signifiers and signified, between tenors and vehicles' (1980: 35–36). In the case of 'Tristesses de la lune', however, this undecidability appears intimately bound up with the making-poetic of the events recounted.

18. It is perhaps also worth imagining that this carrying forward into the future of Baudelaire's nostalgia, and its translation onto Buñuel's film, is also an anticipatory act. The double-movement of intertextuality, which is such that it is able to work against the linear time of historical influence, creates the possibility of reading 'Tristesses de la lune' as a dream of cinematic visions to come. I thank Marguerite Johnson here for reminding me of that poem's particularly cinematic quality.

REFERENCES

Balides, Constance (2016), 'Intertext as archive: Méliès, *Hugo*, and new silent cinema', in P. Flaig and K. Groo (eds), *New Silent Cinema*, New York and London: Routledge, pp. 135–58.

Barnouw, Erik (1981), *The Magician and the Cinema*, New York and Oxford: Oxford University Press.

Baudelaire, Charles (1997), *Complete Poems* (trans. W. Martin), Manchester: Carcanet.

Baudelaire, Charles (1998), *The Flowers of Evil* (trans. J. McGowan), Oxford: Oxford University Press.

Gibb, Dirk (2019), 'The return of the 1920s: An examination of the twenty first century revival', Ph.D. thesis, Newcastle, Australia: University of Newcastle.

Johnson, Barbara (1980), *The Critical Difference: Essays in the Contemporary Rhetoric of Reading*, Baltimore and London: The Johns Hopkins University Press.

Lanzoni, Rémi Fournier (2002), *French Cinema: From Its Beginnings to the Present*, New York and London: Continuum.

Marie, Michel (2003), *The French New Wave: An Artistic School* (trans. R. Neupert), Malden, MA and Oxford: Blackwell.

Niemeyer, Katharina (2014), 'Introduction: Media and nostalgia', in K. Niemeyer (ed.), *Media and Nostalgia: Yearning for the Past, Present and Future*, Houndmills: Palgrave Macmillan, pp. 1–23.

Scott, Clive (2006), 'Translating Baudelaire', in R. Lloyd (ed.), *The Cambridge Companion to Baudelaire*, Cambridge: Cambridge University Press, pp. 193–205.

Williams, Linda (1981), *Figures of Desire: A Theory and Analysis of Surrealist Film*, Urbana: University of Illinois Press.

6

Breathless in Paris

Christopher Falzon

The aim of this chapter is to consider the significance of the city of Paris for Jean-Luc Godard's New Wave classic *Breathless* (*À bout de souffle*, 1960). Paris is not just the place where the film happens to be mostly set. It is a city that has a special importance for film as such. Paris is after all the fabled birthplace of cinema, said to have begun in 1895 in the basement of the Grand Café in the Boulevard des Capucines, with the films projected on a screen by the Lumière Brothers. Moreover, as France's cultural and educational capital, Paris also brought the developing film industry into contact with literature and philosophy. French filmmakers often emerged from literary circles, and artists and philosophers took a serious interest in film almost from the start (see Brody 2009: 3–4). Most importantly for present purposes, Paris brought together the post-war philosophical and literary movement of existentialism, with its key figures Jean-Paul Sartre and Simone de Beauvoir, and the luminaries of the New Wave cinema that was to flourish in the late 1950s, François Truffaut, Jacques Rivette, Claude Chabrol, Éric Rohmer, Agnès Varda and Godard himself. Though the Paris-born Godard was absent from Paris during the war, he returned in 1949, drawn by the lively film culture of a city that was also buzzing with the new existentialist philosophy. Ten years later, he would make *Breathless,* his first feature film.

Paris has an important role to play in the genesis of the film, but the city also appears in the film, and not just as a setting for the action. There is an engagement, indeed a dialogue, between the film and the city as it is portrayed in the film. *Breathless* is a kind of documentary of Paris, capturing the everyday life of the city, and this in turn frames and sets into relief the film's cinematic artifice. As such, the city plays a key role in one of the film's most distinctive features – a radical realism in which the film goes so far as to acknowledge its own artificiality, reminding the viewer that it is, after all, just a movie. But, it is also a movie that captures a real city, Paris as it was in the late fifties. And from the standpoint of the present, the film has become a remembrance of a Paris that has in many ways ceased to exist.

Existentialism and Breathless

To explore the relationship between the city and the film in more detail, it is useful to say a few things about the existentialism that is part of the film's immediate historical background. After the rigours of the war and the German occupation of the city, there was a resurgence of creative and intellectual life. More or less at the centre of this resurgence were the figures associated with the new existentialist philosophy, above all Sartre and Beauvoir. The physical epicentre of this cultural activity was the Left Bank, especially Saint-Germain-des-Prés, where many of those involved lived and worked (see Poirier 2018). Sartre himself, after a brief internment in a POW camp, had spent the war in Paris. His monumental *Being and Nothingness*, a definitive formulation of existentialist philosophy, appeared in 1943. After the end of the war, in 1945, Sartre gave his popular lecture 'Existentialism is a Humanism', at the Club Maintenant, which was filled to overflowing, with people reportedly fainting in the crush. After this, existentialism became all the rage in Paris. In 1945, Sartre and Beauvoir also started the journal *Les Temps Modernes* to publish new philosophical and literary work. French existentialism itself found expression not only in philosophical texts but also in literature. Sartre wrote novels including his debut work *Nausea* (1938), along with short stories and plays. We also have Beauvoir's novels, including *The Mandarins*, a fictionalized portrayal of the Parisian intellectual scene after the war.

Existentialism offers an exhilarating vision of human beings as capable of wholly creating themselves, giving their existence meaning and purpose. It makes this claim against the background of a world understood as being absurd, without any pre-given meaning or purpose. As Roquentin, hero of Sartre's *Nausea*, says at one point, 'if I knew the art of convincing people, I should go and sit down next to that handsome white haired gentleman and I should explain to him what existence is […] here we all are, all of us, eating and drinking to preserve our precious existence and there's nothing, nothing, absolutely no reason for existing' (Sartre 1963: 162). In the novel, this sense of things having no meaning and not mattering leads the protagonist to intermittent bouts of nausea, feelings of anxiety, dizziness and despair. In 'Existentialism is a Humanism', Sartre suggests that an important part of this sense of life's meaninglessness is that we have been 'abandoned by God', and so no longer have any God-given plan or set of values that might give our lives purpose and direction. Here, existentialist thought reflects the decline of religion as a significant force in European culture over the last 300 years. We are on our own, unable to justify our values and goals by reference to a supreme being. The sense that all the old frameworks of values were collapsing was no doubt reinforced by the chaos and upheaval of the war years.

However, the response of Sartre and the existentialists to this situation was not to fall into nihilism and despair. The proper conclusion to draw from absurdity, Sartre argued, is to recognize that it is we who give meaning to the world. Through our freedom, we choose the goals and values that give our lives purpose. To that extent, existentialism is a positive philosophy of freedom, the central message being that people are capable of taking responsibility for their existence. This is perhaps why existentialism was so appealing to the people of post-war France. Against the background of the war's upheaval and destruction, existentialism came along with the idea that people had the power to create their world anew, from scratch. The collapse of the old world could now be seen as an opportunity for people to construct a new world and a new future. In envisaging human beings as able to create themselves through their choices, Sartre makes freedom central to human existence, as that which sets human beings apart from the rest of the world, and this is a very radical conception of freedom. For Sartre, nothing determines us to do, be or become what we are or will be. We are absolutely free to 'make ourselves', to choose the sort of person we want to be. Certainly, there are aspects of ourselves that are determined, our 'facticity', but morally, in terms of our values and goals, we are free to make ourselves. We may always exist in a situation, a set of concrete circumstances, but nothing in our situation determines what we are or do. We are always free to choose ourselves in relation to our situation.

There are negative aspects to this freedom. In an absurd universe, the only meaning or purpose my life can have is the meaning I give to it through my choices. I and I alone am responsible for the values I have, the goals I pursue. This is an enormous burden, and I experience my freedom as 'anguish', a fundamental anxiety before the necessity of having to choose, to take total responsibility for my existence. This is why people often attempt to hide from their freedom in various forms of bad faith. In *Being and Nothingness*, Sartre says 'man, being condemned to be free, carries the weight of the whole world on his shoulders; he is responsible for the world and for himself as a way of being' (1958: 553) and 'it is precisely thus that the for-itself [Sartre's term for the conscious self] apprehends itself in anguish, that is, as a [...] being which is compelled to decide the meaning of being [...] one realizes in anguish one's condition [...] but [...] most of the time we flee anguish in bad faith' (1958: 556). We might, for example, pretend that we are merely a product of our environment or upbringing, that there are God-given values we can appeal to for guidance, or, tellingly in the immediate aftermath of the war, that we were 'only following orders'. But even if freedom is burdensome and a source of anguish, Sartre insists that existentialism is a positive, optimistic philosophy because it does not see human beings as condemned or determined by a past to be a certain way. Whatever they have done in the past was freely chosen, and they are always free to make themselves anew. Existentialism is a humanism because it puts the human being at the centre, as the legislator of moral value (Sartre 1975: 369).

When Godard returned to Paris in 1949, he came under the influence of Sartre's writings. As Godard says, 'I had encyclopaedic tendencies. I wanted to read everything. I wanted to know everything. Existentialism was at its peak at the time. Through Sartre I discovered literature, and he led me to everything else' (quoted in Brody 2009: 18). Godard also frequented the Saint-Germain-des-Prés area, including the Café de Flore and other cafés popular with Sartre's followers (Brody 2009: 75; Fairfax 2017). In addition, Godard immersed himself in the city's film culture. He watched a huge number of movies at the 'ciné-clubs' that were popping up around Paris, including Henri Langlois's *Cinémathèque Française*, whose attendees included Sartre and Beauvoir. Here, Godard met other future New Wave directors including Truffaut, Chabrol and Rivette. In the fifties, Godard turned to film criticism. Along with Truffaut and others, he became a regular contributor to the *Cahiers du Cinéma* movie journal, founded in 1950 by the critic André Bazin. Sartre's influence is visible in Godard's film criticism, being 'one of a vast constellation of writers, philosophers and artists frequently evoked in his playfully allusive prose' (Fairfax 2017).

Breathless is based on a story suggested by Truffaut. The film's plot is relatively straightforward. Petty criminal Michel Poiccard (Jean-Paul Belmondo), who idolizes Humphrey Bogart, steals a car in Marseilles and drives it to Paris. On the way, he is stopped for speeding and shoots the traffic cop. In Paris, he steals money from an old girlfriend, meets American Patricia Franchini (Jean Seberg) an aspiring journalist whom he likes, on the Champs-Élysées, and tries to collect some money from a friend. About one-third of the movie is shot in Patricia's hotel room, while Michel tries to convince her to sleep with him and run away with him to Italy. After he has driven Patricia to the airport to interview a famous novelist, they head down to a Swedish model's apartment in Montparnasse. When it looks like the trip to Italy is a real possibility, she turns him in to the police. Instead of running away, he waits around. When the police arrive, a friend throws him a gun in an attempt to save him. The police shoot him dead.

There are some similarities between *Breathless* and Sartre's *Nausea*. Godard was certainly familiar with the novel. Daniel Fairfax notes that in a 1958 film review, Godard refers to the 'cheap, sordid pessimism reminiscent of *La Nausée*' (Godard 1972: 84; Fairfax 2017). Both Sartre's novel and Godard's film are debut works; and as Fairfax also points out, there are similarities between the sequence in Patricia's hotel room, where she and Michel talk and flirt, and the scene in the novel where *Nausea*'s hero Roquentin visits his former lover Anny in her Paris hotel room. However, Michel is also unlike Roquentin in significant ways. Roquentin feels the absurdity of the world. His world has become disordered, strange and nauseating. At this point, Sartre had not yet fashioned his positive response to absurdity, which would emerge five years later in *Being and Nothingness* – the idea that, in an absurd world, human beings can take centre stage as the sovereign creators of meaning, giving themselves meaning and purpose through their free choices (see Falzon 2005). As we will see, Michel is much more like this heroic subject, the independent, self-determining individual who rebels against traditional norms and creates an identity for themselves.

The existentialist spirit of heroic self-determination is also evident in the film itself. It has an air of freedom, a sense of 'anything goes', as Godard himself put it (1972: 173). It is a film that rebels against the constraints of the existing French cinema. This was the 'Tradition of Quality' identified by Truffaut in his 1954 *Cahiers* essay 'Une certaine tendance du cinéma français' ('A Certain Tendency in French Cinema') (see Truffaut 1976). Indeed, the whole New Wave movement can be understood as a reaction to the safe, conventional, studio-bound films, often literary adaptations, that the French movie industry was turning out in the fifties films, such as Jean Delannoy's *Maigret et l'Affaire Saint-Fiacre* (1959), a poster for which appears fleetingly in *Breathless*. The heroes of the *Cahiers* critics were the auteurs who went their own way, whose films were very much an expression of their personal vision and individual style; older French directors like Jean Renoir and Robert Bresson; or contemporaries who were working outside the studio system, like Jean-Pierre Melville. The very notion of the film director as auteur, promoted by Truffaut in his 1954 essay, seems to be epitomized in the Godard of *Breathless*. Let us turn now to the kind of world that *Breathless* portrays, and how Paris figures in that world.

A documentary of Paris

As befits a rule-breaking, existentialist film, *Breathless* often has an energetic, free-wheeling look about it. Contributing to this are the film's famous jump cuts, where short sections of film are cut out within a scene, interrupting the continuity. As a result, the action jumps abruptly from one moment to another, giving the film a nervy, hyperactive quality suggesting Michel's life as a fugitive on the run. Godard himself indicates that the cutting was originally done for practical purposes, since the film was running too long. But if so, the practical requirement became part of Godard's artistry. Rather than follow fellow director Melville's advice to shorten the film by cutting unnecessary scenes, Godard cut portions within scenes that seemed to him to lack 'vigour' (Godard 2014: 24; Brody 2009: 68).

The film is not all cinematic hyperactivity, however. There are also long periods where Michel and Patricia are just walking, talking or playing around, and there Godard simply lets the camera run on in extended takes. There is the famous stroll down the Champs-Élysées, the long central portion with the two of them in Patricia's hotel room, and the sequence in the Swedish model's apartment at the end. Dramatically, not a lot is happening in these scenes, the story pretty much coming to a halt, but they are nonetheless compelling to watch. We seem to be witnessing something very natural, uncontrived, authentic, a realistic portrayal of two people talking in real time. No doubt with this in mind, Godard described his film as 'a documentary on Jean Seberg and Jean-Paul Belmondo in a film by Jean-Luc Godard' (1987: 166).

It is not that the actors were simply making things up on the spot or that Godard was improvizing scenes as he went along. Commenting in *Le Monde* on his method of directing the film, Godard said:

> I improvised nothing, I had taken numerous notes in no particular order and written some scenes and some dialogue. Before beginning the film I sorted out these notes and I had a general plan of action. This enabled me, every morning, to write the eight pages corresponding to the sequence I had to shoot that day [...] I give [the actors] lots of little indications and I try to find just the essential gestures.
>
> (1987: 165–66)

That said, for some observers, like Godard's cameraman, Raoul Coutard, it did look very much like a film being improvized on the go. Coutard recounts how Godard would write lines of dialogue in an exercise book that no one else was allowed to look at, on the morning of the day's shooting. He would then give the lines to Belmondo and Seberg, have a few brief rehearsals of the scenes involved and film them (see Coutard 2016).

What is clear is that Godard wanted *Breathless* to have a spontaneous, naturalistic feel to it, and in this, he was assisted by some recent technical innovations in cinematography. The availability of the handheld camera, along with faster film stock, allowed the film to be shot outside the studio, in natural locations like the street or a cramped hotel room, with minimum artificial light. No longer tied to shooting platforms and tracks, the camera could move freely in the urban environment. As Phillip John Usher recounts, 'Coutard carried the camera on his shoulder and simply walked around – or was pushed in a wheelchair by Godard or an assistant' (2014: 29). The camera could also be concealed for street scenes. In order to film Michel and Patricia's stroll down the Champs-Élysées, Coutard and his camera were hidden in a mail cart, with a hole for the camera lens, and pushed alongside the actors as they talked (Sterrit 1999: 47).

The result of all this is a naturalistic, documentary-style portrayal, not only of the characters but also of the city they inhabit. The film reveals Paris in its everyday reality, the normal life of a city with all its grittiness, energy and spontaneity. This is in fact a feature of many of the New Wave films: '[t]he Paris that the New Wave directors wanted to represent was the Paris of everyday life. The city that was laid out before them as a kind of immense background, the city that no one paid attention to' (Douchet 1998: 124). In *Breathless*, everyday Paris is everywhere we look. The film documents the Champs-Élysées, the many bustling and car-filled streets, Patricia's tiny hotel room in the Hotel de Suède on Quai Saint-Michel, the Swedish model's upmarket Montparnasse apartment in Rue Campagne Première, along with cafés and bistros, cinemas, newspaper offices, travel agencies and used car yards. The realism of these views is emphasized because Godard also includes a few touristy shots of the city, featuring landmarks like the Louvre and Notre Dame, accompanied by lush music.

This naturalistic portrayal of Paris is another way that Godard breaks with the traditional French cinema. Godard, along with the other New Wave filmmakers, wanted to get away from the artificial-looking, studio-shot portrayal of the city typical of the older cinema. The studio was to be replaced by the street, and instead of extras, there would be ordinary Parisians going about their business. A concealed camera also meant that there would be little in the way of reaction on the part of the pedestrians. In this urban realism there can be detected the influence of the Italian neorealism of the forties and fifties, the films of Roberto Rossellini, Luchino Visconti and others. The Italian directors similarly wanted to get away from studio artificiality, in favour of naturalistic stories in authentic settings. They were much admired by *Cahiers* founder Bazin, mentor to Godard and the other New Wave filmmakers (see Andrew 1973: 64; Sterrit 2000: 6; Sterrit 2002).

However, *Breathless* is not simply devoted to documenting the real. As is evident in the film's jump cuts, Godard is also a fan of cinematic artifice. In this respect, he was at odds with Bazin. For Bazin, what was most important about film was its capacity to photographically capture reality. He favoured the long take and deep focus, which were prominent in Italian neorealist cinema (Andrew 1973: 64); indeed, he believed that film editing techniques 'serve mainly to falsify reality by breaking up space and time', whereas Godard in contrast argued for the importance of editing as a means of expressing psychological reality through its spatial discontinuities (Brody 2009: 14, 28). His disagreement with Bazin on this point was played out in the pages of the *Cahiers*, while Godard was still a film critic. The December 1956 issue featured an article by Bazin called 'Montage Interdit' ('Editing Forbidden') and one by Godard, 'Montage, mon beau souci' ('Editing, My Beautiful Concern').

To put this debate in a more general context, while some theorists like Bazin emphasized film's capacity to possess the real world photographically, others like Eisenstein identified editing as the essence of cinema. But as film theorist

V. F. Perkins argues in *Film as Film*, neither alone is sufficient. Rather, narrative fiction film 'exploits the possibilities of synthesis between photographic realism and dramatic illusion' (1972: 60). Film's conquest of the visual world 'extends in two opposite directions. The first [...] gives it the power to "possess" the real world by capturing its appearance. The second [...] permits the representation of an ideal image, ordered by the film-maker's will and imagination' (1972: 60). In the latter case, the real is transformed into cinematic narrative by means of the various cinema-specific techniques, framing and editing, montage, the close-up, the tracking shot, sound and music and so on. Ordinary life is thereby idealized, turned into cinema, though we might equally say that abstract ideas are being realized, made concrete, brought down to earth. Depending on which aspect, the photographic realism or the artifice, is more dominant, there is a spectrum running from the realist documentary to the wholly constructed cartoon, with narrative fiction film in a compromise position between them.

In *Breathless*, as a narrative film, both these aspects are discernible. The element of photographic realism is evident in the film's naturalistic, documentary-style portrayal of its characters and their city. At the same time, the film makes use of various cinematic devices, such as the audacious editing that adds to the film's energy. There is, however, a further feature of the film that especially distinguishes it. Narrative film may be a hybrid of photographic realism and cinematic artifice, but it still usually aims to present a reality. This 'reality effect' is generally achieved through the completeness of the film's illusion and the invisibility of its editing. A film typically hides its artifice, conceals the fact that it is a movie. *Breathless* explores another cinematic possibility – that one might radicalize the realist aspect of film in order to undermine its reality effect. It is a narrative fiction film that goes so far in its realism as to call attention to the artifice of its own cinematic devices, to remind the viewer that it is just a movie. And here, the Paris so realistically portrayed in the film has an important role to play.

As mentioned, Godard is clearly not afraid to use cinematic artifice. In this regard, *Breathless* reflects the influence of a whole history of film and film technique. Godard has clearly watched a lot of film, especially Hollywood film, in the Parisian *ciné-clubs*. Here, the role Paris played in the film's genesis is evident once again. The influence of American film in particular reflects a definite moment in the city's history. After the war, US economic relief helped France get back on its feet, aid that was given on the condition that the market be opened to, amongst other things, American cinematic imports. Accordingly, Hollywood movies quickly filled the capital's cinemas. Though in his later years, Godard would become aggressively anti-American, in his early critical writings for the *Cahiers du Cinéma*, he championed westerns and B-grade noir crime drama films (see Rolls and Walker 2009: 169; Usher 2014: 25). The *Cahiers* critics in general were enthusiastic advocates of American film, of Hollywood directors like Alfred Hitchcock, Howard Hawks and Nicholas Ray, and of 'low-brow' westerns and films noirs (though Godard and Truffaut use terms like 'B movie' and 'gangster film' rather than film noir).

Breathless features some very obvious elements from the noir world. Michel is the amoral hoodlum who commits a crime, wants to get out of town to avoid the cops and is inevitably killed at the end of the film. As Godard put it, 'as my avowed ambition was to make an ordinary gangster film, I had no business deliberately contradicting the genre: he must die' (1972: 174). Patricia is another recognizable noir figure, the femme fatale who brings about the male hero's downfall. The film explicitly alludes to its Hollywood sources. It opens with a dedication to Monogram pictures, American producers of low-budget gangster films, westerns and horror films. And there are many American films in the film, on movie posters or playing in cinemas. Michel walks past a poster for *10 Seconds to Hell* (Aldrich 1959) with the slogan 'Vivre dangereusement jusqu'au bout' (live dangerously until the end); Patricia hides from the cop tailing her in a cinema playing Preminger's *Whirlpool* (1950); and after she loses him, she and Michel end up in a cinema playing *Westbound* (Boetticher 1959) (see Andrew 1987: 15–16). The appropriation of elements from Hollywood film is also something that Michel himself does within the film. Along with a general obsession with American culture (he only ever steals American cars), Michel is obsessed with Humphrey Bogart. He seems to have fashioned his personality around a tough-guy Bogart persona. We see him stopping outside the Cinéma Normandie on the Champs-Élysées, playing Bogart's film *The Harder They Fall* (1956). Michel also has his Bogart gesture, rubbing the thumb across the lips, which he makes throughout the film, every time he passes a mirror.

The film's appropriation of Hollywood film elements is yet another way in which it distances itself from the older French cinema and announces its status as New Wave. As Barbara Mennel notes in *Cities and Cinema*, 'The film's aesthetics cite film noir of the B-category in stark contrast to the studio-based, high-production value, star-driven, literary adaptation of French cinema that came before the New Wave' (2008: 78). However, the film also subverts its Hollywood borrowings, distancing itself from the Hollywood cinema it is drawing on, and setting its noir story in an everyday Paris plays an important role in this subversion. An American film would have had Michel spending his time in dimly lit nightclubs and shadowy alleyways. *Breathless* is a film noir set in the city of light, mostly in daytime and in the middle of summer (Monaco 1980: 118; see also Levy 2010; Ezell 2014). It is also a very ordinary, naturalistically portrayed Paris, and this realistic urban setting has the effect of showing up the artificiality of the film's Hollywood elements[1]. Here in particular, we can see the engagement or dialogue that is going on between the film and the city as it is portrayed in the film. As

Nathan Heller puts it, '*Breathless* is an orchestrated dialogue between two worlds – a world of stylized Hollywood romanticism, and the everyday world of banal, uncinematic life. The film is Godard's idea of a fast-paced Hollywood gangster movie transplanted to the Paris streets' (Heller 2010).

In this mundane setting, we cannot take the noir plot entirely seriously. A case in point is the sequence where cops are tailing Patricia, hoping she will lead them to Michel, and she loses them by ducking into a cinema. The whole movie-style routine looks unrealistic and comical when played out on the bustling Avenue Mac-Mahon. Heller points out another scene earlier on, where Michel's gangster friend Tolmachoff (Richard Balducci) is tracked down by some cops looking for Michel, not in a dingy bar but in a well-lit travel agency. The cops are inept and overweight, while the gangster leans nonchalantly against the counter, playing with a toy plane. The whole meeting looks a bit absurd (see Heller 2010). Later, in the sequence in Patricia's hotel room, she and Michel are shown doing ordinary things, washing up, teasing one another, chatting about music and literature. In the midst of this, we cut to a composed frame of the two kissing in sunglasses, a real 'movie kiss' that against this background looks especially contrived.

Godard has suggested that this air of contrivance is another aspect of the film that was not originally intended. His avowed ambition was to make a normal gangster film, but 'one never does exactly what one intended. Sometimes one even does the opposite [...] I realized that [*Breathless*] was not at all what I thought. I thought I had made a realistic film like Richard Quine's *Pushover*, but it wasn't that at all'. The film turned out looking disingenuous because he 'didn't have enough technical skill' (Godard 1972: 175). Even if so, Godard has turned this into one of the film's most distinctive features. And, this air of contrivance is not at odds with the film's realistic portrayal of ordinary life. Rather, in calling attention to its cinematic elements, the film's realism is intensified. As David Sterrit puts it, in contrast to the Italian neorealists, Godard 'welcomed a different kind of realism – a realism that grows from a cheerful acknowledgement that cinema is in fact cinema' (1999: 6). For Godard, 'true realism [...] is not simply the attempt to perfectly capture the world as it is. It is the effort to mobilize the true power of the cinematic apparatus to reveal *the reality that film itself is an artifice*' (Rockhill 2010: 115).

It is thus apt to refer to this as a cinematic 'hyperrealism'. Precisely by calling attention to its artifice, the film comes across as more realistic, more honest, more authentic. As Nathan Andersen points out in *Film, Philosophy, and Reality*, the film's reminders that the scenario it depicts is fictional 'do not so much distract from its power as enhance it. Rather than make it feel fake, they lend it greater authenticity' (2019: 142). Andersen points to the influence here not just of Italian neorealism but also the documentary filmmaker Jean Rouch. In films like *Moi, un Noir* (1958), Rouch called attention to the artifice involved even in documentary filmmaking, highlighting in his documentaries the presence of the camera, and the editing in particular. *Moi, un Noir* also made pioneering use of the jump cut. For his part, Godard reportedly thought of calling his film *Moi, un Blanc* (see Brody 2012).

The use of noticeable editing devices like the jump cut, rather than invisible continuity editing, is another way that *Breathless* calls attention to its cinematic workings, reminding the viewer that they are watching a movie. In fact, there are multiple ways Godard does this at the level of editing. He will sometimes refuse a smooth fit between sight and sound. For example, when Michel shoots the cop at the start of the film, we see him aim a gun, the cop falls down and we hear gunshots on a soundtrack that is obviously post-synched (see Romney 2000). A couple of times Godard uses the incongruous device of irising in to close a scene, a technique borrowed from the silent cinema era. Another sort of alienating device that Godard makes use of is having his characters break the fourth wall and directly address the audience, as Michel does while driving down to Paris at the start of the film, with the memorable speech: 'If you don't like the sea, if you don't like the mountains, if you don't like the town, get stuffed'. Addressing the audience is the classic alienation device that Bertolt Brecht talks about, the result being that: '[t]he audience can no longer have the illusion of being the unseen spectator at an event which is really taking place' (1964: 91).

This is all very different from the Hollywood filmmaking where one is supposed to forget that one is watching a film, to be taken in by the illusion. It is the opposite of someone like Hitchcock, for example, who is a master of audience manipulation. Nonetheless, Hitchcock himself was not averse to disrupting the illusion a little, making his famous cameo appearances in his films. And there is a Hitchcock touch in *Breathless* along these lines. There is a scene where Patricia and Michel pull up in a car opposite Patricia's workplace, the *New York Herald Tribune* office in Rue de Berri, on their way to her airport interview. The man in dark glasses reading the paper and checking Michel out, then running off to inform the cops, is Godard himself. In *Breathless*, the role of the director cameo is not designed so much to interrupt the proceedings as to get the story going again, after the long pause in Patricia's hotel room. As Andersen points out, Godard's informer not only alerts the police to Michel but also to Patricia, whom they will use to eventually corner Michel (2019: 145ff). But by including himself at a critical juncture to move the plot along, Godard can also be seen as calling attention to the film's cinematic contrivance. Plot, whether a Hollywood noir movie plot or otherwise, is itself something artificially imposed by the filmmaker.

It is worth adding that along with the director himself, many of Godard's friends and colleagues from the Parisian film world make an appearance in various roles in the film, alerting the knowledgeable viewer at least to the milieu out of which it has emerged. The director Melville plays Parvulescu, the smug male chauvinist novelist that Patricia is going to interview at the airport. Earlier in the film, in the travel agency, Michel makes a passing reference to a certain Bob Montagne, who is the hero of Melville's film *Bob le flambeur* (1956). Fellow New Wave director Jacques Rivette plays the victim of a car accident that Michel witnesses. *Cahiers* film critic Jean Douchet is the one kicking Rivette to see if he is still alive. Another *Cahiers* critic, Jean Domarchi, is the man Michel beats up and robs in a cafe toilet shortly afterwards. The *Cahiers* journal itself makes an appearance at one point, as a student approaches Michel in the street trying to sell him a copy, which he pointedly refuses to buy.

Freedom and situation

Let us now turn the focus onto the film's two main characters and consider their relationship not only with the film they are appearing in but also the city that appears in the film. This is also an opportunity to explore further the film's relationship with Sartrean existentialism.

Clearly, these characters cannot be reduced to the types required for a Hollywood noir movie. As we have seen, the film subverts its borrowed genre elements and not only by transplanting a Hollywood noir movie to an ordinary, commonplace Paris, but it also spends a lot of the time ignoring its noir movie plot altogether. For example, the action comes to a complete halt in the long hotel room sequence, where Patricia and Michel just do ordinary things in an unaffected way. When cinematic elements appear, like the movie kiss, they come across as artificial and contrived. The film can also be seen as subverting the Hollywood plot by having it enacted by 'ordinary' people. They do from time to time act in the sorts of ways required to move the plot forward, but generally speaking, when they are most acting according to type, things are least convincing. As Jonathon Romney (2000) points out, when Michel shoots the traffic cop at the start of the film and runs off, it looks very much like the actor impersonating the getaway in an American thriller; and when Patricia brings about Michel's downfall, reporting him to the police, it seems less a betrayal and more a 'generic tragic gesture'. This is partly because even if these actions are pivotal for the plot, the characters seem to perform them almost as an afterthought, in the midst of pursuing more ordinary human concerns. They are above all interested in being free spirits, which in turn brings to mind the existentialism that celebrates freedom as a central feature of human existence.

Michel seems very much the heroic existentialist subject, the independent, self-determining individual. He certainly does not seem to be concerned with social conventions. He constantly breaks the rules to satisfy his desires. He shoots cops, steals cars, mugs people, pilfers money from old girlfriends and in general does whatever he wants. He does want to have a relationship with Patricia, but spends a lot of time trying to cajole her into going along with his plans. Like Michel, Patricia sees herself as a free spirit and is very concerned to preserve her freedom of action. This is evident in her relationship with Michel. She says to him: 'I want you to love me; but at the same time I want you to stop loving me – I'm very independent you know'. Hubert Dreyfus suggests that this is ultimately why Patricia betrays Michel to the cops because she feels that her independence will be threatened if they become a proper couple and go off to Italy, something that by the end of the film has become a real possibility. So, she betrays him to stop that happening and also to prove to herself that she does not love Michel. As she says, 'I stayed with you to see if I was in love with you […] and since I'm being cruel to you, it proves I'm not in love with you' (see Dreyfus 2012).

On Dreyfus's reading, what Godard shows us in *Breathless* is the world according to existentialism, a world that is amoral, senseless and empty, in short absurd. The values and justifications that ordinary people cling to in order to give their lives purpose and meaning are illusions, and Michel is one of those who recognizes the situation. He no longer looks for ultimate justifications for what he does. This might be the significance of the word on the wall of his old girlfriend Liliane's apartment, 'pourquoi' (why?) spelt out in cigarette packets. It is posing the existentialist question: why do anything? There is no objective reason or justification for anything that one does (see Dreyfus 2012).

For Sartre, as mentioned, this lack of any ultimate justification for what we do does not leave us without values or direction, but means that human beings alone are responsible for the values and goals they pursue. And, Michel seems to take advantage of the lack of any externally dictated meaning to create his own meaning for himself. He invents a past for himself as he goes along. He claims that his grandfather drove a Rolls, that his father was a brilliant clarinettist and that he can only stay at the Claridge, an expensive hotel, among other things (see Dreyfus 2012). Above all, he fashions his own identity, drawing on American popular culture, especially Bogart movies, to create a tough-guy persona for himself. Patricia also recognizes there is no preordained path for her to follow. She does not see herself as bound by the constraints of a traditional female role, living instead a relatively liberated life in a foreign city. Dreyfus suggests that she differs from Michel in that where he takes the breakdown of meaning as an opportunity to freely invent himself, freedom for her is primarily negative, freedom from anything that might tie her down, including becoming part of a proper couple with Michel. However, this might be to underestimate the extent to which she is also making a different kind of life for herself and inventing her own persona.

Where Michel draws on American film, Patricia draws on models from European high culture – the Renoir poster, and the story of Romeo and Juliet, in particular (see Sterrit 1999: 58).

Dreyfus's contrast also underestimates the extent to which Michel also seeks a negative kind of freedom. He does what he wants without regard for other people. 'Never mind the pedestrians', he says to a taxi driver, 'step on it. That's all I ask'; and 'Don't use the brakes. Cars are made to go, not to stop!' In one interview, Godard refers to Michel as 'a bit of an anarchist' (Godard 1987: 165), but this is clearly not the progressive sort of anarchism that aims to abolish the state in order to replace all forms of government authority with free associations of individuals and groups. Michel is not interested in bettering society or fostering the freedom of others. He only cares about his own freedom from interference by others. This was picked up on by critics at the time, who accused Godard's film of 'bourgeois anarchism', a reactionary celebration of the individual who revels in their individuality, to the exclusion of broader social issues (Martin 2003). The concern was that the film failed to appreciate the extent to which individuals exist in social relations and are shaped by them. Similar criticisms were made of Sartrean existentialism by the communists in the forties. A later, more politicized Godard would come to agree with these criticisms, decrying *Breathless* as 'fascist' (Godard 2014: 28), the fascism residing in the film's 'refusal of the reality of social relations and the propagation of the myth of an existence outside those relations' (McCabe 1980: 33–34).

Despite such criticisms, Michel and Patricia are socially located in the film – at least in the sense of living in Paris. It is true that they are living a somewhat dislocated existence there. As Mennel notes, they are both without family, living transitional lives in the city. They are often on the move, walking through the streets, driving or being driven in cars and taxis. Even the interiors that the characters inhabit are transitional places, like Patricia's hotel room. Michel is even more rootless than Patricia, who at least has a room, a job, appointments with work colleagues and press conferences she needs to go to. Michel is unemployed, has no fixed abode and spends a lot of time wandering the Paris streets (see Mennel 2008: 79). For all that, Paris is more than a series of public and private spaces the characters pass through. It is also the framework that brings the characters together, giving unity to their meandering adventures. Moreover, it provides a cultural framework, the cultural materials on which the characters draw for their apparently anarchic personalities.

This is a point pursued by Sterrit, who argues that for all its celebration of the individual, *Breathless* is in fact questioning the idea that Michel and Patricia are totally free agents, and that Godard is challenging the existentialist position that individuals can entirely make themselves (1999: 56ff). On Sterrit's reading, the film is in laying bare the influences that have gone into the construction of these characters. Michel the Frenchman has absorbed a lot of his character from American films, mastering the American movie tough-guy attitude. He has a whole catalogue of tough-guy macho behaviours. His habit of making faces suggests that he is embedded in social role-playing. Patricia, the American woman who wants to become French, seems to be fashioning a persona from European high culture. Sterrit suggests that far from being free spirits, these characters are playing roles that existed long before they came on the scene. Michel even seems to be aware of this at one point when he says, in the car as they are driving down to Montparnasse, that 'informers inform, burglars burgle, killers kill, lovers love' (Sterrit 1999: 60). Such fatalism could not be further from the existentialist position, which Sartre sees as optimistic precisely because it rejects the view that human beings are doomed by their past or situation to any role or set of behaviours (see Sartre 1975: 359–60).

Still, it is hard to see the characters as no more than products of their situation, as Sterrit's reading suggests. While they certainly depend on and are circumscribed by cultural roles, they are also actively taking them up and performing them, and we feel we know them through these performances because they make them their own. The Bogart tough-guy image may be there in the culture, but Michel is actively drawing on it, using it to fashion a distinctive style of living for himself. He is very much playing his own version of Bogart. It is not clear that Bogart, in any of his films, ever made the lip-rubbing gesture that Michel effects. Michel even acts out his tough-guy death in inimitable style, melodramatically drawing it out as he staggers along the Rue Campagne Première, and closing his own eyes at the end. Patricia, in trying on various masks, is also striving to be her own person. She more than holds her own with Michel in the extended exchange in her hotel room. And, it is believable that she would betray Michel in order to preserve her independence. In the very last scene, she also picks up the Bogart lip-rubbing gesture from the recently departed Michel, as if he has handed his tough-guy persona on to her for her own use. She is not playing Bogart so much as playing a Frenchman playing Bogart. And because the lip-rubbing gesture is a little different when she does it, she also makes it her own.

There is a parallel between the way the characters both depend on and actively transform their cultural influences, and what is happening at the level of the film itself. Godard's film is certainly drawing on existing cinematic norms, including the conventions of the American film noir cinema that provides elements for the plot. Beyond that, there is the influence of the many films Godard has watched in the ciné-clubs. Steeped in film history and technique, *Breathless* is thoroughly traditional, not modernist at all. At the same time, it is utterly modernist in the way it breaks with tradition and challenges the rules of film-making. Dudley Andrew may hold that 'Godard, for all his belief in authenticity, doubts the possibility of radical originality' and that 'the theme of the film, like the essence of its hero, is the futile struggle to be original' (1987: 12), but for all that, *Breathless* remains a film of prodigious invention. The originality of the film, as Brody (2008) points out, lies in its relationship with the inherited material. Like Michel with the Bogart persona, Godard is actively using his Hollywood sources, turning them to his own purposes. He is introducing Hollywood elements to effect a break with traditional French cinema and, in subverting them, also distancing himself from Hollywood cinema, and indeed from film itself as it had traditionally been made. In the process, he has transformed these borrowed elements and made them his own.

Godard's own label for what he is doing in *Breathless* was 'a cinema of reinvention': 'What I wanted to do was to take a conventional story and remake, but differently, everything the cinema had done. I also wanted to give the feeling that the techniques of film-making had just been discovered or experienced for the first time' (1972: 173). A later, more political Godard was to become critical not only of the individualism of the film's characters but also of his own role as the rule-breaking New Wave auteur. As Andrew notes, the later Godard 'abandoned all vestiges of commercial filmmaking in the climate that produced the events of 1968. In his subsequent Dziga Vertov Group period, he recanted the aesthetic libertarianism that had made *Breathless* complicit, he intimated, with Michel Poiccard's rightwing anarchism, and thus unwittingly an effect of bourgeois capitalist ideology' (2014). But even here, in this subsequent condemnation of both character and film, the parallels between the two are preserved.

Conclusion

Overall, *Breathless* and Paris have an involved relationship. The city plays a significant role in the film's emergence, and the film in turn presents a documentary of a commonplace Paris that frames and sets into relief the film's cinematic artifice. One final point is that while the Paris so realistically portrayed in the film is still recognizable, it is like any other city subject to change and transformation over time. It has undergone its own modernist reinvention. In that respect, the film, as a documentary of late-fifties Paris, preserves a city that no longer exists. It has become the remembrance of a Paris past. We see Patricia and Michel strolling down the Champs-Élysées as it was back then, before the commercialization took over. Fifty years later, we can only look on with a certain nostalgia at the Paris of *Breathless*. But Godard has anticipated this development. This process of transformation is alluded to in the film itself, when Michel during a taxi ride expresses nostalgia for an older Paris, the nineteenth-century architecture that he thinks is being ruined by ugly 1950s buildings: 'Look at the house where I was born. Across the street they put up a horrible house'. The modernization is real enough, even if all comments Michel makes about his past have to be taken with a grain of salt. Along with the city, the film also captures people who no longer exist, who only remain as memory. The final scene, where Michel dies in front of Patricia, is just around the corner from the Montparnasse cemetery, where Jean Seberg is buried, and where can also be found the gravesite of Jean-Paul Sartre and Simone de Beauvoir.

NOTE

1. A small qualification is necessary here. The soundtrack contributes significantly to the film's realistic portrayal of Paris, often just consisting of the natural sounds of Paris life, the car horns, engines, brakes, police sirens and other noises typical of a large modern city (van Ruymbeke 2013). But for the actors to be audible above the din of the city, the film had to be shot mute, with sound and dialogue dubbed in afterwards in the studio. So, they may still be natural city sounds, but they are being intentionally imposed, even when they drown out bits of dialogue, as occasionally happens in the hotel room scene (see McCabe 2003: 119; Brody 2009: 75). So even the film's realistically portrayed Paris can be said to conceal a certain artifice in its portrayal, a certain idea of Paris.

REFERENCES

Andersen, Nathan (2019), *Film, Philosophy, and Reality: Ancient Greece to Godard*, London: Routledge.

Andrew, Dudley (1973), 'André Bazin', *Film Comment*, 9: 2, pp. 64–68.

Andrew, Dudley (1987), '*Breathless*: Old as New', in D. Andrew (ed.), *Breathless*, New Brunswick and London: Rutgers University Press, pp. 3–20.

Andrew, Dudley (2014), '*Breathless* Then and Now', Criterion DVD notes, https://www.criterion.com/current/posts/526-breathless-then-and-now. Accessed 27 January 2021.

Brecht, Bertolt (1964), 'Alienation effects in Chinese acting', in J. Willett (ed.), *Brecht on Theatre: the Development of an Aesthetic*, New York: Hill and Wang, pp. 91–99.

Brody, Richard (2008), An Interview with Richard Brody, interview by Bijan Tehrani. *Cinema Without Borders*, 14 May, https://cinemawithoutborders.com/1582-an-interview-with-richard-brody-writer-of-everything-is-cinema-the-working-life-of-jean-luc-godard/. Accessed 27 January 2021.

Brody, Richard (2009), *Everything Is Cinema: The Working Life of Jean-Luc Godard*, New York: Picador.

Brody, Richard (2012), 'Jean Rouch and D. W. Griffith', review in the *New Yorker*, https://www.newyorker.com/culture/richard-brody/jean-rouch-and-d-w-griffith. Accessed 27 January 2021.

Coutard, Raoul (2016), 'Interview with Raoul Coutard', in Claude Ventura and Xavier Ville-tard, *Chambre 12, Hôtel de Suède*, Criterion DVD of À bout de souffle.

Douchet, Jean (1998), *French New Wave* (trans. R. Bonnono), New York: D.A.P./Distributed Art Publishers.

Dreyfus, Hubert (2012), 'Lecture 20, Discussion of Godard's Breathless', https://archive.org/details/Phil7-ExistentialisminLiteratureandFilm-Spring2012/Lecture+20+Disussion+of+Godards.mp3. Accessed 27 January 2021.

Ezell, Brice (2014), 'Boundaries Are All Fictions in Godard's *Breathless*', https://www.popmatters.com/180736-breathless-a-director-with-a-newspaper-2495669380.html. Accessed 27 January 2021.

Fairfax, Daniel (2017), 'Models of the public intellectual: Cinema and engagement in Sartre and Godard', *Senses of Cinema*, 84, http://sensesofcinema.com/2017/sartre-at-the-movies/cinema-and-engagement-in-sartre-and-godard/. Accessed 27 January 2021.

Falzon, Chris (2005), 'Sartre's *Nausea* and meaningful existence', in A. Rolls and E. Rechniewski (eds), *Sartre's 'Nausea': Text, Context, Intertext*, Amsterdam and New York: Rodopi, pp. 105–20.

Godard, Jean-Luc (1972), *Godard on Godard* (ed. and trans. T. Milne), New York and London: Da Capo.

Godard, Jean-Luc (1987), 'Interview with Yvonne Baby', in D. Andrew (ed.), *Breathless*, New Brunswick and London: Rutgers University Press, pp. 165–66.

Godard, Jean-Luc (2014), *Introduction to a True History of Cinema and Television* (trans. T. Barnard), Montreal: Caboose.

Heller, Nathan (2010), 'Go See *Breathless*', https://slate.com/news-and-politics/2010/06/how-jean-luc-godard-s-breathless-reinvented-the-movies.html. Accessed 27 January 2021.

Levy, Emanuel (2010), '*Breathless*: Godard's Seminal Film Part 2', http://emanuellevy.com/review/breathless-godards-seminal-film-part-two-8/. Accessed 27 January 2021.

Martin, Adrian (2003), 'Review: *À bout de souffle*', http://www.filmcritic.com.au/reviews/a/aboutdesouffle.html. Accessed 27 January 2021.

McCabe, Colin (1980), *Godard: Images, Sounds, Politics*, London and Basingstoke: Macmillan.

McCabe, Colin (2003), *Godard: A Portrait of the Artist at 70*, London: Bloomsbury.

Mennel, Barbara (2008), *Cities and Cinema*, London and New York: Routledge.

Monaco, James (1980), *The New Wave: Truffaut, Godard, Chabrol, Rohmer, Rivette*, New York: Oxford University Press.

Perkins, V. F. (1972), *Film as Film*, Harmondsworth: Penguin.

Poirier, Agnes (2018), *Left Bank: Art, Passion, and the Rebirth of Paris, 1940–50*, New York: Henry Holt & Co.

Rockhill, Gabriel (2010), 'Modernism as a misnomer: Godard's archaeology of the image', *Journal of French and Francophone Philosophy*, 18: 2, pp. 107–29.

Rolls, Alistair and Deborah Walker (2009), *French and American Noir: Dark Crossings*, Houndmills: Palgrave.

Romney, Jonathan (2000), 'Breathless, again', https://www.newstatesman.com/node/151646. Accessed 27 January 2021.

Sartre, Jean-Paul (1958), *Being and Nothingness* (trans. H. Barnes), London: Methuen.

Sartre, Jean-Paul (1963), *Nausea* (trans. R. Baldick), Harmondsworth: Penguin.

Sartre, Jean-Paul (1975), 'Existentialism is a humanism', in W. Kaufmann (ed.), *Existentialism from Dostoevsky to Sartre*, New York: New American Library, pp. 345–69.

Sterrit, David (1999), *The Films of Jean-Luc Godard*, Cambridge: Cambridge University Press.

Sterrit, David (2000), '40 Years Ago, *Breathless* Was Hyperactive Anarchy. Now It's Part of the Canon', https://www.chronicle.com/article/40-Years-Ago-Breathless-Was/31498. Accessed 27 January 2021.

Sterrit, David (2002), 'Breathless', in J. Carr (ed.), *The A List: The National Society of Film Critics' 100 Essential Films*, Cambridge, MA: Da Capo, pp. 43–48.

Truffaut, Francois (1976), 'A certain tendency of the French Cinema', in B. Nichols (ed.), *Movies and Method*, Berkeley: University of California Press, pp. 224–37.

Usher, Phillip John (2014), 'À bout de souffle: Trials in new coherences', in T. Conley and T. J. Kline (eds), *A Companion to Jean-Luc Godard*, Chichester, West Sussex: Wiley-Blackwell, pp. 21–43.

van Ruymbeke, Laura (2013), 'Paris as seen by the French New Wave', https://www.myfrench-life.org/2013/06/19/paris-as-seen-by-the-french-new-wave/. Accessed 27 January 2021.

7

As Sedate as Swans: The Parisian Side of Jean-Paul Sartre's *La Nausée*

Alistair Rolls

At a certain point quite early in *La Nausée* (*Nausea*), Jean-Paul Sartre's novel of 1938, at a point at which the novel is still self-consciously grappling with the importance of writing (itself as) a diary and resisting the almost inevitable pull of its own (ostensibly as yet unformed) ending, which will of course make of it the literary output that it is always destined to be and which arguably it is from its very outset, the story's protagonist, Antoine Roquentin, refers rather curiously to some of the pieces of paper that, he reveals to the reader, he likes to pick up from the muddy ground as swans: 'D'autres tout neufs et même glacés, tout blancs, tout palpitants, sont posés comme des cygnes, mais déjà la terre les englue par en dessous [Others which are new and even shiny, white and palpitating, are as sedate as swans, but the earth has already ensnared them from below]' (2002: 25 [2000: 21]).[1] There are two prior mentions of pieces of paper in this paragraph: first, '[j]'aime beaucoup ramasser les marrons, les vieilles loques, surtout les papiers [I am very fond of picking up chestnuts, old rags, and especially pieces of paper]', and second, '[d]'autres feuillets, l'hiver, sont pilonnés, broyés, maculés [o]ther pieces of paper, in winter, are pulped, crumbled, stained' (2002: 25 [2000: 21]). French here alternates between the nouns *papier* and *feuillet*, which are both easily rendered in English as paper. Certainly, *un feuillet*, perhaps especially because it signals its etymological source in the kinds of leaf litter (*une feuille* is a leaf in French) that make up much of the muddy ground where Roquentin finds his pieces of paper, seems particularly appropriate here. The pieces of paper, the reader is repeatedly told, are rotting, dead. The allusion is inevitable: the written word is dead, cut-off from the context of its production. Even rotting, its ink blurring into dirty smears, its words are, however, there to be deciphered and traced back to an original meaning, which is itself unalterable. Such pieces of paper, it is made clear at this stage of the novel, are not what Roquentin is endeavouring to produce; instead, he wants to write a living diary that will reflect his daily existence as he lives it – in real time, therefore, and subject to change. His living text is to be contrasted with this dead matter, as it is not predestined by the fatality of a fixed ending.

The term *feuillet* has, however, been used before in the text. Famously, the words 'Feuillet sans date [Undated Sheet]' (2002: 9 [2000: 13]) are given as the title of the text at that point where the paratextual apparatus, which is significant in *La Nausée* (it has not only a cover and title page, as is typical of any novel, but also a dedication, an epigraph and, most deceitfully, a page with a publishers' note), gives way to the text itself.[2] Thus, these other pieces of paper, which Roquentin finds in the mud, are precisely not different from those pieces of paper that the reader of *La Nausée* is holding. Or rather, they are other and also the same. Clearly, this is a deliberate move on Sartre's part, if not necessarily on Roquentin's: this internal reference, in a paragraph that appears designed to stress the otherness of pieces of paper not carrying the words that Roquentin is directing at us (and to whom Roquentin may be said to be writing is an important question), points to a title given to a sheet that has no author's mark or date. Roquentin did not write the words *feuillet sans date*, but he does use the term *feuillet* later, at a point where any number of words are available to him. Here, the question is whether the publishers (who are, of course, not the real ones at Gallimard in 1938, but the fictional ones in Sartre's novel) are referencing a very small quotation from Roquentin, embedded some pages into the text, or whether, as appears more likely, Roquentin is referencing the publishers, or his own text as it transforms into exactly the kinds of published literature that he enjoys picking up, which is to say, dead, and this in the properly poststructuralist sense of coinciding with its own meaning and thus transparently meaningful. If Roquentin is quoting Roquentin here, then he is quoting himself as Other, or Sartre (as Roquentin). In other words, the self-alterity of the pieces of paper is also the self-alterity of Roquentin (who is precisely undergoing an existential crisis) and of Sartrean Existentialism itself.

What I propose to examine in this chapter is whether it is possible to challenge the geographical location of this text, or perhaps, more properly, to read it allegorically as a text about an urban space other than those typically associated with it. For, while the sheet that opens Roquentin's diary is famously 'undated' and thus the story lost to a certain degree in time,[3] it appears to locate itself unmistakably in a place called Bouville. In his introduction to the Penguin Classics edition of the novel, James Wood rightly notes that Bouville, or *Mudtown*, is 'possibly based on Le Havre, where Sartre taught for several years' (2000: viii).[4] Wood's attenuation of the link between Le Havre and Bouville in the form of the adverb 'possibly' attests to the mix of sources of influence. Anne Quinney, for example, who considers *La Nausée* to be the closest that Sartre came to writing an autobiographically inspired novel, also sees elements of La Rochelle in the descriptions of provincial life in Bouville (2008: 71).[5] It is equally possible for us to explore other sources of inspiration for *La Nausée*'s setting. And, it is precisely in order to change the parameters of this search that I wish to return to the description of those pieces of paper 'as sedate as swans'.

It is quite possible that one of the reasons why the reader is not struck by the incongruity of this simile is that its intertextual pull is outmuscled by the paratextual echo of the *feuillet*. Indeed, intertextual allusions tend to be overlooked by readers of *La Nausée*, and this for two principal reasons: first, Sartre's overweening authorial presence casts the whole text in a philosophical light (retrospectively of course, as he did not have the same philosophical stature at the time of the novel's publication that he did after the Second World War); second, the paratextual apparatus, which I have mentioned, tends to dominate the text's status as literature and thus to rein in the full extent of its meaningfulness.[6] In a posthumously published essay in which a poetic hypertext is compared to its Baudelairean hypotext, the late Ross Chambers has this to say about the paratext:

> Not only titles and explanatory notes, but also epigraphs, dedications, author-interviews, publisher's blurbs and other forms of jacket-copy, along with later mentions of the title in question in authorial writing (author-interviews, memoirs and the like) – all these are understood to form the paratext of a given text. The concept, therefore, tends to be author-, and publisher-, centred […].
>
> (2018: 229)

It is easy to see how much of this description pertains to *La Nausée*, both in terms of the way that it presented itself to the reader in 1938 and how it has since been framed in public debate (by the author and, if we push the envelope in Chambers's direction, the broader field of French studies). It seems fair to say that the text of *La Nausée* has at times become secondary to its paratext. Chambers continues as follows:

> I've never seen a newspaper review, say, or a critical essay in a scholarly journal, counted as paratextual, even though the function of such texts, very much like authorial/editorial supplementation, is to guide the reader's interpretive choices. In the end, the careful distinction made between 'intertext' and 'paratext' turns out to be based, then, on the concept of authoriality, and for that reason is not really a distinction at all, but merely a (deconstructible) difference. For, as the function of intertextuality itself demonstrates, to sign a given text, let alone to publish it, does not constitute sole ownership of that text, which can give rise to as much interpretive commentary of all kinds as the many and varied 'sources' on which it draws.
>
> (2018: 229)

As we have seen, *La Nausée*, as text, works hard to confuse this matter of ownership, and precisely as Chambers notes, the paratextual debate over whether words such as *feuillet* were authored by Roquentin or Sartre, or indeed by publishers (real or fictional) or even Simone de Beauvoir (again, if we push things a little, either the *real* friend who carefully reads the text or the paratextually liminal figure of *le Castor* to whom the work was dedicated, and towards whom it intends), overshadows other literary sources. In this case, the source, as would not have been lost on Chambers, is Baudelaire.

In an attempt to follow this distinction between what the text presents and what the author presents via the text, I intend to explore a typically Baudelairean chiasmus. There are two principal movements in the paragraph that we have been looking at and also in the novel more broadly: on the one hand, there is the paratextual movement that sees the text constrained by pieces of paper and the relative degrees of ownership that pertain to them; on the other hand, there is the intertextual movement that sees the text expressing a relationship to another text. Both movements have a connection to Baudelaire. My argument here is that the paratextual connection lies in the essay that Sartre wrote on Baudelaire, which was published in 1946. Interestingly, this may not be considered paratextual in the framework of Baudelairean studies, as Chambers's point about scholarly articles makes clear. Yet, *Baudelaire* turns out to be very much a 'Sartrean' work of its time, and as such it expresses the philosophy with which Sartre was then, and still is, associated, which is to say, Existentialism as discussed in *L'Être et le néant* (1943, *Being and Nothingness*).[7] The intertextual connection to Baudelaire, to which the reference to sedate swans attests, suggests an underside to *La Nausée*, or *another* other side (something in the novel that is not just about the Nausea, in other words something textual), over which Sartre's authorial control is a subject for debate.

Insofar as I am a reader predisposed to seeing Baudelaire everywhere and one whose own recent rereading of *La Nausée* came on the heels of some close reading of Baudelaire's poem 'Le Cygne' ('The Swan'),[8] the reference to swans immediately resonated with me. In Riffaterrean terms, I was struck by the phrase's 'syntactical ungrammaticality' (Riffaterre 1978). For Michael Riffaterre, this kind of phrase is ungrammatical because it, and the text of which it is part, cannot be (completely and, it is sometimes suggested, properly) understood without knowing from which other text, or intertext, it originates. In this case, the simile 'as sedate as swans' can be said to be a Riffaterrean 'dual sign', as it functions in two specific places at once, within one broader singular–plural space that is the Intertext. In the original French, there is something of a double duality at play, for in the phrase 'posés comme des cygnes' (Sartre 2002: 25), the word *cygnes* (swans) is a homophone for something more typically associated with pieces of paper, especially in the context of semiotics, that is, *signes* (signs). In this way, these new, shiny and white pieces of paper are perhaps 'palpitants [palpitating]' (Sartre 2002: 25 [2000: 21]) by virtue of their ungrammaticality; they are, in other words, signs pointing beyond the limits of the text and, as such, work against those other pieces of paper ('feuillets') that point back, internally, to the borders of the text, to the limits that make it what it is and protect it, albeit ambivalently, from what it is not.

Chambers is right to be cautious in his discussion of the distinction between the intertext and the paratext, and the question of what is within and what beyond the control of the author. Riffaterre, for his part, seems to point to the problematic nature of this distinction by predicating his notion of ungrammaticality (and the complete or proper meaning that it signs) on reader response. Whether the reader can pick up the author's signs depends on what the former has read. What Chambers is pointing to, it seems to me, are those intertexts that call out to the reader but that were not necessarily intended as such by the author. The breadth and depth of Sartre's reading of Baudelaire are one thing; what strikes me as a more powerful argument for reading these swans as double signs in the strictly Riffaterrean sense, and thus as 'obligatory intertexts', is the similarity between Sartrean understandings of the human condition, or the being for-itself (*l'être pour-soi*), and poststructuralist theories of textuality. Human consciousness for Sartre is something that continuously pours out of the body, beyond the limits of our physical being, onto the world. Sartre wanted to postulate the human ego as something at work in the world, not a kind of spirit locked up inside the body or mind. At the same time, however, consciousness is always already repatriated, continuously recoiling into the body. This way of understanding the world, not by digesting it, but by pouring (literally vomiting) onto it, has a dual effect that can be likened to the paratext: the barrier of our bodily self not only separates us from the world (such that I am not the computer that I am using to write this), but it also joins us to it (in this sense, I understand the computer by projecting myself onto it and, therefore, as Sartre puts it, *existing it*). This is why what distances us from the world is the same negating strip that joins us to it: nothingness. Similarly, the text has a thingness about it, a form specific to it that allows us to distinguish, say, *La Nausée* from 'Le Cygne', but part of its DNA is necessarily open to and shared with other text. All texts are therefore intertexts; they are all themselves and all joined with others, and thus all both themselves and Other.

In the remainder of this chapter, I want to do four things: first, I will review Sartre's *Baudelaire*; second, I will discuss some specific ways in which 'Le Cygne' can be seen to demonstrate what Chambers calls 'kinship' with *La Nausée*; third, I will review the ways in which Baudelaire represents Paris in his poetry and last, I will conclude by outlining some of the ways in which *La Nausée* represents Paris.

Sartre's Baudelaire

As has been argued throughout this volume, Paris is considered the capital of any number of things, from the nineteenth century, through Modernity, to no less than the world. Proponents of such notions tend to consider Paris to be a city divided between itself as an existential site evolving in real time and an ahistorical, mythical self, which stands as an essential city, a set of values to which the existential Other aspires. The present volume is concerned *inter alia* with the ways in which Paris present remembers Paris past, with the caveat that this latter Paris never really existed, at least not as it is understood objectively, or from the perspective of the present.

In his study of the poet whom we consider central to the divide that sees Paris present divorced from Paris remembered, Sartre largely neglects Baudelaire's Parisian situation, focusing instead on the primal dyad that he formed, as a child, with his mother. It is in the union of mother and son, which Sartre goes as far as to label 'incestueux [incestuous]' (1947: 18[9]), that Baudelaire felt protected from the conflictual space of the world and thus himself unconflicted. As Sartre puts it, 'il se fond avec l'absolu, il est justifié [he forms one with the absolute; he is justified]' (1947: 19). His existential crisis, or *prise de conscience* (awareness of the reality of his own autonomous existence in the world), comes in 1828 when his widowed mother remarries. The rupture caused by this is described by Sartre as 'sa fameuse fêlure [his famous *fêlure*]' (1947: 19), which is a term for a crack in one's personality.[10] It is at this point that Baudelaire, according to Sartre, 's'est *fait* un autre [*made* himself another]' (1947: 21, original emphasis). Once he is another, his recollection of his initial state of oneness must necessarily be experienced as nostalgia: 'C'est de la sécurité absolue de l'enfance que Baudelaire a la nostalgie [It is for the absolute security of childhood that Baudelaire is nostalgic]' (1947: 60).

The sense of being stranded from the childhood condition that Sartre describes here – that time when the poet's truth was known (by his parents, seen reflected in their eyes) and when the world that presented itself to him in its newness came with meanings attached (by them) and with which it coincided – is of course one part of critical modernity's double view of the world, and it is one half of the twin perspectives that we have seen in the prose poems. In my analysis in Chapter 1 above, however, this dual view that sees the world simultaneously presented (through childlike eyes) *and* represented (with the objectivity of adulthood) is shown to be allegorical of Paris; it is a world view founded on a primal trauma, but it is one, I argue, that comes in response to the city. In Sartre's study, which founds its existential analysis of Baudelaire on something almost psychoanalytical, the trauma is Baudelaire's; Paris, by contrast, is (merely) the situation in which it occurs. Sartre often stated that Nausea was not a metaphor (we do not feel sick because we cannot face contingency) but a fundamental aspect of our being in the world (we experience the world emetically, pouring ourselves out onto it). It is likely therefore that Sartre would caution against seeing Baudelaire's *fêlure* as a metaphor for Paris, or indeed *vice versa*.

Certainly, *Baudelaire* explains its poetic subject in terms that echo closely the philosophy of *L'Être et le néant*, the seminal Sartrean essay beneath whose weight his works of literature have struggled to assume their full textual mobility. 'L'homme baudelairien [Baudelairean man]', Sartre writes, 'n'est pas un état: c'est l'interférence de deux mouvements opposés mais également centrifuges dont l'un se porte vers le haut et l'autre vers le bas [is not a state; he is the coming together of two opposed, but also centrifugal, movements, one of which is upwards and the other downwards]' (1947: 44). This chiastic meeting of contrary movements appears to be a contextual adjustment of Sartre's existentialist view of the human condition, which sees transcendent movement outwards always already resisted by the inertia of corporeality.[11] As a chiasmus, however, this description appears itself something of a metaphor: the double movements meeting here are also the becoming-Sartrean of Baudelaire and its unsaid other, the becoming-Baudelairean of Sartre.

What then, if anything, does Sartre have to say about Baudelaire's Paris? Basically, Sartre denies that Baudelaire was affected by his environment (1947: 190). This denial of the importance of situation, while consistent with Sartre's own philosophical thinking at this stage of his career, can be tempered by his focus on the period of the 1840s. Critics like Chambers, for whom Baudelaire and Paris are almost synonymous, typically consider 1848 as something of a watershed moment.[12] In fact, for Sartre, Baudelaire's obsession with dissolution and death at a time when the French were predominantly forward-looking, inventing the future, saw him 'vivre le temps à rebours [living against his time]' (1947: 190). Baudelaire hated progress, Sartre concludes, because it privileged long-term projects, which the poet could simply not bring to fruition (1947: 191). Nonetheless, as Sartre concedes, the times caught up with Baudelaire, and by 1852, the poet found himself aligned with the Zeitgeist:

> [L]e Progrès à son tour est devenu un rêve mort du Passé. Dans la société *piétinante* et funèbre de l'Empire, toute soucieuse de maintenir ou de rétablir, hantée par des souvenirs de gloire et par de grands espoirs disparus, il a pu mener paisiblement son existence stagnante, il a pu continuer à son aise sa marche lente et chancelante à reculons. [Progress in turn became a dead dream, a thing of the Past. In the *stumbling*, funereal society of the Empire, intent on maintenance and re-establishment, haunted by memories of glory and by great hopes now gone, he was able to lead his stagnant existence in peace and continue, as he was wont, to walk slowly and falteringly backwards.]
>
> (1947: 194–95, emphasis added)

It is just possible here to read into this passage a glimpse of Baudelaire's time, and also his place, his Paris, catching up with Sartre. Although I am conscious of the subjectivity of my own reading lens, it is my contention that the use of the adjective *piétinante* here to describe the stumbling, wallowing of society at the beginning of the Second Empire can be considered an intertextual ungrammaticality, or stumbling block, for it is precisely this term that Baudelaire uses to describe the 'negress' in 'Le Cygne': 'Piétinant dans la boue [Treading in the mire]' (1998: 176 [177]). Individually, of course, this resonance of what is quite an appropriate term in Sartre's passage could be dismissed as coincidental. It forms part of a nexus, however, of swans, mud, staggering and enigmatic black artistes that conjoins Sartre's *La Nausée*, Baudelaire's 'Le Cygne' and now Sartre's study of Baudelaire.

In addition to being an independently wealthy, jobless bourgeois (1947: 33), the young Baudelaire resembles Roquentin by dint of the objects that Sartre has him observe:

> Pour nous autres,[13] c'est assez de voir l'arbre ou la maison; tout absorbés à les contempler, nous nous oublions nous-mêmes. Baudelaire est l'homme qui ne s'oublie jamais. Il se regarde voir, il regarde pour se voir regarder; c'est sa conscience de l'arbre, de la maison qu'il contemple et les choses ne lui apparaissent qu'au travers d'elle, plus pâles, plus petites, moins touchantes, comme s'il les apercevait à travers une lorgnette. [For people like us, it is enough to see the tree or the house; caught up in our contemplation of them, we forget about ourselves. Baudelaire is the man who never forgets about himself. He watches himself seeing; he watches to see himself watch. It is his consciousness of the tree, of the house, that he is contemplating, and things only appear to him through it, paler, smaller, less touching, as though he was seeing them through opera glasses.]
>
> (1947: 25)

Here, 'the house' appears added on, as if to draw our attention away from (after he has already drawn our attention to) the tree. The latter cannot but remind the reader who is familiar with *La Nausée* of the famous chestnut tree scene, which has become the very symbol of the author's philosophical and paratextual hegemony over the novel's will to mean. Put simply then, *Baudelaire* serves, paratextually, to delimit *La Nausée*'s literary freedom; intertextually, on the other hand, it betrays this other side. Even as it represses Paris's influence on, and symbolic presence in, Baudelaire's poetry, the essay speaks, *almost* unconsciously, of another side.

'Le Cygne'

In 'Le Cygne', Chambers writes,

> the 'I' of the poem reflects on the way history – history understood in light of the adage that the more things change the more they stay the same – produces winners

and losers, whose lives intersect without meeting because their experience of that history differs radically, the winners being optimists, celebrating change as good, while the losers are in the grip of a paralysing nostalgia for former times, even as they survive painfully among the ruins of the present.

(2006: 107)

This is Baudelaire's 'I' of one remove, to which Sartre refers as looking through opera glasses. It also reflects the fractured 'I' from the same essay. Sartre would doubtless consider that the multivocal expression of grief that is 'Le Cygne' also contains a sort of self-satisfaction, as though the time for grieving has finally swept up all those around the poet, forcing him into some kind of kinship with others in the crowd. In this way, he might be a winner (he is the author of what will be recognized, albeit posthumously, as one of the greatest works of French poetry) as well as a loser in history's relentless onward march.

More ostensibly, however, Baudelaire positions himself on the side of history's losers, and it is in the framework of this nostalgic hankering for the past that Chambers has the most interesting contribution to make for our present purposes. The poem presents three figures that at face value seem utterly dissimilar: Andromache, who in Greek mythology was the grieving widow of the Trojan hero Hector; a swan, escaped from its cage, waddling in the dust of a desolate building site but craning its neck towards the skies (including, via a simile, to classical poetry – Roman this time, in the form of Ovid) and a 'negress' trudging through mud and looking towards far-distant Africa (Baudelaire 1998: 172–77). These three figures, who represent different ages and spaces, are brought together, presented in synchronicity and, crucially, in the same place. Although the poet represents Andromache and the 'negress' in his mind's eye, whereas the swan is present to him as he crosses 'the modern Carrousel' (in Paris, near the Louvre), and although the negress paddles in mud, while the swan is pitifully dry, this is a poem about making the historically disparate synchronous and bringing together the distant and dispersed in one space. The movements, of course, are double: the poet thinks himself away to distant lands, but Paris causes him to summon these exotic locales to his immediate vicinity. And the name that overarches these movements in space and time is that of the swan, the eponymous figure. All the poem's striving for equivalence notwithstanding, the real, present swan trumps, paratextually at least, the two represented figures. This is, then, a poem about Paris as much as it is about grieving, as the statement 'Paris change ! [Paris may change]' (1998: 174 [175]) makes clear.

Chambers stresses this point: the present and the past are co-present. In the poem, a chiasmus neatly demonstrates Paris's ability in this case to be two places at once: 'Comme je traversais le nouveau Carrousel. / Le vieux Paris n'est plus [As I was walking through the modern Carrousel. / The old Paris is gone]' (2006: 174 [175]). For, despite the presence of the new and the absence of the old, poetically what counts is the chiastic conjunction of these opposites at this (real *and* poetic) crossroads, and of course the convergence again of these opposite movements. For Chambers therefore, nostalgia cannot be the whole story:

> For a modern to regret the past as having been crucially different from and preferable to the present is to fall victim, therefore, to a form of illusion, specifically the form of self-deceit known as nostalgia. A truly modern consciousness [...] is one for which nostalgia is made impossible by the knowledge that no essential difference separates past from present even though a crucial change has taken place.
>
> (2006: 107)[14]

We may well think of the criticism levelled at Gil by his fiancée's pedantic friend in Woody Allen's *Midnight in Paris* (2011). What of course happens in that film is that Gil's nostalgia for Paris past is eventually diffused when he meets a kindred spirit who longs for the same thing. What also happens is that Paris past is brought into the present and Gil is transported into the past from the present (the two movements meeting in another Parisian chiasmus). In this way therefore, nostalgia itself is challenged. Gil learns that the present and past (which Allen brings together in one singular–plural cinematic space) are the same insofar as people have always looked back to previous golden ages, which logically means that these better days have always been myths. Gil is arguably suffering from a bout of melancholy therefore, and this is resolved through his ultimate romantic success.

In Baudelaire's poem, Paris is subject to radical change, but the melancholia of the poetic 'I' does not move. As Chambers notes, melancholia of this kind is 'a permanent mental disposition' (2006: 108). While there is almost no specific mention of Paris in *La Nausée*, an unchanging melancholia pervades the novel as a result of the Baudelairean intertext, which surfaces here and there in echoes of 'Le Cygne'. (Roquentin's one actual visit to Paris takes the form of a brief visit to Anny, but the episode has a dreamlike quality.[15]) As Brian Larkin states in relation to national allegory, it 'is not always a feature immanent to a text but is something texts have placed upon them through the act of circulation across cultural difference'; he notes further that '[a]llegory, in this mode, is not tied to the imagination of writer or director but is derived externally from the movement of the text in and out of different publics' (2009: 164–65). In this case, whether Sartre is conscious of the references to the Baudelairean intertext is of secondary importance; the movement of the text, between, in this case, different readerships, causes *La Nausée*'s allegorical potential to emerge.

Baudelaire's Paris: Three modes of representation

In terms of the relative presence or absence of what Larkin calls 'immanent features', I consider there to be three basic modes of representing Paris in Baudelaire's poetry. The first is found predominantly in his verse poetry, in poems like 'Le Cygne'. In this mode, Paris is explicitly present and doubly so: there are clear references to the city ('immanent features') as it presents itself to us (poet and reader) as a real urban space; and there are also metaphors for the city, that is, signs of the city as myth (figures like Andromache and the negress in 'Le Cygne'). In this way, Paris is presented (as a real city) and represented (as a mythical city) simultaneously, and clearly, in the one place, for this is the key to critical modernity, in which we not only encounter the present but also understand it through overarching values already set in the past. In poems like 'Le Cygne', metaphors (city as absent) serve to mark the distance between our real experience and our mental perception, imagination and memories.

The second mode of representing Paris is the type expounded in Chapter 1 above: it is a fetishistic mode, and it is most clearly seen in the prose poems. In these poems, there are hardly any immanent features that we can recognize as Parisian. While there are plenty of things on display, the close-up view that we have of the city streets prevents a more global perspective or objective means of navigation. Paris is present, then, but only as much as it is absent. This absence–presence depends, like the fetish, on contiguity for its signification. Paris is metonymically absent–present in every object on display, as opposed to being in turn absent (through metaphors) and present (through clear place markers). In this way, Paris is not named in the individual prose poems. The poems' overarching Parisianness is given, however, *paratextually*, in the form of the collection's title (albeit one that was only definitively fixed after Baudelaire's death, when the prose poems were published). The Paris of the prose poems is therefore never entirely absent; rather, it is disavowed, which in Freud's scenario means that it is not entirely repressed (French psychoanalysts discuss the fetish as a form of 'partial repression') because it is always signified, albeit indirectly, partially, contiguously.

The third mode is the representation of Paris through the total absence of immanent features. This mode functions allegorically by being, as Larkin describes, 'derived externally'. Clive Scott has commented at length on the ways in which the poems of various writers, including (but not limited to) those who have translated

Baudelaire's work, are for him, to his readerly ear and eye, eerily reminiscent of Baudelaire. When in the grips of such an uncanny experience, Scott may find himself unable to tell whether what he is reading is Baudelaire or not; as he puts it, 'I do not know exactly what the linguo-literary status of these lines is' (2006: 196). An example that I have used elsewhere to expose a Parisian allegory in a text otherwise unrelated to Paris also hinges on the presence of swans: Edgar Wright's 2007 film *Hot Fuzz*. Set entirely in England, and in the countryside for the most part, *Hot Fuzz* presents certain similarities when viewed by someone seeped, like Scott, in Baudelaire; these range from its incongruous and curiously singular–plural swan to its reduplication of hooded figures of Death (Rolls 2020). This mode is, as Scott admits, difficult to define in linguo-literary terms, as it hinges on something close to intuition. I should argue, however, that Riffaterre's notion of ungrammaticality can usefully enable us to call this third mode 'intertextual representation'.

Paradoxically, in terms of our intertextually oriented investigation into the way in which Paris is represented in *La Nausée*, what the reader encounters predominantly in the text is the second of these modes. It is true that Roquentin does travel to Paris in the novel in order to pay a visit to Anny; yet, this scene is so oneiric in feel, and importantly so similar to the (disavowed) verses of 'Some of These Days' as to become a retelling of that other story of loss (see Rolls 2003), that it is debatable whether Roquentin can be said to be present to the city as real space. Thus, the mode of representing Paris is not the same in *La Nausée* as it is in 'Le Cygne'. Anny is the link to Paris in the text: Anny as lost love, Anny as the call of the city from the other end of the railway line. And Anny is also the key to unlocking the novel's fetishism: while Roquentin tells the reader of his sexual liaisons with the *patronne*, the moment of intimacy itself is veiled by her request to keep her stockings on (2000: 17, 2002: 21). The fact that their sexual relations depend on only partial unveiling sends the text immediately into a screen memory, in the precise form of Anny: 'Autrefois – longtemps même après qu'elle m'ait quitté – j'ai pensé pour Anny [In the past – even long after she had left me – I used to think about Anny]' (2002: 21 [2000: 17]). In the framework of the present Parisian reading, the fact that Anny's textual presence is predominantly as a figure of mourning – someone who has long since, and perhaps always, been someone to think of, to remember – suggests a fundamental melancholia similar to that unshakeable type described by Chambers. Roquentin's not being in Paris – his changing of place – is, in light of this melancholic disposition, a metaphor, or arguably, via the contiguity of the intertext, a metonym, for Baudelaire's Paris as capital of modernity, the Paris that changes.

The importance of fetishism notwithstanding, what is of especial interest to me here is the third, intertextual mode of representing Paris that comes through in ungrammaticalities like the simile of the sedate swans.[16] For it is this mode, reliant as it is on the reader to make the connection, that speaks most powerfully to Paris's inescapable textual presence in texts that, at face value, have travelled as far as they can to escape it.

La Nausée's *Parisian side*

At the end of the 'Feuillet sans date [Undated Sheet]', we read that there could only be one condition under which a diary could be written and that it would be if ... And then the text ends (2002: 16 [2000: 11]). In light of Roquentin's desire for his life to be meaningful, it is possible that the condition is this (impossible one): if the author were dead. A person's life is only transparently meaningful when the person is no longer able to change its course through free actions enacted in real time. To be able to savour one's life's meaningfulness is a paradox, as it would involve being alive and dead at the same time.

This is the explanation given for Roquentin's obsession with 'Some of These Days': he considers the 'Negress' to be saved by the recording of her voice, which can be infinitely played back (not only brought to life but also celebrated in and as death, or at least as completion). It is easy to conflate the 'Negress' with the various black singers who have interpreted this song (we might think of Ethel Walters or Ella Fitzgerald), but it is not clear that this is the version that he is listening to throughout the novel, as the only lyrics transcribed are the chorus. The most likely singer is Sophie Tucker, whose recordings included the original 1911 version (with its verses that recall love lost and trains missed) and the best-selling 1926 version, which she recorded with Ted Lewis and his band (Carroll 2006: 401). Both these versions predate the composition and diegesis of *La Nausée*. Given, as mentioned previously, that Sophie Tucker is white, it is easy to read the 'Negress' as a figure of inversion (on which the novel, which is so markedly *not* the diary whose form it nonetheless performs, is predicated).

It is equally possible, on the other hand, to read the 'Negress' as an intertextual figure. As he waits, we assume, at the railway station in Bouville for the train to Paris, Roquentin hesitates. He is unsure whether or not to write a novel. But, other hesitations suggest themselves. His last thoughts are not for Anny, but for the 'Negress'. He writes of those people who might read his novel and what he would mean to them: 'ils penseraient à ma vie comme je pense à celle de cette Négresse [they would think about my life as I think about the life of that Negress]' (2002: 250 [2000: 252]). In 'Le Cygne', we read: 'Je pense à la négresse, amaigrie et phthisique [I think of a negress, thin and tubercular]' (Baudelaire 1998: 176 [177]). The poet, for his part, thinks of this 'negress', and of the swan, and again of Andromache, as he stands before the Louvre; and from here, his thoughts spread outwards, centrifugally, from Paris to alight finally on shipwrecked sailors and 'à bien d'autres encor! [many others more!]' (1998: 176 [177]). As Paris conjures metaphors, causing itself to be mapped onto exotic images of elsewhere that are only ever reflections of itself (of its autodifferentiation), so too Roquentin becomes one of those many other stranded victims of melancholia. His looking to Paris from Bouville echoes Baudelaire's looking from Paris outwards across the same figure. It is therefore in Paris's tendency always to be itself in otherness that *La Nausée* allows glimpses of its Parisian (other) side – almost but not quite, between the lines, uncannily.[17]

Roquentin's other pieces of paper, those that he likens to sedate swans, are shiny and white (hence, one assumes, the simile), but they do not long remain so: 'mais déjà la terre les englue par en dessous [but the earth has already ensnared them from below]' (2002: 25 [2000: 21]). Thus, the pieces of paper are both swan and 'negress', for it is the latter who is described as 'Piétinant dans la boue [Treading in the mire]' (Baudelaire 1998: 176 [177]). Black and white, swan and 'negress' are arguably not so much inversions of each other as interchangeable figures, figures of interchangeability. The weight of the intertext, which allows us to read these figures in this way, is categorical, however: all such figures, fundamentally, represent Paris.

The epigraph that follows the dedication to 'le Castor', or Simone de Beauvoir, takes on an interesting light if considered as part of a single paratextual strategy. Beauvoir's role in rereading (and potentially rewriting) the manuscript of *La Nausée* is well known. It is equally well known that the manuscript sent to Gallimard, and indeed accepted by them, was entitled not *La Nausée* but *Melancholia*. And if the latter title is attributed to Simone Jollivet, the title finally chosen was found not by Sartre, who had entirely given up in the face of Gallimard's refusal to publish the novel as *Melancholia*, but by none other than Gaston Gallimard himself (Cohen-Solal 1999: 223–24). If the final publication of the novel is, in Cohen-Solal's words, 'déjà à lui seul tout un roman [a novel in and of itself]' (1999: 218), then it is a story that is not only Parisian but also an entirely collective endeavour (Cohen-Solal uses the term 'accouchement collectif', or collective birth [1999: 222]). The epigraph from Céline, which stands as a denial of 'importance collective [collective significance]' (2002: 9 [2000: 7]), simply puts in play the power shifts between individual and collective responsibility: the very title, *La Nausée*, that first paratextual sign, belies Sartre's authorial power over his text, and the dedication that follows cedes it to his life-long friend.

This abandonment of authorial power and the spreading of literature, almost like something contagious, in the form of Roquentin's penchant for picking up dirty paper, come together in the scene of the final visit to Bouville's municipal library.

This scene presents itself to the reader, albeit metaphorically, as a dirty piece of paper. The dirty story here is that of an act of paedophilia, a kind of honey trap for the Autodidact that turns out, when read reflexively, to be a trap for the reader. The tension expressed by the intensity of the stares of those present in the library builds not only in Roquentin but also, and especially, in us. Roquentin, we learn, has finished reading, and his eyes now flit from the scene of the Autodidact's hand and the contiguous boys to the newspaper (2000: 232–34, 2002: 230–31). This scene recalls Roquentin's own early experience of nausea of the hands that brought together the sight of his hands on a pebble and children on a beach. It is therefore as if the Autodidact has caught this same strand of nausea. The attendant fascination with young boys is a form of textually transmitted disease, which has been passed on from the undated sheet. Alternatively, Roquentin's experience at the beach can be read as a prescient act, with the dirty stone standing in for his long-seated fascination for dirty sheets of reading matter. Seen in that light, the episode on the beach anticipates this concluding scene in the library. Either way, Roquentin has finished reading, and when he fitfully returns to his newspaper, his heart, or at least his own hand, is no longer in it. The fat lady has also put down her book and turned her gaze to the consummate reader, the reader *en abyme*: the Autodidact (2000: 234, 2002: 232). But, of course, that reader is no longer reading; he has taken up his role in a dirty story, whose pages only we readers of *La Nausée* are now turning. The copy of *La Nausée* that we have in our hands is now a living embodiment of the nausea of the hands. No one is innocent here, as even the Corsican librarian likes to keep his eyes on the boys and plays his own games with them. And yet, it is the reader alone who can cause the scene to stop by putting down the dirty pages. The ineluctability of the novel's end-orientation causes us not to read between the lines, not to notice that all the readers in the library, the very pages of the book itself, are looking at us, and so we read on. We have been trapped by *La Nausée*: in Sartrean terms, which is to say, in terms of the inter-personal interactions laid out in *Being and Nothingness* (1993: 364–68), we have assumed the position of the beloved and have given our love freely (by choosing to read on) to the novel as lover. We have adopted an amorous attitude towards the sheets of paper and invested them with life, made living text out of inert matter. The ending may well be set in stone; it is nonetheless our decision to read it.[18]

The question here is whether this paratextual ploy, which sees the novel's existentialist philosophy and seemingly proto-poststructuralist mechanics ensnare the reader in such a way as to make enamoured readers of us and text of inert matter, joins with the novel's intertextual Parisianness. By refusing to put down our own paper, thereby forcing the Autodidact's hand, and not just figuratively, we muddy our hands, taking our own part in the movement of the 'objet brun et velu [brown hairy object]' and its hesitant approach (2002: 232 [2000: 234]). And yet, what this dark figure of disgrace approaches is itself described in terms that recall the sedateness of the swan: it is none other than a small white hand: 'elle reposait sur le dos, détendue, douce et sensuelle, elle avait l'indolente nudité d'une baigneuse qui se chauffe au soleil [it was lying on its back, relaxed, soft, and sensual, it had the indolent nudity of a woman sunning herself on the beach]' (2002: 232 [2000: 234]). Indeed, successively, the young boy and then the Autodidact are struck both still and pale. To this extent, they are both soiled and sedate as swans.

The library scene progressively turns into a space where people have *finished reading*, which is to say, the library as both embodiment of and memorial to itself, and where their gazes become focused on an event that is about to happen. In other words, this privileged site of thoughts recorded, sayings set down on paper and immortalized, is disrupted and transformed into an event being made (not only made real but also made literature) in real time. In this sense, like the Parisian site of 'Le Cygne', the library is both a place of recollection and anticipation, of stasis and imminent, violent departure. In this light, the touching of hands that happens here is both an act of textual memory, reflecting back on and repurposing the paper-as-swan simile, and an intertextual instance of ungrammaticality, a further (de)composition of the reference to Baudelaire's 'Le Cygne', and specifically to that poem's eponymous figure.

Although the triad of Andromache, the swan and the 'negress' cannot be mapped neatly onto *La Nausée*'s conclusion, there are a number of ungrammaticalities that suggest that Sartre's ending is designed to look back, with nostalgia, on Baudelaire's famous figures of modernity. Following the scene at the library, which can be placed under the sign of the swan, Roquentin recalls that he is due to leave Bouville, to return to Paris, in just two hours. The impending sense of being up against the clock immediately conjures an image that appears, in light of this intertextual grammar, a condensation of the experience of 'Le Cygne': 'je me promène dans la rue Boulibet. Je *sais* que c'est la rue Boulibet, mais je ne la reconnais pas [I am walking along the rue Boulibet. I *know* that it is the rue Boulibet, but I don't recognize it]' (2002: 237 [2000: 239]). One might suggest that *le vieux Bouville* (of which this street looks curiously metonymic, with its partial homophony) is no more: just like Baudelaire's Paris, it is there, but it has changed beyond recognition. Roquentin ponders over this, stating that he has in a sense already left Bouville without having left it; he notes, indeed, that he is 'entre deux villes [between two towns]', one of which knows nothing of him, while the other knows him no longer (2002: 238 [2000: 240]). A coded reference to Anny ('une lourde jeune femme, à Londres [a plump young woman in London]') immediately serves, as references to Anny do throughout the novel, to send thoughts, both Roquentin's and the reader's, elsewhere. In this case, however, the references to London and then to Egypt serve to unsay the passage's underlying intertextual grammar: this urban space that is itself and other (including Africa), and which is marked so emphatically at this point in the text, is, of course, Paris.

The conjuring of Anny, as a figure of another time (now older, changed – Roquentin thinks of her as fat) and another place (London now, not Paris), makes her present, meaning that she is seen by Roquentin here in this temporally and spatially fractured place. Thus, Anny is *La Nausée*'s Andromache, a figure of grief, now as she ever was, and more importantly, intertextually, a figure of Parisian autodifferentiation.

Anny in turn conjures the lines of 'Some of These Days', which take Roquentin into the next space of the conclusion, which is the café, the *Rendez-vous des Cheminots*, where he says goodbye to the *patronne*. This space is synonymous with his listening to the voice of the 'negress'. Here, Roquentin's very act of announcing his departure is made paradoxical by its association with the request for the song to be replayed, for the song is nothing if not a symbol of infinite replay. The very words 'Juste une fois, avant que je ne parte [Just once, before I leave]' unsay themselves, as Roquentin's final request for the record to be replayed is itself a replay of Madeleine's offer, a few pages before, to play the song ('voulez-vous l'entendre pour la dernière fois ? [do you want to hear it for the last time?]') (2002: 248 and 243 [2000: 250 and 246], respectively). Roquentin's final song is therefore always already a replay of a replay. Its expression in French also draws on the expletive *ne* of high-register syntax in order to couch the act of leaving in the semi-negative (something caught between the positive and the negative): 'avant que je *ne* parte' (2002: 248, emphasis added). The suggestion is that, on some level, Roquentin is *not* about to leave. That level may be unconscious, but it is also textual, as the novel will run out before the countdown to the Paris train's scheduled departure. Intertexually, this is logical, as Roquentin cannot leave Bouville in order to return to Paris, for the simple reason that Bouville and Paris are the same place, both expressions of Paris as itself and Other. The café is therefore the space of not only Roquentin's singer but also Baudelaire's 'negress', who treads in the mud (the famous *boue* of *bou*ville) but who thinks back to Africa.[19]

The three figures (Andromache, swan and 'negress'; Anny, white hand and the voice of 'Some of These Days') are ultimately combined in two spaces, for Roquentin does not in fact make it quite as far as the station. It nonetheless constitutes the last thing that he sees (before he leaves and before he does not leave). The novel's famous last words, 'demain il pleuvra sur Bouville [tomorrow it will rain over Bouville]' (2002: 250 [2000: 253]), when placed in the context not only of the whole final sentence, which describes the train station seen, not from its platforms but from the street beyond, but also from a new context of Roquentin's hope for a future as a writer of fiction, embody the entirety of Baudelaire's 'Le Cygne':

> Le chantier de la Nouvelle Gare sent fortement le bois humide: demain il pleuvra sur Bouville.

[The yard of the New Station smells strongly of damp wood: tomorrow it will rain over Bouville.]

(2002: 250 [2000: 253])

The word *chantier*, which Baldick translates here as the station's 'yard', also means a building site, which is an accurate description of the space in which the poet sees the three figures of 'Le Cygne'. The station's name 'la Nouvelle Gare' does more than simply attest to its replacement of a previous, older station; here, it references Baudelaire's building site, 'le *nouveau* Carrousel'. Even the hesitating dampness that is the smell of the station echoes the dual conditions of 'Le Cygne''s Paris, which is by turns dust-dry (for the figure of the swan) and muddy (for the negress). And finally, *La Nausée*'s famous last words, 'demain il pleuvra sur Bouville', answer a question posed, or so the poet imagines, by the swan: 'Eau, quand donc pleuvras-tu? [Water, when will you rain?]' (Baudelaire 1998: 174 [175]). In this way, the future of Roquentin's project is opposed uncertainly not only to his recent past, which he has spent almost entirely (with the exception of that one especially oneiric-feeling trip to visit Anny in Paris) in Bouville, but also to memories of years spent travelling extradiegetically to exotic locales, which are located textually in the spatial and temporal uncertainty of the diary's beginning. In this light, these locales are echoes of Baudelaire's (Paris as) lost Africa.

This grammatically veiled development of 'Le Cygne' at *La Nausée*'s conclusion completes the Baudelairean framing of this novel that began with the paper-as-swan simile. A call-and-response is set up between the figures of the swan, which, as in Baudelaire's poem, corral the immediacy, and urgent temporality, of the present and the timelessness of the past in one place. And as in Baudelaire's vision of modernity, all roads lead away from and back to (or, rather, never actually leave) Paris. Even as Roquentin prepares to leave Bouville, with all the hesitation of someone poised just as likely to stay, a fat lady putting down a book and looking on, a negress singing in lieu of another, absent fat lady, white hands making swan signs (*signes d'un cygne*) and, finally, the building site of a station performing one last swan song, all these call across the paratextual limen of the undated sheet and join with Baudelaire's figures of Parisian melancholy (the anonymous 'many more' summoned in the final lines of 'Le Cygne').

What might remain so many freely transcendent similes and metaphors in the textual confines of *La Nausée*'s Bouville become metonyms of Parisian self-alterity when read through the intertextual grammar of 'Le Cygne'. Paris, then, like Anny, is absent-present, for Roquentin as it was for Baudelaire's poet. If Roquentin ends up in bad faith, almost ecstatically fantasizing about his future as a writer (while Andromache is left, some of these days and forever, to miss her honey), he is arguably making amends with the past.[20] At last knowing when the rain will fall, Roquentin, sedate as a swan, turns his back on melancholia and allows himself a little nostalgia.

NOTES

1. I shall throughout use the original French title when referring to Sartre's novel. Quotations from it will be given in the original and in translation. I shall refer to Robert Baldick's translation, which was first published in 1963. The editions I am using are the 2000 Penguin Classics edition of *Nausea*, with its introduction by James Wood, and the 2002 Folio edition of *La Nausée*, which was originally published by Éditions Gallimard in 1938. The translations of Sartre's other texts are my own. I continue to refer to James McGowan's translation of Baudelaire's 'Le Cygne [The Swan]'.

2. For a detailed analysis of the difficulty of locating the beginning of what we might call the 'diegesis proper' in a text that, much as does Italo Calvino's *If on A Winter's Night a Traveler* (*Se una notte d'inverno un viaggiatore*, 1979), struggles wilfully to get going *for real*, to become in some way itself as opposed to the literary trappings that it claims to want to escape but that hold it prisoner, see Rolls and Vuaille-Barcan (2011).

3. In the 'Avertissement des éditeurs' (which Baldick translates in what may be considered a translation error as the 'editors' note' [2000: 8, 2002: 11]), the publishers fix the writing of the diary at the latest in January 1932, some three years after Roquentin's arrival in Bouville after his lengthy travels around the world. This is an interesting part of the note, as it plays into the double role of the *avertissement*, which ostensibly informs readers that what they are reading is a diary *and thus not a novel,* whereas, as a literary conceit, such a note is typical of a novel, especially in the eighteenth-century epistolary tradition (Laclos's *Les Liaisons dangereuses*, for example, warns its readers in just such a note that it is a novel rather than the series of letters that it appears to be). The date may well refer to Louis Ferdinand Céline's *Voyage au bout de la nuit* (*Journey to the End of the Night*), which was published in 1932 (and thus six years before *La Nausée*, but, if we believe the publishers, after Roquentin has finished his own journey). Importantly, Céline's novel is and is not a journey around the world, for, importantly, it is (also) a dream.

4. It is easy to forget that there are three villages named Bouville in France: one in the department of Eure-et-Loire, a second in Essonne and a third in Seine-Maritime in Normandy. The first two are closer to Paris than Le Havre or La Rochelle; the third is close to Rouen, where Simone de Beauvoir was located while Sartre was teaching in Le Havre. Cohen-Solal notes how Sartre's pupils would enjoy watching their philosophy teacher running out of school to catch the train to Rouen and thus to meet 'le Castor', on Wednesday afternoons (1999: 170). The image is strikingly reminiscent of the second verse of the original 1911 recording of 'Some of These Days' (which is, of course, the version that the soldiers would have had in mind as they whistled in the streets of La Rochelle, as Roquentin recalls in the novel). That verse tells the story of a lover rushing down to the station only to see his beloved leaving on the departing train, which will also of course be Roquentin's experience in what I argue is his dream of seeing Anny in Paris.

5. According to Cohen-Solal, Sartre, while a young boy living in La Rochelle, would often play rather roughly with his cousin Annie, leaving her bruised. On one occasion, Sartre's

145

mother, Anne-Marie Schweitzer, wrote to Annie, saying 'Il ne t'a pas oubliée [...] malgré les malices qu'il a pu te faire, en grand polisson qu'il est ! [He has not forgotten you [...] in spite of the horrid things he may have done to you, naughty little chap that he is!]' (Cohen-Solal 1999: 102). In the novel, Anny bears a name that is an anglicized version of that of the cousin with whom Sartre shared these tumultuous childhood memories. And, Roquentin certainly has not forgotten Anny.

6. I have often taught *La Nausée* in its English translation to Honours students at the University of Newcastle, Australia. These students, who have mostly majored either in English (literary studies) or in Creative Writing, approach the novel unburdened by the large philosophical part of the paratextual apparatus that I am discussing here. For this reason, they are often drawn to passages such as that of the two people colliding into each other at the train station, which ends with the potentially memorable, but often neglected, line: 'Il y avait donc là, en même temps, cette palissade qui sent si fort le bois mouillé, cette lanterne, cette petite bonne femme blonde dans les bras d'un Nègre, sous un ciel de feu [So there, at one and the same time, you had that fence which smells so strongly of wet wood, that lantern, and that little blonde in a Negro's arms, under a fiery-coloured sky]' (2002: 22 [2000: 18]). This passage stands out, I should argue, at least in part because of its intertextuality: it tells the story of the absent–present verses of 'Some of These Days', and in particular the paratext of that song, which was in reality penned by a black male composer (Shelton Brooks) and sung by a white Jewish female performer (Sophie Tucker), whereas in the novel its origins are given in reverse (a white Jewish male composer and a black female singer). This is the technicolour production of the intertext, against which the text's version is the negative. It is also a powerful sign of the role played by reversal in the mechanics of the novel. For essays that draw on this image, see *Sartre's 'Nausea': Text, Context, Intertext* (Rolls and Rechniewski 2005), which resulted in part from discussions produced by this English literature course.

7. In his review of the essay, Édouard Roditi accuses Sartre of being more focused on his opinions on existence than on Baudelaire, and specifically of neglecting the complexity and paradoxes of the poet's work (1950: 100). It is true that Sartre's study relies more heavily on paratextual materials (notably Baudelaire's correspondence) than on poetic analysis. It is also possible to see in Roditi's review an accusation of overreliance on a Germanic approach that is of its time: Sartre's preoccupation with Husserl and the city of Berlin coincided, as Cohen-Solal documents (1999: 188–98), with the lead-up to the Second World War, and Roditi's review is written at an early stage in the post-war period.

8. For a more detailed reading of dual signs, swans and seeing Baudelaire everywhere, see Rolls (2020). It might be noted here that Stéphane Mallarmé also wrote a poem about (and sometimes known as) 'Le Cygne', with which Sartre was without doubt familiar. I hope in the course of this reading to make a strong case for this intertextual ungrammaticality's pertaining to Baudelaire's swan, but this other poem, which is often considered to be a metaphor for writer's block and which describes the contrast of a swan's white plumage against the horrors of the ground, remains a good candidate for comparison.

9. Perhaps despite himself, Sartre represents this union in terms both incestuous and divine, which is, of course, a typically Baudelairean oxymoron.

10. A more famous instance of a *fêlure* can be found in Émile Zola's *La Bête humaine* (*The Beast Within*), in which it describes an hereditary trait from which man cannot escape. For a reading of *La Nausée*'s paradoxical similarity to Zola's famous tale of hereditary psychopathy, see 'Roquentin's Primal Scene, Or What is and What is Not Seen in *La Nausée*' (in Rolls 2014: 109–41).

11. Sartre considers both these movements to be transcendent, however: all is movement in Baudelaire. As he writes, these movements are 'deux formes de la transcendance que nous pouvons nommer, après Jean Wahl, transascendance et transdescendance. Car cette bestialité de l'homme – comme son angélisme – il faut l'entendre au sens fort: il ne s'agit pas seulement de la trop fameuse faiblesse charnelle ou de la toute puissance des bas instincts [two forms of transcendence, which we can name, following Jean Wahl, transascendance and transdescendance. For this bestiality of man's, as too his angelism, is to be understood in the most literal terms: it is not just the weakness of the flesh for which [Baudelaire] is so well known or the omnipotence of base instincts]' (1947: 44). Like nausea then, Baudelaire's carnality is a fundamental assumption of being in the world.

12. As noted in Chapter One above, Mary Gluck describes the flâneur of the 1840s as a 'popular' figure, whereas after this watershed, in the 1850s, he is an 'avant-garde' one (2005: 65–107). In this second phase, the flâneur is much more in line with Baudelaire's imaginative observer, whose gaze is writerly, to map Barthes's term onto this kind of urban reading, rather than simply readerly.

13. It is interesting to speculate as to whom Sartre has in mind with his reference to 'nous autres' (literally, 'us others'). Certainly, it is difficult to believe that he who was perhaps the most famous phenomenologist of the twentieth century would look at any object quite like most other people. On the other hand, he famously described that he and Roquentin were one and the same person ('J'étais Roquentin [...] en même temps, j'étais *moi*' [Sartre 1965: 210]), so he may well have himself and Roquentin in mind, in a kind of royal first-person singular-plural.

14. It should be noted that for scholars like Lauren Rosewarne, on the other hand, nostalgia is considered to encompass this kind of melancholy. As she notes, '[n]ostalgia is underpinned by the longing to return to a time and place previously inhabited while simultaneously recognizing the impossibility of it, hence why the sentiment is so often tinged with melancholy'; indeed, as she argues further, '[w]e know that going backwards and reliving our pasts is impossible', yet, '[t]his knowledge [...] doesn't obliterate the desire' (2020: 81). In *La Nausée*, Sartre uses the intertext of 'Some of These Days' to enable the impossibility of the past to remain alive, partially at least, which has precisely this effect of interlacing desire with melancholy.

15. I not only wish to remain focused on the Baudelairean intertext here for reasons of space but also because I have written extensively elsewhere on Anny's role as a fetishistic portal out of textual reality into another, oneiric space. See, for example, Rolls (2003).

16. And neither should this Parisian angle be considered merely a device for avoiding other more self-evident modes of presentation and representation, such as the famous Sartrean modes of being (the *in-itself*, which speaks to immanence; the *for-itself*, which strikes a tension between immanence and transcendence; and the *for-others*, which suggests a mode of existing in necessary and inevitable relation to other human beings that is not dissimilar from the intertextuality that connects all text to other texts); rather, these Parisian modes speak of an alternative, but equally powerful, source of *La Nausée*'s development.

17. In *Baudelaire*, Sartre offers an interesting commentary on Baudelaire's final departure from Paris, which sees him ending up in a caricature of that city. Roquentin's departure at the end of *La Nausée* might be considered a negative image of this movement: 'C'est lui qui a délimité la géographie de son existence en décidant de traîner ses misères dans une grande ville, en refusant tous les dépaysements réels, pour mieux poursuivre dans sa chambre les évasions imaginaires [...] et qui, blessé à mort, n'a consenti à quitter Paris que pour une autre cité qui en fût la caricature [It was he [Baudelaire] who delimited the geography of his existence by deciding to haul his misery around a big city, by refusing all real changes of scenery, in order all the better to pursue in his bedroom journeys of the imagination [...] and who, at death's door, only consented to leave Paris for another city that resembled it like a caricature]' (1947: 222–23).

18. To this extent, we readers invest *La Nausée* with consciousness. Its novelistic ambition to have the self-founding immanence of an *in-itself* being is therefore always already undercut by that parallel, philosophical underside, that is, the inevitability of being *for-itself*, of freedom.

19. It is worth noting that Anny's corpulence stands opposed to the emaciation (through tuberculosis) of Baudelaire's 'négresse', as though Anny was conceived as a parallel figure but also as her opposite.

20. In terms of nostalgia, it is arguably of no matter whether Roquentin's future is attainable or whether it is merely an illusion. One of the cures of nostalgia, when it was first diagnosed among soldiers fighting overseas, included, according to Katharina Niemeyer, not only returning the patient home but also, quite simply, 'the promise of doing so'; to this, she also adds exposure to 'music that evokes images and memories of the homeland' (2014: 9). Beneath the images that Roquentin conjures of the conception and first performances of 'Some of These Days' in New York, for him, it seems clear, the song evokes personal, Parisian memories.

REFERENCES

Baudelaire, Charles (1998), *The Flowers of Evil* (trans. J. McGowan), Oxford World's Classics, Oxford: Oxford University Press.

Carroll, Mark (2006), '"It Is": Reflections on the Role of Music in *La Nausée*', *Music and Letters*, 87: 3, pp. 398–407.

Chambers, Ross (2006), 'Baudelaire's Paris', in R. Lloyd (ed.), *The Cambridge Companion to Baudelaire*, Cambridge: Cambridge University Press, pp. 101–16.

Chambers, Ross (2018), 'Significant others, or textual congress: Concerning Baudelaire and Tranter', *Australian Journal of French Studies*, 55: 3, pp. 223–36.

Cohen-Solal, Annie (1999), *Sartre. 1905–1980*, Paris: Gallimard.

Gluck, Mary (2005), *Popular Bohemia: Modernism and Urban Culture in Nineteenth-Century Paris*, Cambridge, MA: Harvard University Press.

Larkin, Brian (2009), 'National allegory', *Social Text 100*, 27: 3, pp. 164–68.

Niemeyer, Katharina (ed.) (2014), *Media and Nostalgia: Yearning for the Past, Present and Future*, Houndmills: Palgrave Macmillan.

Quinney, Anne (2008), '"Il faudrait qu'elle soit belle et dure comme de l'acier": Sartre and The problem of writing', *Dalhousie French Studies*, 83, pp. 69–79.

Riffaterre, Michael (1978), *Semiotics of Poetry*, Bloomington, IN: Indiana University Press.

Roditi, Édouard (1950), 'Baudelaire', *Poetry*, 77: 2, pp. 100–03.

Rolls, Alistair (2003), '"This lovely, sweet refrain": Reading the fiction back into *Nausea*', *Literature and Aesthetics: The Journal of the Sydney Society of Literature and Aesthetics*, 13: 2, pp. 57–72.

Rolls, Alistair (2014), *Paris and the Fetish: Primal Crime Scenes*, Amsterdam and New York: Rodopi.

Rolls, Alistair (2020), 'Saving Paris from Nostalgia: Jumbling the urban and seeing swans everywhere', *Australian Journal of French Studies*, 57: 1, pp. 66–77.

Rolls, Alistair and Rechniewski, Elizabeth (eds) (2005), *Sartre's 'Nausea': Text, Context, Intertext*, Amsterdam and New York: Rodopi.

Rolls, Alistair and Vuaille-Barcan, Marie-Laure (2011), 'Paratextuality, self-alterity and the becoming-text', in A. Rolls and M.-L. Vuaille-Barcan (eds), *Masking Strategies: Unwrapping the French Paratext, Modern French Identities*, vol. 92, Oxford: Peter Lang, pp. 159–85.

Rosewarne, Lauren (2020), *Why We Remake: The Politics, Economics and Emotions of Film and TV Remakes*, London and New York: Routledge.

Sartre, Jean-Paul (1947), *Baudelaire*, Paris: Gallimard.

Sartre, Jean-Paul (1965), *Les Mots*, Paris: Gallimard.

Sartre, Jean-Paul (1993), *Being and Nothingness: An Essay on Phenomenological Ontology* (trans. H. Barnes), London: Routledge.

Sartre, Jean-Paul (2000), *Nausea* (trans. R. Baldick), London: Penguin.

Sartre, Jean-Paul (2002), *La Nausée*, Paris: Gallimard.

Scott, Clive (2006), 'Translating Baudelaire', in R. Lloyd (ed.), *The Cambridge Companion to Baudelaire*, Cambridge: Cambridge University Press, pp. 193–205.

8

'La forme d'une ville/Change plus vite, hélas! [...]': Translation and the Changing Modes of Urban Cognition

Clive Scott

> *Le chercheur est un passeur. Il n'a rien d'un douanier veillant à la surveillance des frontières (disciplinaires) mais est plus volontiers un contrebandier. C'est un traducteur.*
> [The researcher is a ferryman. He has nothing about him of the customs officer monitoring (disciplinary) border-controls but has real affinities with a smuggler. He is a translator.][1]
>
> (Laplantine 2018: 25)

The converse of this observation is the proposition that the translator is like a ferryman, someone for whom borders are a challenge, are for crossing, with smuggled goods. This chapter argues that translation is not merely designed to cross borders between languages but also to cross borders within the work being translated, to use the former to achieve the latter. And when we speak of crossing borders within the work itself, we are thinking primarily of those works which cannot decide which/what world they wish to belong to, so that within them, different worlds either confront each other or are porous to each other. I have suggested, for example (Scott 2007: 25–26), that Manet, in *La Musique aux Tuileries* (1862), in which Baudelaire is portrayed, juxtaposes a regime of portraiture, of posing, of returned look, of the spectatorial gaze, of stilled time, of serried verticals, with a loose confusion of figures, animation, turned-away, unselfconscious activity, a glimpsing, glancing spectator, passing time, distributive and relational horizontals. Not surprisingly, J. A. Hiddleston has explored Baudelaire's own ambiguous attitudes to Manet's ambiguities (1999: 223–51), because Baudelaire's writing is similarly caught in unresolved and unresolvable contradictory impulses. The relative force of such impulses is by definition impossible to compute, but as a necessarily experimental writing, translation can develop and redistribute such impulses. Translation transforms what cannot be done with one language into what can be done with another language.

But, translation has other preoccupations, too. It is not just a linguistic matter of texts on the page; it is also about the reading experience, where the text on the page expands into a life, the life of the reader in all its multi-sensory and associative ramifications. We assume too readily that the reader's function is to serve the text and too easily overlook the reverse: that the text exists to serve the reader. This does not necessarily entail the text finding a new lexicon – though it must do so to a certain extent, as a translation – but more essentially perhaps, it entails the text finding a new form, in order that its words can mean differently, with a different kind of expressive energy, with an expanded experiential range, can suit, in short, a new cognitive idiolect.

This notion of expanding text has in fact two senses, of equal importance. The text expands in the process of reading, as we have just argued, expands into the proliferating psychosensory responses of the reader. But, equally, the source text (ST) expands, through the number of translations it attracts, into its own textual totality. As it is translated again and again, the ST becomes an increasingly small fraction of its total potential self, of all the versions of itself that might be elicited. Let us insist: in translating, we are not trying to find our way back to the ST; we are trying to find a way forward for it, into a multiplicity of possible idiolects.

Proust writes, of his Impressionist painter Elstir: 'si Dieu le Père avait créé les choses en les nommant, c'est en leur ôtant leur nom, ou en leur donnant un autre qu'Elstir les recréait [if God the Father had created things by naming them, it is in removing their names or giving them others that Elstir created them anew]' (1988: 191). Only if we enter language without pre-empting its meanings, by letting words return to a kind of mutism, will language come back to us with revitalized sense. Texts are already filled with muteness, with their invisible. From the given text, translation extracts a set of senses which is made possible by, but is lacking in, the ST, senses which are not so much choices (decisions of limitation) as parts of an experiential totality we shall never have done with. Words make an impact on us, an impact which we, in return, make visible. The ST is a first draft, a first step in a dialectic, or a script which will constantly beget different kinds of performance. But we must emphasize that the ST is not an inert and unchanging raw material – it is in dialogue, that is to say, it is an initial proposition which, in response to countless counter-propositions reveals ever more of itself, reveals itself to be more than it was. And we must further remember that the disposition of text in the space of the page is to be counted as an expressive resource peculiarly enjoyed by poetry. *Mise-en-page* explores the free-variational plurality of writing as a spatial art, highly sensitive to expressive perspectivism and perceptual modality.

REMEMBERING PARIS

* * * * *

The last four lines of Baudelaire's 'Le Crépuscule du matin [Morning Twilight]'[2] in the 1861 edition run:

L'aurore grelottante en robe rose et verte
S'avançait lentement sur la Seine déserte,
Et le sombre Paris, en se frottant les yeux,
Empoignait ses outils, vieillard laborieux.

In the 1857 edition, we would have read:

L'Aurore grelottante en robe rose et verte
S'avançait lentement sur la Seine déserte,
Et le sombre Paris, en se frottant les yeux
Empoignait ses outils, – vieillard laborieux!

We tend to treat variants as glitches in composition, or abandoned options, particularly if they concern only punctuation and capitalization, as here; we rarely think of them as re-educations of vision or palimpsestic texts. But variants tell us about the underlying malleability of text, about potential directions for the composing mind. Here, Baudelaire quietens his burst of dawn light, both because its entry is so tentative and because the personification, already in the metaphorical description, has lost its larger allegorical ambitions. This is a leap forward in time, from the matinal crepuscular, across the unmentioned 'aube' (that period when light is still below the horizon), to a daybreak now endowed with an illuminating '/ɔR(ə)/'. But there is also, in the shift to lower case, a gesture of assimilation: it is as if the dawn is drawn into the urban condition, is another member of the urban population, and, correspondingly, as if the poet, abandoning a transcendental, moralistic position, joins the bleary-eyed crowd.

The removal of the dash has a somewhat similar effect. In Baudelaire's work, we associate the dash with the indication of the poem's imminent closure; sometimes that dash covers a whole final stanza or the last line or lines, but sometimes it occurs within the final line as here or as in another couplet poem, 'Allégorie':

Elle regardera la face de la Mort,
Ainsi qu'un nouveau-né, – sans haine et sans remords.

In this sense, the dash is a gesture of self-dissociation, a shift from the discursive to the meta-discursive, the ritual allocation of a meaning. Remove the dash, and the poet is still caught up in the volatile flux of discernment; 'vieillard laborieux', no longer a proclamation, an ironic ceremonial designation (the exclamation mark), recovers itself as a sympathetic and unassuming appositional adjunct, a product of existential circumstance.

What one would want to suggest is that Baudelaire's writing is prey to a psycho-perceptual uncertainty, is likely at any point to reset its psycho-perceptual coordinates, particularly as a shift from the rhetorical to the genetic, from a *repertoire* of expressive effects to the generation of an associative weave of sense(s). My translation tries to capture that change of perceptual position:

Day	a
is breaking	b also a (a)
garbed in pink and green	c
its teeth	c (a)
chattering	
making	b also a (a)
its slow way	a
across the deserted Seine	a (a)
and sombre Paris	d
grabs	d (a)
hold of its tools, rubbing its eyes	e
a labourer long past his prime	e (a)

[Note: (a) = half-rhyme or relation of assonance; thus, 'making' forms a full rhyme with 'breaking' but a half-rhyme with 'Day/way/Seine']

The assonantal trail relates to what Henri Meschonnic would call *récitatif*: 'par quoi j'entends toute la sémantique sérielle dans le continu du discours, et qui court à travers le récit, qui est l'énoncé [it is what I call the recitative, by which I mean the whole serial semantics in the continuum of discourse, which runs through the narrative, which is the enunciated]' (2007: 114). The assonantal chain is the generator of *énonciation* within the *énoncé*, that is, not an acoustic pattern in the service of the eurhythmic, or of the consolidation of meaning, but the reaching of the tongue for sources of sense in the materiality of language, language in the very process of coming to sense, of finding its sources of life. We might think of this sequence as a meshwork (lines of flow and interwovenness), a term borrowed by Tim Ingold from Henri Lefebvre, to set against a rhetorical network (lines of connection). Elsewhere, Ingold speaks of 'the *meshwork* of entangled lines of life, growth and movement' and associates it with animistic ontology in which 'beings do not propel themselves across a ready-made world but rather issue forth through a world-in-formation, along the lines of their relationships' (2011: 63). Translation here acts against the ST's notion of rhyme as a network of points, by transforming jumps between like-sounding words into the morphing of the acoustically oblique or transverse, sound itself in motion.

I choose this formal mode because it cultivates a susceptibility to the leakage of one element into another, to metamorphoses which in other contexts would be identified as metaphors, figures of speech, but which here are natural synaesthetic, cross-category perceptual mergings. The reading eye is here persuaded by the text to see not contours and perspectival hierarchies, in an even white light, but rather prismatic decompositions, such that '[i]l arrive à voir la réalité dans l'atmosphère vivante des formes, décomposée, réfractée, réfléchie par les êtres et les choses, en incessantes variations [it comes to see reality in the living atmosphere of forms, decomposed, refracted, reflected by beings and things, in incessant variations]' (Laforgue 1903: 136).

Our concern, then, is with that too little studied subject, the psycho-perceptual experience of forms. The pair of 'Crépuscule' poems are in *rimes plates* [couplets], a rhyming mechanism as if specifically designed for stichic – that is, non-stanzaic – verse, a verse that pulls towards self-sufficient, evenly distributed episodes and undetermined limits. We are aware of its indispensability to the continuities of classical drama. But in the nineteenth century, and in the hands of Baudelaire, it serves 'le paysage des grandes villes', 'c'est-à-dire la collection des grandeurs et des beautés qui résultent d'une puissante agglomération d'hommes et de monuments, le charme profond et compliqué d'une capitale âgée et vieillie dans les gloires et les tribulations de la vie [the landscape of cities: that is to say, the ensemble of splendours and beauties which grow from a powerful conglomeration of people and monuments, the profound and complex charm of a capital, aged and grown old in the glories and tribulations of life]' (1976: 666). Charles Marville's photographs of old Paris (1865–68) remind us above all of a city unamenable to the *flâneur*, given over to labyrinthine and confined spaces. The poem in stichic couplets may generate something of the same feeling, the spaces created by rhyme-pairs uncomfortably cheek by jowl, compressed. And it is the agglomerative capacity of the couplet which seems to preside in 'Le Crépuscule du matin', with its readiness to drift into the plurals of multiple isolations. This process of isolating each of the many is engineered by the insistent use of the definite article, accompanied by an inescapable possessive adjective which chains them to their condition:

Et les agonisants dans le fond des hospices
Poussaient leur dernier râle en hoquets inégaux.
Les débauchés rentraient, brisés par leurs travaux.

While	a
the dying	a (a)
laid out	b
in the poorhouse	b (a)
wards	
expel their final breaths	

'LA FORME D'UNE VILLE/CHANGE PLUS VITE, HÉLAS! [...]'

in deep uneven	c
gasps and those greedy	c (a)
for a sniff of skirt	d
toil home	e
broken	e (a)
by their night's exertions	d (a)

But how to turn the multiple isolations, the agglomerations, that cities seem to nourish, into the 'croisement de leurs innombrables rapports [intersection of their innumerable connections]' (1975: 276), as Baudelaire puts it in his dedicatory letter to Arsène Houssaye which acts as a preface to *Le Spleen de Paris*? How to turn the identitarian into the relational? This shift is fundamental to the Haussmannian project: 'Le principe de la ville haussmannienne repose sur l'idée de circulation: le commerce prend le pas sur l'industrie, le mouvement et l'échange sur le logement [The principle of the Haussmannian city rests on the idea of circulation: trade overrides industry, movement and exchange supplant dwelling]' (Thézy 1994: 29). If the couplet is inclined to count things off, to create but little space in its enumerated units, the quatrain in *rimes croisées* creates narrative weave, give-and-take, forward propulsion; the rhyme partners are as if delayed, not already in view, as if recovered from memory:

Je vois s'épanouir vos passions novices;
Sombres ou lumineux, je vis vos jours perdus;
Mon cœur multiplié jouit de tous vos vices!
Mon âme resplendit de toutes vos vertus! ('Les Petites Vieilles')

In place of multiple isolations, we have the promise of isolated but restored multiplicities, thanks to the poet's own capacity to imaginatively and empathetically multiply.

Rhyme in the couplet may appear to be the vice in which the subject is caught, a destiny predicted by language itself, already imprinted in the edicts of homophony, a structure of repeated closure. This amounts to a knowledge of the world which the poet, as a master of language, has prior access to: 'pourquoi tout poète qui ne sait pas au juste combien chaque mot comporte de rimes est incapable d'exprimer une idée quelconque [why any poet who does not know exactly how many rhymes each word has at its disposal is incapable of expressing any idea whatever]' (1975: 183). But, in other circumstances, rhyme is something of a lottery and is an elusive prey that the poet has to go looking for:

Flairant dans tous les coins les hasards de la rime ('Le Soleil')

Suddenly, we are faced with the poet as ragpicker, searching for the detritus of the city in its dark corners, looking to recycle discarded materials. In place of the master of rhyme comes the *bricoleur* of rhymes, and rhyme is no longer an inevitable destiny but a route to the unpredictable, to a more mercurial future, to fantasy. In Baudelaire's writing, there begins a shift from the identity of the perceived to the performance of perception itself, where we are constantly released from the pressures of an iconographic tradition into our own perceptual autobiography, into our own perceptual duration and into our own re-setting of perceptual relations. We no longer perceive what is given, what is impressed on us, by the collective memory, but rather what is possible, or made possible, by the free exercise of an associative memory, acting achronologically (we remember the present in the past).

So what sense do we want to make of the distribution of verse-forms in 'Tableaux parisiens' as a whole? Of the eighteen poems, six are in stichic alexandrine couplets, one in stanzaic couplets with a syllabic pattern of 7.7.7.4, seven are stanzaic, in *rimes croisées*, with six in alexandrines and one in octosyllables ('Rêve parisien'), one is stanzaic, in *rimes embrassées* and octosyllables ('Le Squelette laboureur') and three are sonnets, all in alexandrines but one of which – 'Brumes et pluies' – has a couplet-orientated structure. What does this look like as a cityscape for Paris? One that is not embarrassed by the discontinuities and promiscuity of its cognitive structures, but equally one that creates new connections between them. Eloquent cases have been made for the sequential cohesiveness of *Les Fleurs du mal*, a cohesiveness of fabric woven by lexical and thematic continuities (see, for example, Runyon 2010); but we also need to see the connections, the cognitive/perceptual roadways, between different versions of the poetic self, different attitudinal postures.

Haussmann's analogous objective – to create connections between left and right banks of the Seine, between centre and periphery, between quarters, railway stations and parks – has its echo on the pavements themselves. 'A une passante', for example, seems to take place in an urban space opened up by a Haussmannian 'percée' [cut-through]. What is released, we might argue, is the subjunctive, the realm of the optative and the hypothetical, of the imaginary, of a blind field of possible relationships:

> Car j'ignore où tu fuis, tu ne sais où je vais,
> Ô toi que j'eusse aimée, ô toi qui le savais!

Language, in its conditionals, its suppositionals, its optatives, is where individuals, and the societies they constitute, make imaginative space for themselves, give themselves options on alternative existences and escape the predictions of history; as George Steiner puts it: 'Through language, so much of which is focused inward to our private selves, we reject the empirical inevitability of the world. Through language, we construct what I have called "alternities of being"' (1998: 497).

'LA FORME D'UNE VILLE/CHANGE PLUS VITE, HÉLAS! [...]'

Free-roaming pedestrians generate dramas of brief encounter, a passing by which might release an electricity.

We know that, for Baudelaire, much of the force of futurity, of alternity, of the aspirational, lies in fashion and make-up and that what pushes this force to the surface, what characterizes its activity, is its 'qualité essentielle de présent [essential quality of presentness]' (1976: 684), its speed and the pressures of the instant. Make-up is an overflowing of being in desire: eyeshadow and rouge 'représentent la vie, une vie surnaturelle et excessive' [represent life, an excessive and supernatural life], while eyeshadow ('le noir') more particularly gives the eye 'une apparence plus décidée de fenêtre ouverte sur l'infini [the more defined look of a window opening on to infinity]' (1976: 717). But to capture the expressive charge of fashion or make-up, one needs 'un moyen expéditif [expeditious means]': 'mais il y a [...] dans la métamorphose journalière des choses extérieures, un mouvement rapide qui commande à l'artiste une égale vélocité d'exécution [but there is [...] in the daily metamorphosis of external things, a rapidity of movement which requires of the artist an equal speed of execution]' (1976: 686). We cannot tell if the 'passante' is wearing eye-liner ('je buvais [...]/Dans son œil, ciel livide [...]'). But she is in the latest fashion: 'Soulevant, balançant le feston et l'ourlet' has a parallel in the reference, in *Le Peintre de la vie moderne*, to 'toute autre étoffe de nos fabriques, soulevée, balancée par la crinoline ou les jupons de mousseline empesée [every other material from our factories, given lift and swing by crinoline or underskirts of starched muslin]' (1976: 695). And speed is an essential part of the encounter's intensity: 'Un éclair', 'Fugitive beauté', 'soudainement renaître'.

* * * * *

Baudelaire's generous use of the exclamation mark and of apostrophe finds its justification in his essay on Théodore de Banville (1861), in which he remarks: 'Tout d'abord constatons que l'hyperbole et l'apostrophe sont des formes de langage qui lui [à la Lyre] sont non seulement des plus agréables, mais aussi des plus nécessaires, puisque ces formes dérivent naturellement d'un état exagéré de la vitalité [First of all, let us note that hyperbole and apostrophe are forms of language which are not only among the most agreeable to the lyric spirit, but also among the most necessary, since these forms derive naturally from an exaggerated state of vitality]' (1976: 164–65). He immediately goes on to say that the lyric eschews the particular and exceptional in favour of 'les traits principaux, généraux, universels [the dominant, general and universal features]'. What I want to suggest is that, for Baudelaire, standard means began to serve new purposes. If, in the Banville essay, exclamation and apostrophe are seen to serve melodramatic moralism, to inflate the image to allegory, common noun to personification, they can equally belong to other kinds of inflationary impulse, other kinds of 'état exagéré de la vitalité', as is suggested in the term 'surnaturelle' applied to make-up, a term more fully explained in *Fusées, XI*:

> Deux qualités littéraires fondamentales: surnaturalisme et ironie.
> [...] Le surnaturel comprend la couleur générale et l'accent, c'est-à-dire intensité, sonorité, limpidité, vibrativité, profondeur et retentissement dans l'espace et dans le temps.
> Il y a des moments de l'existence où le temps et l'étendue sont plus profonds, et le sentiment de l'existence immensément augmenté (1975: 658).
> [Two fundamental literary qualities: supernaturalism and irony.
> [...] The supernatural comprises general colour and accent, that is, intensity, sonority, limpidity, vibrativity, depth and resoundingness in space and in time.
> There are moments in existence in which time and space have more depth and the feeling of existence is hugely increased].

In Baudelaire's Janus-faced view of vitality, hyperbole might just as well serve heightened sensitivity to sensory contact and the expansion of synaesthetic encompassment, as the looming spectres of moral fallenness. And about apostrophe, multifaceted though it is (see Culler 2015: 186–243), we might suggest that, in Baudelaire, it shifts from ritual invocation, the plea to be heard, an engagement with the unseen forces of the universe, to a form of address which sets the addressee in the now of writing, in (temporal/spatial) close-up, and begins to find a kinship with reactive exclamatories like 'Oh!' and 'Ah!'. Furthermore, when we look at the sestet of 'A une passante' as a whole, we may feel that Baudelaire is now using the arts of punctuation not for grammatico-syntactic purposes but as a graphism, as expressive marks, justified by perceptual, affective and modal considerations, the nervous expectancies of *points de suspension*, the peremptory break and perceptual re-orientation of the dash, the existential irradiation and 'retentissement', rather than vocal loudness, of the exclamation mark. Let us remember that, in the visual arts, the 'moyen expéditif' is to be found among the graphic arts: drawing, etching, pastel, lithograph; Baudelaire is using punctuation as a set of graphic gestures. This suggestion may seem a little fanciful, but we have plenty of evidence of Baudelaire's sensitivity to punctuational issues in his manuscript revisions and variants.

In the first quatrain of the sister sonnet 'Les Aveugles',[3] Baudelaire uses a punctuational strategy of a very different kind: semicolons to mark off the elements in a sequence of predominantly verbless notations:

> Contemple-les, mon âme; ils sont vraiment affreux!
> Pareils aux mannequins; vaguement ridicules;

Terribles, singuliers comme les somnambules;
Dardant on ne sait où leurs globes ténébreux.

We see this same punctuational practice in his enumeration of the motifs which Constantin Guys, his painter of modern life, has harvested from Turkey (1976: 704). But it reminds us, too, of a notational capacity in Baudelaire, not necessarily attached to the semicolon, which surfaces in interior monologue in, for example, 'A une heure du matin' (*Le Spleen de Paris*). These poems – 'Les Aveugles', 'A une passante', 'A une heure du matin' – as indeed 'Les Sept Vieillards', present an observer who has spent his day in urban perambulation, but who cannot sustain a moral independence, who is drawn into the midst of the urban predicament and/or for whom the room is no longer a refuge but rather a space inhabited by the continuing repercussions and infiltrations of the street. The attempted interposition of the dash, which guarantees self-extrication and creates distance enough to deliver a concluding judgement in the ante-penultimate stanza of 'Les Sept Vieillards':

– Mais je tournai le dos au cortège infernal.

is irremediably nullified by the stanza following:

Exaspéré comme un ivrogne qui voit double,
Je rentrai, je fermai ma porte, épouvanté,
Malade et morfondu, l'esprit fiévreux et trouble,
Blessé par le mystère et par l'absurdité!

And just as Baudelaire removes the dash at the end of 'Le Crépuscule du matin', so equally he removes it from the penultimate line of 'Les Aveugles', which in *L'Artiste* read:

– Moi, je me traîne aussi, mais, plus qu'eux hébété

It is as if the dash of cool identification and self-dissociation has been replaced by the exclamation marks not of allegorization but of 'le sentiment de l'existence immensément augmenté', albeit in the direction of self-exposure:

Vois! Je me traîne aussi! mais plus qu'eux hébété

Some of the distinctions I have so far made correspond to the distinction between urban documentary photography and the newly developing genre of street photography (see Scott 2007). The authority of the documentary derives from the agreement it can produce in the spectatorial community, by the specimen-like targeting of the individual who has become his *métier* (see, for example, Eugène Atget's *chiffonnier* (1899–1900) [Szarkowski and Hambourg 1985: 59]). Street photographs, on the other hand, look to disperse authority by inviting a diversity of individual input. And while the documentary imprisons its subject in the iterative and durative aspects of tense, the perceptual experience of street photography takes place in ever-eventful time, the punctual present. For present purposes, we might propose that couplets gravitate towards the documentary, whereas *rimes croisées* enact the spirit of the street photograph. In suggesting these distinctions, I want to turn back to my earlier translations of 'Les Aveugles' and 'A une passante'. The documentary photograph does not interest itself in the reverse shot, that is to say, in what the subject might think of the spectator, in unconscious or suppressed dialogue; street photography is altogether more alert to participatory activity and the notion of shared spaces, spaces shared by the heterogeneous, the often ill-assorted, the menagerie. My translation of 'Les Aveugles' (2000: 141–46) is an experiment in reverse-shot translation, to draw the accusative into the nominative, to relieve the blind of their exemplarity and restore them as volatile consciousnesses. I quote the first lines and the last lines:

They watch us with derision and distaste,	10
compare us	3
to tailors' dummies	5
and sleepwalking freaks.	5
What can the movement of our eyeballs mean?	10
What do we look like, we who cannot see?	10

* * * * *

But what does he	4 (x / x x)
really want?	3 (/ x /)
To give us walk-on parts	6 (x / x / x /)
in a fancy masque of his	7 (x x / x / x /)
about the *deus absconditus*?	9 (x x x / x x / x x)

The early lines hold the blind, even as they speak, in an orderly representative community, keep them in check, by binding them to an underlying iambic pentameter. But as the poem proceeds, the blind increasingly occupy a free verse which prevents the 'culture' of regular verse-forms dictating their locutionary options and makes their speech an origin rather than a compliance.

For my versions of 'A une passante' (2000: 97–105), I chose the villanelle, first (a) in its strict 19-line English form (I quote the final three stanzas) and then (b) as a 16-line free-verse form, still in tercets with a final quatrain (I quote the final two stanzas):

(a)   Her eyes full of storm and so hauntingly strygian.
     Was she grieving *grande dame* or a whore on her beat,
     Her motion elastic, her furbelows Stygian?

     And then she was gone, slick-fast as a widgeon,
     To beyond all beyond, to where none ever meet.
     My whole self convulsed as she passed callipygian,

     Too late, but she knew, this canny Parisian,
     That love at last sight puts the city on heat,
     Her motion elastic, her furbelows Stygian.
     My whole self convulsed as she passed callipygian.

(b)   Then she was gone. Nowhere to be seen.
     Yet I've been jolted
               back to life.
     Somewhere the traffic rumbles on and on.

     Missed trains, missed friends,
               and other chances missed.
     These little pains disturb,
               whip up the blood,
     And still the street-noise dins inside my head
     And still her hand lifts up her swinging hem.

Verse-forms, as I have already argued, have their own cultural memories, a sedimentation that passing time may only add to, memories which are not ours, but those of a literary tradition. But the writer can inflect those memories by, as it were, remembering forward, outlining for memory a future path. The villanelle, I suggested, because of its interwoven repetitions, is 'reminiscent' both of Eadweard Muybridge's chronophotography, 'a series of frames slightly differentiated from each other', and of minimalist music, 'a kind of Nymanian experience designed to accompany the theatrical spectacularity of Greenaway cinema' (2000: 99). The free-verse version allows the different elements to drift across the poem in looser fashion, with more marked mutations and more diversity in their relating, as though the specifics of the encounter were gradually dispersing across the urban setting, but ever bubbling up as questions in the memory.

As we trace this shift from a moralistic hyperbole to an existential hyperbole of sensory expansion, from an apostrophe of plea to one of confrontational complicity, we must remember what Baudelaire tells us in 'Le Poème du hachisch' (*Les Paradis artificiels*, 1860): that our distinction between the moral and the existential is too sharp, that allegory is less didactic than cognitive, less an amplification of lesson and more an amplification of the powers of apprehension, and thus no enemy of the symbolic: [4]

> L'intelligence de l'allégorie prend en vous des proportions à vous-même inconnues; nous noterons en passant que l'allégorie, ce genre si *spirituel*, que les peintres mala-droits nous ont accoutumés à mépriser, mais qui est vraiment l'une des formes prim-itives et les plus naturelles de la poésie, reprend sa domination légitime dans l'intel-ligence illuminée par l'ivresse.
> [The understanding of allegory takes on proportions unfamiliar to you; we will note in passing that allegory, this genre so full of fine-mindedness, which clumsy paint-ers have accustomed us to hold in contempt, but which is truly one of the primitive and most natural forms of poetry, recovers its legitimate dominion in an intelligence illuminated by drunkenness.]
>
> (1975: 430)

* * * * *

It is the projective, future-orientated nature of translation that should be empha-sized, the 'constant margin of incompletion, of arrested potentiality which chal-lenges fulfilment' (Steiner 1998: 227). I want to propose that translation creates this forward-directed alternity of being, by itself acting as the agent not of transfer but of hypothesis: the ST admits the 'dreaming' reader[5] and thus begets the target text as optative, or conditional, or suppositional. Translation *justifies* the diversity of languages by itself pursuing alternity (not to be confused with alterity). Trans-lation refuses to accept the world (ST) as it is; foreign languages are invitations to reimagine or reconfigure reality, to reset perceptual coordinates and to change the chemistry of consciousness. And that is because reading itself is not a careful hermeneutic, is not driven by a teleology of Q.E.D.s or by obligations to chronol-ogy, but is the anarchic play of the totality of the reading mind. We read Baude-laire in order to destabilize him because reading itself is a destabilizing activity, and always in excess of what it reads. Put another way, it is translation's task to re-inscribe the ST in the eco-system of its reading.

As we investigate the significance of translation for the ecological re-embed-ding of the ST, there are three founding positions that I should reiterate: first, our argument that translation works within a world of the relational rather than the identitarian: this is the distinction that Baudelaire himself comes round to making in 'Les Foules', where 'l'égoïste, fermé comme un coffre [the egoist clamped shut like a chest]' is set against the mutable and freely transferable subjectivity of the poet-*flâneur*, able to inhabit any being, and addicted to that 'sainte prostitution de l'âme qui se donne tout entière, poésie et charité, à l'imprévu qui se montre, à l'inconnu qui passe [sacred prostitution of the soul which offers itself in its entirety, poetry and charity, to the unforeseen as it manifests itself, to the unknown as it passes by]' (1975: 291); second, that, in this sense, the function of translation, inasmuch as it is about engaging language with the situated world of the here and now, is to lead language back from the symbolic to the indexical/deictic, from sensory representation to synaesthetic involvement; and third, that the reciprocity which informs the relational, the dialogic, the dialectical, is a reciprocity of *symbiotic* difference, that is to say, a difference which is not of mutual exclusion, but of mutual supplementation, diversification, multiplication.

Reading and translation encourage us to adopt an ethos which is that of the ferryman, who can take us across borders and relate territories which lie alongside each other. Translation is a continuation of Baudelaire's own self-amplifying mental and imaginative activity, that 'vaporisation [...] du *Moi* [evaporation [...] of the *Self*]' (1975: 676) which is the expansion of self into the multi-sensory and into a time and space suddenly endowed with extra dimensions. But translation also serves Reading in its struggle against the critical obligations of History. Within the understanding of literary criticism as an institutional discipline, Reading works with History to assess and interpret the literary work within a given context and set of literary affiliations, within, that is, what we might roughly call a tradition. Reading left to its own devices, however, operates with the idiosyncratic, associative memory and imagination of the reader, unfettered by chronology or any duty to probabilities of sources, influences, repercussions and so on. This kind of Reading, that richly and freely re-filters the givens of a text, is one that translation can exploit, in order to uncover in the ST those experiential possibilities it is on the brink of.

NOTES

1. All translations are my own.
2. Because of the nature of the analysis in this chapter, I have preferred to leave the poetic texts referred to here unaccompanied by a translation. Translations for sense are, if necessary, readily available for readers, including online.
3. These two sonnets appeared together from the start, in *L'Artiste* of 15 October 1860.
4. In the sentence prior to this one on allegory, Baudelaire makes mention of '*analogies*' and '*correspondances*', which themselves grow out of a preceding assertion: 'Cependant se

développe cet état mystérieux et temporaire de l'esprit, où la profondeur de la vie, hérissée de ses problèmes, se révèle tout entière dans le spectacle, si naturel et si trivial qu'il soit, qu'on a sous les yeux, – où le premier objet venu devient symbole parlant [Meanwhile there develops this mysterious if temporary spiritual state in which the depths of life, bristling with their problems, reveal themselves whole in the sight, however natural and trivial it is, that is before one's eyes – in which the first object to come along is a speaking symbol]' (1975: 430). These words parallel, often verbatim, a similar observation made in *Fusées, XI*.

5. Baudelaire describes Guys's graphic manner as 'saisissante, suggestive et grosse de rêveries [intense, suggestive and brimming with daydreams]' (1976: 701).

REFERENCES

Baudelaire, Charles (1975), *Œuvres complètes*, vol. 1 (ed. C. Pichois), Paris: Gallimard.

Baudelaire, Charles (1976), *Œuvres complètes*, vol. 2 (ed. C. Pichois), Paris: Gallimard.

Culler, Jonathan (2015), *Theory of the Lyric*, Cambridge, MA: Harvard University Press.

Hiddleston, J. A. (1999), *Baudelaire and the Art of Memory*, Oxford: Clarendon Press.

Ingold, Tim (2011), *Being Alive: Essays on Movement, Knowledge and Description*, Abingdon: Routledge.

Laforgue, Jules (1903), *Mélanges posthumes*, Paris: Mercure de France.

Laplantine, François (2018), *Penser le sensible*, Paris: Pocket.

Meschonnic, Henri (2007), *Éthique et politique du traduire*, Lagrasse: Verdier.

Proust, Marcel (1988), *À la recherche du temps perdu*, II (eds. J-Y. Tadié, with D. Kaotipaya, T. Laget, P.-L. Rey and B. Rogers), Paris: Gallimard.

Runyon, Randolph Paul (2010), *Intratextual Baudelaire: The Sequential Fabric of the 'Fleurs du mal' and 'Spleen de Paris'*, Columbus: Ohio State University Press.

Scott, Clive (2000), *Translating Baudelaire*, Exeter: University of Exeter Press.

Scott, Clive (2007), *Street Photography: From Atget to Cartier-Bresson*, London: I. B. Tauris.

Steiner, George (1998), *After Babel: Aspects of Language and Translation*, 3rd ed., London: Oxford University Press.

Szarkowski, John and Hambourg, Maria Morris (1985), *The Work of Atget, IV: Modern Times*, London: Gordon Fraser.

Thézy, Marie de (1994), *Marville: Paris*, with Roxane Debuisson, Paris: Hazan.

9

Paris, Capital of the Australian Poetic Avant-Garde: Christopher Brennan's 'Musicopoematographoscope', John Tranter's 'Desmond's Coupé' and Chris Edwards' 'A Fluke' and *After Naptime*

David Musgrave

One could forgive a visitor to the northern end of Sydney's Hyde Park for thinking that the city was, in fact, at one time some kind of colonial outpost of France. The Archibald Fountain[1] is a splendid example of Art Deco by the French sculptor François-Léon Sicard (1862–1934), complete with mythological figures in a complex allegory of peace in a memorial designed to commemorate association between Australia and France in the First World War. It was bequeathed to the citizens of Sydney by J. F. Archibald (1856–1919), co-founder of the *Bulletin*, with the stipulation that it was to be designed by a Frenchman. Archibald was an ardent Francophile who let it be known that his first and middle names were Jules François, with French and Jewish blood on his mother's side, and not John Feltham, his baptismal names (Kirkpatrick 2007: 32). That the co-founder of the *Bulletin* and promoter of an emerging literary nationalism (often more closely associated with bush poetry and social realism) was so enamoured of all things French should not be seen merely as a charming quirk of an influential editor: his cosmopolitanism was shared by the editor of the *Bulletin* Red Page, A. G. Stephens (1865–1933), who 'encouraged the reading and discussion of French literature with missionary zeal' (Kirkpatrick 2007: 35). One of the Australian writers associated with the *Bulletin* during this period was the poet and scholar Christopher Brennan (1870–1932), whose articles on the newer French poets, published by Stephens in the Red Page in 1899, offered 'some of the best-informed discussion of the achievements of the Symbolists and Parnassians available anywhere in the English-speaking world' (Kirkpatrick 2007: 35). In this chapter, I will focus on Brennan as the originary influence on a particular avant-garde poetic tradition in Australian literature which, I will argue, has persisted in situating itself in an imaginary, post-colonial realm of which Paris is its chimerical, post-Symbolist capital.

Christopher Brennan occupies a peculiar place in Australian letters. Stephens acknowledges Brennan as the major literary figure of the period (cited in Hawke 2009: 6), yet his contribution as a poet has, at times, been overlooked (Smith 2008: 355), and Farrell notes that 'Brennan's reputation is, though generally conceded, unstable: swinging through deep ambivalence from positive to negative extremes' (Farrell 2015: 139). His life ended in scandal and poverty, yet his erudition was legendary[2] and his influence was significant and long-lasting. While his poetry was widely read and discussed during his lifetime, it took around thirty years after his death from stomach cancer in 1932 for volumes of his collected verse and prose to appear, 'his major work, *Poems*, having been out of print for nearly half a century' (Ellis 2009: 1). Despite the fitfulness of his published legacy, Hawke notes that 'the influence of Brennan can be seen in two contemporaneous traditions in Australian intellectual life which often intersect' (2009: 7). The first of these is a 'metaphysical' tradition which includes leading poets such as Kenneth Slessor and Judith Wright, and which Wallace-Crabbe also characterizes as 'the main Sydney tradition of French symbolism' (2002: 32–33). The second is 'the Brennan tradition amongst French scholars, whose writings in Australia were considerably ahead of their time' (Hawke 2009: 7), particularly as they followed Brennan's interest in the poetry of Mallarmé, and also in his attempts to formulate and systematize a theory of Symbolism. To these can be added a third tradition, originating in pastiche and parody, which I will discuss in further detail below.

Brennan's interest in Mallarmé needs to be understood against the backdrop of late colonial Australian literary culture, which was dependent on British culture in obvious ways, such as the importation of books and magazines from London being the main source of reading material (Kirkpatrick 2007: 31). The acquisition of French was then, as it often is now, a marker of belonging to the middle class, yet Francophilia was by no means a wholly anodyne index of refinement and sophistication, particularly for those who positioned themselves apart from the bourgeoisie. Kirkpatrick notes that

> [t]he Francophilia of Australian bohemians at best reflected a utopianism that rebelled against oppressive British cultural and social legacies; at worst, the studied eccentricity of the poseur.
>
> In an Anglo-Saxon colonial culture such as Australia's, the adoption of French customs or habits of thought could have a subversive edge to it. Politically, France

was the land of revolution and democratic hope, and stood as a symbol of republicanism: ideals directly opposed to what many by the end of the nineteenth century considered the dead weight of British influence [...]. Seemingly more frank and sensual, Gallic culture constituted a familiar exotic, a ready alternative to High Victorian stodginess and hypocrisy.

(2007: 32)

For Brennan, the attraction to French and German languages and literature was partly stimulated by his Irish Catholic background, which Clark describes as 'the common Irish feeling of being a permanent outcast or outsider' (1980: 6). In a letter to Stéphane Mallarmé,[3] he wrote of his lifelong feeling of being an alien 'in the society of the majority' and that he felt that 'English culture and even the English language [...] were "foreign", and thus increased for him the attractiveness of European languages and literature' (Clark 1980: 6). Although Brennan excelled in French at school, he later claimed that his French was 'self acquired' during his time in Berlin, where he elected to undertake study in fulfillment of the James King of Irrawang travelling scholarship from 1892 to 1894 (Clark 1981: 13, 56). This somewhat autodidactic approach to learning the language did not seem to have been a hindrance in reading widely in French literature and speaking French with some fluency. Whatever personal and intellectual motivations Brennan had for reading extensively and conversing in French, it should be noted that he achieved his proficiency in the language at a significant geographical, and perhaps emotional, remove from his homeland: it was one of the languages of his self-mythologized exile.

Brennan first encountered the poetry of Mallarmé in the northern summer of 1893 when 'he started to read in earnest contemporary French writers, especially the Symbolists', as well as Flaubert, Baudelaire and Gautier (Clark 1980: 68). He took to Mallarmé immediately and set about collecting and reading as much of his work as he could, even writing to Mallarmé for bibliographical information and receiving in reply a formal letter from the poet on 9 January 1894 with a list of his publications drawn up by his daughter (Clark 1980: 70). It is somewhat surprising, particularly in the light of how Mallarmé and Symbolism were to become lifelong intellectual projects, that Brennan never visited Paris, nor indeed France, and his only visit to a French-speaking city in his life was a quick dash to Brussels on the trip home to Australia in May 1894 (Clark 1980: 69, 76–77). Brennan's biographer Axel Clark notes that this 'may simply have been a result of the lassitude and lack of ambition, the disinclination to carry a plan out, that he manifested often in his life' (1980: 77), but he was also engaged to his landlady's daughter and this, combined with impecuniosity, may have been sufficient reason for the lack of a visit; nevertheless, Andrew Taylor finds this missed opportunity a 'double exile', arguing 'that Brennan's life in Australia was also a time in exile, a time spent as an expatriate from the countries and cultures [French and German] whose literatures he had chosen to adopt as his own, his birthright' (Taylor 1987: 37). Even though Clark's portrayal of Brennan in Berlin seems to reasonably explain why he did not make it to Paris, Taylor's thesis nags with its suggestion that Brennan somehow preferred to have the world of Paris and its literature remain solely as a republic of letters of the mind. In 1896, Brennan received 'a communication from Stéphane Mallarmé through a mutual acquaintance, Gustave Neymark, a French painter then staying in Sydney'. Brennan's reply reveals 'how deeply he was pleased by the favour shown him' (Clark 1980: 97):

Dear Sir,
Our friend Mr Neymark has delivered to me your notice of Madame Morisot – which, in effect, it would have been difficult for me to obtain – enriched, for me, personally, by the fact that it came, signed, from your hand and the kind expressions of your letter.

I pray you to believe in the sincere gratitude for your gift (not merely the printed pages) which this letter endeavours to express, but which still remains a debt – a part of that larger debt of gratitude (may I be permitted to make allusion to it?) which I, with some others, must ever owe to you.

Believe me, Sir,
most respectfully and
cordially yours,
Chris: Brennan

(Mallarmé, *Correspondance: VIII* 1983: 217)

While it is unclear what prompted Mallarmé's letter, which does not survive, the effect of it was to be one of the most important on Brennan's intellectual and poetic development. His commitment to Mallarmé and Symbolism intensified and deepened, and a correspondence with the poet continued.

It is in this context, then, that we can appreciate the production of two tribute/parodies by Brennan of Mallarmé which he composed in 1897 and which constitute a third influence of Brennan in Australian poetry not directly mentioned by Hawke. The tribute/parodies are of Mallarmé's 'Un Coup de dés' and were written for Brennan's closest friend, Dowell O'Reilly, in late 1897, seemingly in response to a hectic argument between the two about 'the relation between a poet and his public, and about their own work' (Clark 1981: 4). These two works, 'Prose-Verse-Poster-Algebraic-Symbolico-Riddle Musicopoematographoscope ("Musicopoematographoscope")' and 'Pocket Musicopoematographoscope', were not really made available to a wider reading public until Clark edited the facsimile reproduction of them for publication in 1981. They are interesting in their own right, for they seemingly reveal a deep ambivalence that Brennan harbours for the influence of Mallarmé. The MS is handwritten, employing a variety of calligraphic styles, in imitation of different typographical styles; the title page, in the form of a poster, contains the following mocking references to its French origins:

Maisong de PAREE
[...]
by M.M.S. Armong-Bahick
[...]
direct from Paree
Invented
by the well-known
Hieratico-byzantaegyptic-Obscurantist
MALAHRRMAY

(Brennan 1981: i [9])

Fagan notes that 'Brennan's crude phonetic versions of Australian pronunciations ("Paree", "Malahrrmay") effect a kind of satirical distance from anxious Anglo-colonial readings that might relegate Australian literature to a second rung after transplanted European models' (2012: 3). It can also be argued that these crude phonetic versions are a self-directed mockery and are a performance of the very anxiety which Fagan supposes: for example, 'Armong-Bahick' indicates a high degree of knowledge of Symbolist publishing, with 'Armong' referring to the French publisher of *Cosmopolis*, Armand Colin, and 'Bahick' an exaggerated rendering of the surname of Edmond Bailly (1850–1916), an editor friend of Mallarmé and the Symbolists who had a reputation for knowledge of esoteric music and was a leading light of the Theosophical Society.[4] Combined with the 'Hieratico-byzantaegyptic-Obscurantist' description of Mallarmé, the compound name of the imaginary publishing house (or possibly editorial collaboration) emphasizes in a self-directed way a kind of defiance of critical opinion through appropriating it (similarly, perhaps, to the way in which Les Murray used the title *Subhuman Redneck Poems* for a collection published nearly a century later). Ostensibly, Brennan is responding to charges of obscurantism in his own poetry by adopting the persona of his admired correspondent and responding defiantly to Brennan's critics, such as A. G. Stephens, who damned his work *XXI Poems*, with 'I DON'T GIVE A TINKER'S DAMN FOR THE PUBLIC' in a typographical reference to Mallarmé's statement in 'Un Coup de dés', 'UN COUP DE DÉS

JAMAIS N'ABOLIRA LE HASARD' (Mallarmé 2006: 139–59). Yet, the work has a coherence in its own right and is far more than a mere joke: as Katherine Barnes has pointed out, 'the care taken in the production of the various styles and weights of lettering indicates that the work was not simply dashed off on the spur of the moment' (2007: 46). The work is as much an homage to Mallarmé as it is a parody, and this ambivalence gives the work a significant complexity.

Among the themes which Barnes discusses in her reading of the work, she notes that 'Brennan develops at some length notions of ancestry and legacy that are to be found in the "Coup de dés"' (2007: 48). In particular, the 'misty ideas' of which A. G. Stephens writes in the *Bulletin* are claimed by Brennan as a 'descendant/of them that ruled of old my Danaan isle/ Thule of mist/& dreams' (Brennan 1981: 4 [14]), thus laying claim 'to poetic credibility through his Irish ancestry' (Barnes 2007: 48). Brennan goes on to state of these rulers that 'by them / honour'd / the singer /Ollamh / among the greybeards set the law / holding / in silences' lucid gaze / the viewless code' (Brennan 1981: 4 [14]). An Ollamh was a member of the highest rank of filí, which itself was an elite rank of poets in Ireland before the Renaissance. 'Ollamh' could be seen as referencing the name 'Mallarmé' through being partially contained by it as a kind of hypogram,[5] similar to the way in which the repeated 'O' references not just 'the perfect circle of exclamation' (Brennan 1981: 3 [13]) and the 'high rais'd / puff'd bubble' of public opinion, the 'emptyness / of mouths / whose rondure / affects / the zeros that would mimic speech' (Brennan 1981: 10 [20]), but also hypogrammatically (or perhaps just synecdochically) references the name of Brennan's supposed interlocutor, O'Reilly;[6] moreover, 'by speaking of Ollamh in terms elsewhere reserved for Mallarmé, Brennan implicitly confers upon Ollamh the status of poetic antecedent of Mallarmé' and 'by making Mallarmé the symbolic inheritor of the Irish tradition to which Brennan belongs, the Australian poet inserts himself into the line of descent' (Barnes 2007: 49). This is a crucial point about not just the themes of 'Musicopoematographoscope' but also about lines of inheritance and influence, which Brennan establishes in this ambivalent manner. The apparent use of the hypogram or the anagram suggests a certain aleatory quality in Brennan's work, insofar as it appears to derive from wordplay, a suggestion that is given more force through the seemingly haphazard arrangement of words on the page. I use the term 'aleatory' here as meaning 'dependent on chance', and I distinguish this from 'contingency', which is an event which may involve chance or accident, but which may be dependent upon a prior event or something uncertain. As I shall show later in relation to other, similar works, the seemingly aleatory quality of aspects of 'Musicopoematographoscope' is better understood as instances of contingency, dependent more upon uncertainty than pure chance. These aspects of the work introduce the theme of indeterminacy, with contingency mitigating the unalloyed authority of the figure of the author, which is a prevalent trope in much avant-garde poetry (see Perloff 1981: 3–44). It may be that this indeterminacy in Brennan's work accounts for its appeal to later poets; in addition, it may be that 'one reason why *Un Coup de dés* has spawned a number of mirror images, or mistranslations, in the Antipodes – it resonates with Australian sensibilities of the outsider or the reject' (Fitch 2019: 19). I will return to the theme of mistranslation and influence in the following sections, but there are two other themes in 'Musicopoematographoscope' which I would like to discuss further.

The first of these is the hieratic character which Brennan assumes and which is a theme in the work. This is primarily an ambivalent elaboration of Mallarméan Symbolism with an emphasis on mystery and on the signifying properties of white space and silence: 'the fair white page / whose candour / illumes / the mythic signs / Abracadabra' (Brennan 1981: 7 [17]). Barnes argues that the point 'that he is overtly alluding to the notion of writing-as-spell as it appears in *Prose (pour des Esseintes)* is absolutely clear because he speaks earlier on the same page of "a parchment without Anastasius' name"'. She goes on to argue the significance of a pun on 'parchemins' and 'par Chemins' in the second last stanza of *Prose (pour des Esseintes)* (2007: 49), claiming that, for Brennan, his critics are only capable of viewing work like his as mere 'parchment' devoid of any 'resurrection'. While it is unclear whether Brennan is referring to what the critics produce or to their responses to his own work, it is clear that he is approaching the question of poetic value from the point of view of a theory of correspondences. Specifically, according to Barnes, Brennan saw that 'part of the calling of the poet is to understand the implication of the doctrine of correspondences for the development of symbolism' (2007: 49); in 'Was Mallarmé a Great Poet?', Brennan refers to 'the corroboration of man's ardours by all those "correspondences" in nature's spectacle, which are the roots of all the myths, the secret of their perpetual newness' (1962: 282). What is interesting here is that this argument proceeds wholly symbolically: in many ways, the figure of the Master as Ollamh is a figure of the poet as visionary to which Brennan's imitators, such as Tranter, subscribe, even if they retain a wholly secular outlook. 'Vision' in this line of descent is metaphorical at best. Thus, the idea of Paris evoked by Brennan and his imitators takes on a quasi-mystical significance in Australian avant-garde poetry which cannot wholly be described as 'influence' – it can be read as a nostalgia for a past that never existed, perhaps, or for traditions, such as Modernism, which apparently failed to fully materialize in Australian poetry.[7]

The other theme in 'Musicopoematographoscope' is the sense of a crisis. Ostensibly, the crisis which precipitated Brennan's parody was the savaging he received by Australian critics for the Symbolist-influenced vagueness of *XXI Poems*. This is manifested at a number of levels: the fragmentariness of the work as evidenced by the inclusion of extracts from those reviews at the end of the work; the sense of departed glory, signified in numerous ways ('discrown'd' (4 [14]), 'Ichabod' (6 [16]), and the work itself 'piled / thrown / heaved / jamm'd / dropp'd / bang'd / slamm'd / slung / chuck'd // together' (12 [22]), to name only a few) and the typographical plurality and the sense of arbitrariness that results. The crisis of receiving poor reviews is elaborated in the work to the extent that it resonates with the larger sense of a Modernist crisis which animates 'Un Coup de dés', and it is this, and other moments in French Symbolist poetry, which Eliot acknowledged as an important source for his own poetry: 'The kind of poetry that I needed, to teach me the use of my own voice, did not exist in English at all; it was only to be found in French' (1952: 198).[8] The immediate appeal which Mallarmé held for Brennan indicates an incipient sensitivity to the crises of consciousness, language and culture, which characterize the Modernity which arose from Symbolism. Henry Weinfield argues that 'one of the fascinating aspects of the Preface [to the *Cosmopolis* edition of *Un Coup de Dés*], in other words, is Mallarmé's awareness that the poem enacts the very crisis of modernity to which it responds' and that 'the poem incorporates contingency at the same time as it attempts to come to terms with it philosophically' (1994: 265, 266). This sense of a reflexive awareness of crisis is also present in Brennan's 'Musicopoematographoscope' and in my opinion forms a large part of its appeal for later generations of Australian poets and critics.

This reflexivity anticipates many aspects of modernity and postmodernity and ramifies well beyond considerations of inheritance and tradition. Michael Farrell's reading of the poem looks at it in terms of 'biodiversity', considering it as an 'exotic' species which enriches the 'field' of Australian poetry: 'Though Brennan's symbolist verse continues to unsettle critics, the agency of the *Musicopoematographoscope* is just beginning its unsettling work' (Farrell 2012: 10). The implication of 'unsettlement' is far-reaching in a post-colonial context, and the claims which Farrell makes for Brennan's parody place it quite centrally in the tradition, if that is not an oxymoron, of the contemporary avant-garde. If Paris is often considered to be metonymic of Modernity (Harvey 2003), then the avant-garde tradition which derives from Christopher Brennan's 'Musicopoematographoscope' evokes this capital of an absent tradition in a nostalgic sense, given that the kind of Modernism which occurred in Australian poetry was very different from that of its Anglophone northern hemisphere counterparts. Northern hemisphere Modernity, at least in terms of poetry, spans the Atlantic with ease, as is evident in the careers of Eliot and Pound, and contains the contradictory elements of a recognition of a moment of cultural crisis and a reflexive, failed attempt to address that crisis. In the Australian context, those elements of Modernism that did appear in the poetry did not include such a wide-ranging attempt at diagnosis, description and cure as may be said to characterize *The Waste Land* and *The Cantos*: that occurred at the 'centre', apparently where it belonged.

The significance of 'Paris' as the source of literary modernity is shared by all Anglophone cultures, and, in this respect, the influence of French poetry on Australian poetry is unremarkable. What does seem worth remarking on, though, is the way in which a number of late-twentieth/early-twenty-first-century Australian poets (and critics) have returned to Mallarmé's 'Un Coup de dés', primarily through Brennan's example and influence, and the degree to which Rimbaud is also held up by them as a paragon of (proto)modernity. Why is it that these two French poets continue to directly influence such poets? The answer, it seems to me, is the position that 'Paris' metonymically occupies in the Australian literary imagination: it is the fugitive capital of an avant-garde tradition that has struggled to find within its own cultural context a suitable zone to claim as its 'home'. It is an alternative to the Anglophone centres of London and New York and can therefore be claimed without a sense of belatedness or inferiority. The reasons for this may be personal (who does one claim as one's poetic ancestor when those nearest to one reject one?) and/or cultural (a particular version of 'the cultural cringe'?). According to Jill Anderson (2002: 7–8), Ross Chambers believed that

> Australians from Brennan onwards have been seduced by Mallarmé's 'Europeanness', yet experience via Mallarmé the contradictory attraction of the 'colonial' (secondary, derived, mimetic) and the 'queer' (both continuous and discontinuous with the object, itself elusive, filigreed etc). This results in a figure of absolute refinement inhabiting a position (both marginal and sacred) in a culture supposedly egalitarian and democratic.

We can see this contradictory attraction at play in the work of John Tranter and Chris Edwards.

In his Doctor of Creative Arts thesis 'Distant Voices', the poet John Tranter included the poem 'Desmond's Coupé', which he terms 'a mainly homophonic translation (or mistranslation) of Stéphane Mallarmé's 1897 poem "Un Coup de dés"' (2009: 117). In a footnote to this identification, he refers to Christopher Brennan's 'Musicopoematographoscope' as a parodic response to reading Mallarmé's poem in *Cosmopolis* and also states that he reviewed Axel Clark's facsimile reproduction of *Musicopematographoscopes* in the *Sydney Morning Herald* of 9 January 1982 (Tranter 2009: 117n). It can therefore be argued that Tranter stands as the next link in the chain of Mallarméan influence on Australian poetry, although it should be stated that Tranter's primary poetic influence was Arthur Rimbaud[9] and that Chris Edwards' homophonic translation of 'Un Coup de dés', 'A Fluke', which was first published by Monogene in 2005 and published by Tranter's online journal *Jacket*, the following year, preceded Tranter's own poetic response by four years.

'Desmond's Coupé' exhibits all of the strengths and weaknesses of which homophonic translation is capable. A trace of the original remains. Mallarmé's title and opening lines (Mallarmé 2006: 139–42)

UN COUP DE DÉS//
JAMAIS//
QUAND BIEN MÊME LANCÉ DANS DES CIRCONSTANCES/
ÉTERNELLES//
DU FOND D'UN NAUFRAGE//
SOIT
que//
l'Abîme//
blanchi/
étale
furieux

are rendered in Tranter's version (2009: 15) thus:

Desmond's coupé is full of jam. He's in a quandary:
a bean lance, or a dance of circumstances.
He's eternally fond of his own naivety.
A swanky beam spells out a white
cranky tale.

Here, we can see an unusual diction, and (not solely) because we know the original, we can see some humour and also some awareness of the Symbolist nature of the original: 'spells' here could well mean 'incants' as well as 'states'; the 'white / cranky tale' could well be the blankness or silence of a white page, which is, of course, a kind of 'crankiness' compared with conventional views of how signification works. These felicitous coincidences appear on the surface to be the result of chance, although on further consideration it becomes clear that homophonic translation is to a certain extent constrained by its original. Tranter admits that

> though there are some tenuous links to the master poem, the employment of homophonic 'translation' causes the vocabulary and topic to vary erratically, leaping from seriousness to crude slang in a single phrase: 'heroic' to 'cough', for example. The only literary decorum is a total lack of decorum, relentlessly imposed.

> (2009: 121)

Homophonic translation appears similar to other experiments which Tranter has undertaken using programmes such as 'Brekdown', written by San Francisco programmer Neil J. Rubenking, which utilizes indexes and frequency tables to combine texts in unusual ways: Tranter gives the example of combining three Matthew Arnold poems with a dozen pages of poetry by John Ashbery (Tranter 1998), although, again, it must be stressed that chance is only one element in composition, if at all. 'Brekdown' utilizes Markov arrays and therefore employs probability as a key element of combination, which is further refined as the poet-composer selects the best of the resulting lines for arrangement in a poem. If the aleatory is to be considered a factor in homophonic translation or in the use of probabilistic programmes such as 'Brekdown', then it can really only be located in the contingency of choice (the use of probability in Markov chains would seem to militate against the element of chance); yet, this contingency is valorized by those inspired by Mallarmé. Toby Fitch, another Australian poet-critic who has written on the influence of Brennan on the contemporary avant-garde in an essay which is structured after Derrida's engagement with Mallarmé,[10] defines mistranslation as follows:

> Mistranslation in poetry, according to many experimenting or procedural poets [...] is a means to an end, a constraint-based, generative practice, whereby a poet 'translates' another poem (usually from a foreign language) into something *newly mistaken*. Transposition from one mode to another, as a practice/praxis, shortcircuits control, bringing chance to the fore – the poet is at the whim of words and their swervings. To double-up (or doubledown) on Walter Benjamin's 'Translation is a mode', let's think of mistranslation – predicated on ceding the initiative to a pre-text – as a *mood* 'in which meaning has ceased to be the watershed for the flow of language and the flow of revelation'.
>
> (Fitch 2019: 17)

In many ways, the appeal of Brennan's 'Musicopoematographoscope' and Mallarmé's 'Un Coup de dés' for Tranter and Fitch is their supposed engagement with the aleatory, which signifies in turn the ambivalent status of modernism in Australian poetry. But to valorize, the aleatory indicates a wilful reading of Mallarmé, ignoring the deep ambivalence of 'Un Coup de dés': for just as Weinfield identifies that the poem is a complex incorporation of, and philosophical response to, contingency, he warns that 'neither should it be regarded as aleatory' (1994: 266). In fact, for Weinfield, Mallarmé's poem is an elaboration of Pascal's Wager, but instead of closing off the Abyss, 'the shipwreck on the shoals of meaninglessness or contingency, is in one sense inevitable and in another a necessary prelude to transcendence of another kind' (1994: 266). Weinfield believes that 'the conception Mallarmé is developing in these lines [the constellation of images in the third folio], vague and oceanic as they are, has something to do with a simultaneity of creativity and destruction, such that the confrontation with the Abyss is fructative also of plenitude' (1994: 268). If Tranter's homophonic translations throw up discoveries which only to a limited extent might be ascribed to chance, the final word Tranter has to say on the subject, that 'the only literary decorum is a total lack of decorum, relentlessly imposed', also implies a simplicity of theme: mere burlesque or inversion, perhaps, for little greater effect. It might be interesting to counter this conclusion with Ross Chambers' readings of Tranter's sequence of poems 'Contre-Baudelaire' from his volume *Starlight* (2010). Chambers suggests that Tranter and Baudelaire can be read paratextually, and utilizing the German notion of poetry as *Dichtung*, or 'thickening', he writes of how two paired poems of Baudelaire and Tranter, 'between them, produce a thickening, the density of which neither poem, dense as each may be individually and in its own way, can equal' (2018: 235). Perhaps, then, the issue with homophonic translation from another language is that the result may be amusing, possibly interesting, but ultimately its method, which is not aleatory but has strong elements of contingency, has little to offer other than apparent difference, even if that difference produces such a 'thickening'. Homophonic translation from the same language, however, might pose a different set of possibilities, perhaps revolving around the question of 'voice' and its relation to the phoneme.[11]

Chris Edwards' engagement with Mallarmé is ostensibly similar to Tranter's, but it has evolved in a different direction. 'A Fluke' seems to employ, or at least arrive at, some of the same techniques as Tranter. Kate Fagan contrasts Edwards' reading of Mallarmé 'as a secular scrap-booker, a joker with a pair of dice "approaching / turbulence hilarity and horror", hanging "vertiginous / over the gap / sans jonquils" and "giv[ing] it the finger"' (Edwards cited in Fagan 2012: 7) with Brennan's who 'believed in a poet's ability to reunify the "complete, perfect, eternal self" through worldly acts of imagination' (Brennan cited in Hawke 2009: 25). Fagan views Edwards' text through a lens of drag or camp, regarding 'A Fluke' as a 'queering'[12] of Mallarmé's poem, but where his version differs from Tranter's is through a kind of adherence to Mallarmé's typographical variety, in particular the inserted title and its distribution through the poem:

> *Un coup de dés jamais n'abolira le hasard*
> A Fluke? Never[!] Noble Liar, Bio-Hazard
>
> (Edwards 2005, 2006: n.pag.)

Fagan (2012: 7) finds that Edwards' translation of Mallarmé's 'folie // N'ABOLIRA' as 'fool // NOBLE LIAR' (Edwards 2005, 2006: n.pag.) refers to Plato's thesis of the noble lie as outlined in the *Republic* which concerns political untruths or allegories that are accepted as true for the sake of maintaining social cohesion, although it could equally be argued that this refers to Plato's poets expelled from the republic because they strayed far from the truth through imitation, or to the depiction of poets against which Sidney offered his *Defence*, with the oxymoron drawing out the contradiction in striving for different kinds of 'truth'. Fagan's reading of this phrase is a tribute to Edwards' considerable wit:

> Seeking the verity of Mallarmé's riddle is a grave folly undertaken by outsiders and textual pirates, and a pursuit that threatens to undercut the magnificent myth of the *polis* when taken to extremes. Edwards' queer rewrite of Mallarmé poses the question: is this poem a fluke, a merely random exercise? The answer of course is *never. A Fluke* is a scrupulous visual, linguistic and ontological collage, a noble jest that generates hazardous outcomes, or more explicitly, bio-hazards – disruptive versions of human subjectivity that are dangerously prankish (*le blague* [sic]) while effecting a serious ontological investigation. Origins themselves including divine sources are scrutinised via the 'noble lie' of Chris Edwards' improper readings. The resulting art object shakes up unified social and aesthetic orders based on ortho-dox heredities and proper names. When reprinting 'A Fluke' in *People of Earth*, Edwards added a question mark to his title page ('A Fluke?') to stress the guiding force of his inquiry. His noble liar is a fool, a mimic, a collagist and a philosopher.
>
> (2012: 7–8)

Comparing 'A Fluke' with 'Musicopoematographoscope', Stephanie Guest notes that 'the two translations studied here parody the high Symbolism of Mallarmé's poem into a sometimes-abject Australian vernacular. In doing so, these trans-lations invert the imagined community of Mallarmé worship – they transform its recondite "universality" into a carnivalised "proximity"' (Guest 2019: 12). Thus, 'Paris' in this sense becomes a kind of foreignized-familiar, ockerized-ex-otic city of the carnivalized imagination in which joyful relativity and ambiva-lence reign.

Edwards' preoccupation with Mallarmé's 'Un Coup de dés' persists into his 2014 collection *After Naptime*. Here, it seems that there is a deepening of the Bren-nan/Mallarmé influence to explore, in a sometimes highly abstract way, issues to do with psychoanalysis, generic stability and physiology. In particular, the hypo-textual statements 'UN COUP DE DÉS JAMAIS N'ABOLIRA LE HASARD', 'I DON'T GIVE A TINKER'S DAMN FOR THE PUBLIC' and 'A Fluke? Never[!] Noble Liar, Bio-Hazard' become in this book an orgasmic 'Ahchoo!' scattered in a similar typographical dispersal across several pages. The significance of the cathectic nature of the sneeze is something I will attempt to sketch in the follow-ing paragraphs.

After Naptime is an innovation on the Brennan-inspired tradition, as it incor-porates the formal qualities of 'Un Coup de dés', 'Musicopoematographoscope' and 'A Fluke', but includes text as images cut up and apparently pasted across the page, as well as images, all sourced from the following books:

> David Astle, *Puzzled*; Birn Brothers Limited, *Once Upon a Time*; clkr.com, public domain clipart; Max Allan Collins, *The History of Mystery* for the Dell Mystery logo; Dennis Cooper, 'The Anal-Retentive Line Editor'; Charles Dickens, *Bleak House*; Charles Dickens, *David Copperfield*; Michael Fallon and Jim Saunders, *Muscle Building for Health: How to Build a Strong, Healthy, Muscular Body*; H. A. Guerber, *The Myths of Greece & Rome: Their Stories, Signification and Origin*; Joscelyn Godwin, *Robert Fludd: Hermetic philosopher and surveyor of two worlds*; Jess, *From Force of Habit*; Lawrence Lessing, *DNA: At the Core of Life Itself*; Michael Newton, ed., *The Penguin Book of Ghost Stories*; Odhams Books Limited, *Adventure Stories for Boys*; Alexander Roob, *The Hermetic Museum Alchemy & Mysticism*; Georges Simenon, *Madame Maigret's Friend*; *The Sydney Morning Herald, The Guide* for the week beginning 17 December 2012; *The Sydney Morning Herald, Good Weekend* 6 January 2007, particularly the articles 'Living Dolls' by Michael Shelden and 'Who You Gonna Call?' by John van Tiggelen; Ward, Lock & Co., *Great Inventors: The Sources of Their Usefulness, and the Results of Their Efforts. Profusely Illustrated* (Edwards 2014: [30])

A cursory read indicates that this poem, like its Symbolist forerunner, cannot be found to cohere in a unitary meaning, yet several significant elements run through it: the detective mystery, magic, boys' own stories, Dickensian Victoriana and human biology, among others. The images can be argued to form emblems with the surrounding text in the manner of the emblem books which were popular in Europe from the fifteenth through to the eighteenth centuries. One of the most prevalent images is that of the nerve cell (see Figures 1 and 2[13]) which is a significant motif in at least two senses: it is an emblem of networking, or communicability, and could be taken to be an icon of intertextuality; it is also an emblem of discharge, for the nerve cell functions, physiologically speaking, through a rise in electric potential which then leads to a discharge of current that allows transmission of the nerve impulse. In this latter sense, each image of dendrite, synapse and axon is metonymic of the discharges that are typographically dispersed through the *livre composé*: 'Ahchoo!'. It can be argued then that one unifying strand of the book is the orgasm, taken not only literally but also symbolically: in Lacanian psychoanalytic terms, it is a *jouissance*, or an excess which has no use value; but equally it could be seen to evoke Roland Barthes' notion of *jouissance* as the pleasure of being lost in the text. Edwards' adaptation of the form and themes of 'Un Coup de dés' is both explicit and extended. The contents page makes clear that the work is divided into 'scenes', which are facing folios, thus hinting at the form

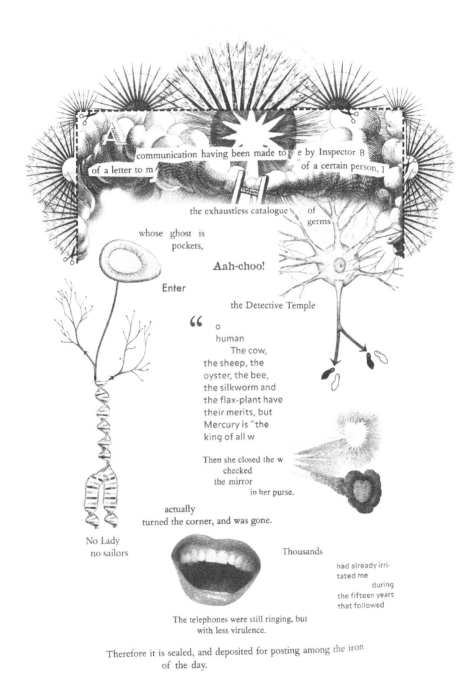

FIGURE 9.1: 'A Communication', (Edwards 2014: [7])

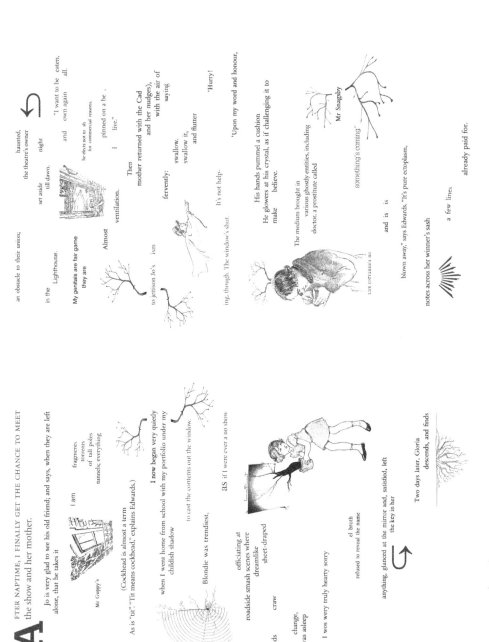

FIGURE 9.2: 'Scene 3', (Edwards 2014: [14–15])

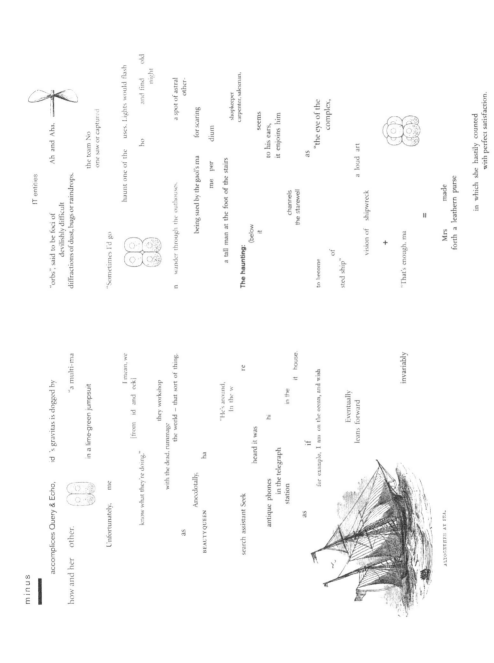

FIGURE 9.3: 'Intermission' (Edwards 2014: [18–19])

of 'Un Coup de dés'. The 'shipwreck' of Figure 3 evokes directly the 'Naufrage' of Mallarmé's poem and, by inference, the 'Damn' of Brennan's parody, and the constellation of images and related words, while suggestive of the quest that is at the heart of all mysteries, forms a complex *livre composé* that is at least equal in scope to its ur-model, 'Un Coup de dés'. To do justice to its complexity is beyond the scope of this essay, but initial considerations would include: *After Naptime* as a twenty-first-century emblem book;[14] intertextual heterogeneity and a 'queering' of Brennan and Mallarmé; a psychoanalytic reading of *After Naptime*; a broader contextualization of the influence of French poetry on Australian poetry, including Baudelaire, Rimbaud and Apollinaire, among others.[15]

Both Tranter and Edwards are avant-garde heirs of Brennan's parody/pastiche of Mallarmé. The former's work is decadent and text-centric; the latter's is more attentive to form and seems the richer development, particularly in *After Naptime*. Both poets seem compelled to repeat the performative nature of Brennan's engagement with Mallarmé as a tribute to his fitful, originary gesture towards literary modernism. In this regard, their works enact a nostalgia for a lost state or a city that never existed: a kind of modernist Paris situated as the symbolic and imaginary capital of an avant-garde, post-colonial poetic enterprise which only came into being belatedly in the Australian tradition. In retrospect, it seems only possible that this could have happened in Sydney, a city named after Viscount Sydney, whose ancestor came to England in the Norman invasion from the town of St. Denis, the same name as the patron saint of Paris, usually depicted in a decapitated state, holding his head in his hands: an apt image, if ever there was one for the post-Symbolic capital of that avant-garde tradition I have just described.

NOTES

1. For a description of this fountain, see 'Archibald Memorial Fountain', https://www.cityart-sydney.com.au/artwork/archibald-memorial-fountain/. Accessed 16 December 2019.

2. 'The story is told of how one evening it was suggested that he turn away from the French poets and make more use of Milton in his verse. Brennan replied, 'I am never without Milton. I don't have to read him, I know him', and proceeded to recite the first four books of *Paradise Lost* from memory. The extempore performance was checked against a text: he made only two small errors' (Kirkpatrick 2007: 45–46).

3. Brennan's letter to Stéphane Mallarmé, 9 August 1897, was published by Randolph Hughes in 'C. J. Brennan: Unpublished Work and Further Discussion', *Australian Literary Quarterly*, 2, 1947, p. 27.

4. The cover of *Australian Divagations*, edited by Jill Anderson, shows an ex libris slip from the library of Christopher Brennan which has on it a couplet, in Brennan's handwriting, which is ascribed to Mallarmé and which Anderson indicates is taken from Mallarmé's 'L'Après-midi

d'un faune': 'Faune, qui te plaignais, ne sois plus assailli par le long désespoir de manquer à Bailly' ['Faun, who used to complain, be no longer assailed by the long despair of being missed by Bailly']. The couplet is not from that poem, nor is it from any other poem in Mallarmé's oeuvre, but appears to be of Brennan's invention, indicating that he was quite familiar with Bailly. My thanks to Bertrand Marchal for his assistance with identifying Bailly as 'Bahick'.

5. See Jean Starobinski (1979) for an extended discussion of Saussure's investigation of hypograms in Latin and French poetry. According to Saussure, 'the *hypogram* is very much concerned with emphasizing a name, a word, making a point of repeating its syllables, and in this way giving it a second, contrived being, added, as it were, to the original of the word' (Starobinski 1979: 18) and is closely related to the anagram, the paragram and anaphony.

6. A similar technique is employed in 'Pocket Poematographoscope', where the repeated phoneme 'CU' appears dispersed across the four pages of this hand-written work. The synecdochic or hypogrammatical qualities of 'CU' are alluded to in the first lines of the work: 'If I were to write C / U / you'd think / would you now / that a wink / upright / or a slot / not such allow me to remark', hints at the obscenity 'cunt', with a secondary meaning as a homophone of 'cul' (or 'arse' in English); yet the conclusion of the work indicates that it is to be read as 'see you' and that the work's hypogram is in fact 'Tomorrow'. The salutation 'Old Fellow', directed towards O'Reilly and which concludes the work, almost resolves the suggested obscenity in a jocular fashion (Brennan 1981: n.pag. [33]).

7. The question of whether there is a Modernist tradition in Australian poetry is vexed; Andrew Taylor gives a brief but useful overview of the argument in the negative in *Reading Australian Poetry* (1987: 100–01); Peter Kirkpatrick (2017) offers a more nuanced account in the positive.

8. This phrase is one of the epigraphs to John Tranter's poem 'Rimbaud and the Modernist Heresy'; the other epigraph is from Mallarmé's commentary on a lithograph by Redon: 'The whole of my admiration goes to the Great Mage, inconsolable and obstinate seeker after a mystery which he does not know exists and which he will pursue, for ever on that account, with the affliction of his lucid despair, for *it would have been* the truth [...]' (Tranter 1979: vii). The view from 2020 is that these epigraphs have the air of a nostalgic gesture, even if Tranter, in the title to his poem, is problematizing 'Modernism' in the Australian literary context.

9. 'Rimbaud has been a long-term influence on my poetry, and on my thinking about tradition and about literary and social roles in their creative and destructive aspects [...] Rimbaud developed a theory of the writer as a person transmuted into a visionary poet, embodied in the phrase 'I is another [JE est un autre]'. As I discuss later, to escape the limits of the individual social being the authorial 'I' of the poetry has to become some other person or thing: In Rimbaud's case the writer seeks to be transformed, through his role as a poet, into a visionary seer whose view of reality is free of the restraints of conventional religion, politics and literature. This sense of displacement and transformation is an important sub-theme of the poetry in this thesis and also of its exegesis' (Tranter 2010: 5).

10. 'Jacques Derrida describes Mallarmé's poetics as "and/or", citing Mallarmé's deft use of homonyms and puns and their chain-like linkages across his oeuvre not as a crisis but as the key to its understanding, and to new possibilities for literature' (Fitch 2019: 13). Fitch structures his essay in paragraphs that mostly alternate with the headings 'aussi' and 'or'.

11. See the second partition of my poetry collection *Anatomy of Voice* (Musgrave 2016). These poems constitute a kind of homophonic translation from English utilizing paragrams and/or anaphony. This technique forms the basis of an enquiry which will be published in my forthcoming *Mishearing* in terms of poems 'misheard' through voice translation software and an accompanying critical essay (Musgrave forthcoming 2021: n.pag.).

12. See Edwards' inclusion in *Out of the Box* (Farrell and Jones 2009). This 'queering' involves the elaboration of a plural self, and in this regard 'A Fluke' bears comparison with Patrick White's *Memoirs of Many in One by Alex Xenophon Demirjian Gray* (see Musgrave 2015).

13. The images in Figures 9.1–9.3 are reproduced here courtesy of Chris Edwards.

14. See, for example, Arthur Henkel and Albrecht Schöne's monumental *Emblemata* (Henkel and Schöne 1996).

15. See examples from recent years: John A. Scott's *Shorter Lives* (Scott 2020) for an account of the lives of Rimbaud, Breton and some other significant French modernists; Toby Fitch's *Rawshock,* which includes Apollinairean calligrammes (Fitch 2012) and his homophonic translations of Rimbaud's *Illuminations, The Bloomin' Notions of Other & Beau* (Fitch 2016), among many others.

REFERENCES

Anderson, Jill (2002), *Australian Divagations: Mallarmé & the 20th Century*, New York: Peter Lang.

Barnes, Katherine E. (2007), 'With a smile barely wrinkling the surface: Christopher Brennan's large *Musicopoematographoscope* and Mallarmé's *Un Coup de dés*', *Dix-Neuf: Journal of the Society of Dix-Neuxiémistes*, 9, pp. 44–56.

Brennan, Christopher (1962), *The Prose of Christopher Brennan* (ed. A. R. Chisholm and J. J. Quinn), Sydney: Angus and Robertson.

Brennan, Christopher (1981), *Musicopoematographoscopes*, Sydney: Hale & Iremonger.

Chambers, Ross (2018), 'Significant Others, or Textual Congress: Concerning Baudelaire and Tranter', *Australian Journal of French Studies*, 55: 3, pp. 223–36.

Clark, Axel (1980), *Christopher Brennan: A Critical Biography*, Melbourne: Melbourne University Press.

Clark, Axel (1981), 'Introduction', in Brennan, Christopher, *Musicopoematographoscopes*, Sydney: Hale & Iremonger, pp. 3–5.

Edwards, Chris ([2005] 2006), 'A Fluke' *Jacket* 9, http://jacketmagazine.com/29/fluke00intro.shtml/. Accessed 27 January 2020.

Edwards, Chris (2014), *After Naptime: A Poem, Profusely Illustrated*, Sydney: Vagabond Press.

Eliot, T. S. (1952), *Selected Prose* (ed. J. Hayward), Harmondsworth: Penguin.

Ellis, Phillip A. (2009), '*Livres composés* and *Musicopoematographoscopes*: Brennan as a new beginning in French influence on Australian Poetry', *Journal of South Texas English Studies*, 1: 1, https://docs.google.com/document/d/1PYfGG4kX2WSMYJ3lDFviIJta13ykkF9rutp-bIQJgpOE/edit/. Accessed 27 January 2020.

Fagan, Kate (2012), '"A Fluke? [N]ever!": Reading Chris Edwards', *Journal of the Association for the Study of Australian Literature*, 12:1, https://openjournals.library.sydney.edu.au/index.php/JASAL/article/view/10175/. Accessed 27 January 2020.

Farrell, Michael (2012), 'Unsettling the field: Christopher Brennan and biodiversity', *Journal of the Association for the Study of Australian Literature*, 12:1, https://openjournals.library.sydney.edu.au/index.php/JASAL/article/view/10179/10077/. Accessed 27 January 2020.

Farrell, Michael (2015), *Writing Australian Unsettlement: Modes of Poetic Invention 1796–1945*, New York: Palgrave Macmillan.

Farrell, Michael and Jones, Jill (eds) (2009), *Out of the Box: Contemporary Australian Gay and Lesbian Poets*, Glebe: Puncher & Wattmann.

Fitch, Toby (2012), *Rawshock*, Glebe: Puncher & Wattmann.

Fitch, Toby (2016), *The Bloomin' Notions of Other & Beau*, Sydney: Vagabond Press.

Fitch, Toby (2019), 'Aussi / Or: *Un Coup de dés* and Mistranslation in the Antipodes', *Cordite 5*. http://cordite.org.au/wp-content/uploads/2019/05/AUSSIOR-CORDITE-TOBY-FITCH.pdf/. Accessed 27 January 2020.

Guest, Stephanie (2019), 'Barbecue sunrise', *Journal of the Association for the Study of Australian Literature*, 18: 3, https://openjournals.library.sydney.edu.au/index.php/JASAL/article/view/11822/. Accessed 24 January 2020.

Harvey, David (2003), *Paris, Capital of Modernity*, New York and London: Routledge.

Hawke, John (2009), *Australian Literature and the Symbolist Movement*, Wollongong: University of Wollongong Press.

Henkel, Arthur and Schöne, Albrecht (1996), *Emblemata: Handbuch zur Sinnbildkunst Des XVI. und XVII. Jahrhunderts*, Stuttgart: Metzler.

Kirkpatrick, Peter (2007), *The Sea Coast of Bohemia: Literary Life in Sydney's Roaring Twenties*, Perth: API Network.

Kirkpatrick, Peter (2017), 'Australian Poetry, 1940s-1960s', in P. Rabinowitz (ed.), *Oxford Research Encyclopedia of Literature*, Oxford: Oxford University Press. DOI: 10.1093/acrefore/9780190201098.013.144/. Accessed 27 January 2020.

Mallarmé, Stéphane (1983), *Correspondance*, vol. 8 (ed. H. Mondor and L. J. Austin), Paris: Gallimard.

Mallarmé, Stéphane (2006), *Collected Poems and Other Verse* (trans. E. H. and A. M. Blackmore), Oxford: Oxford University Press.

Musgrave, David (2015), 'Menippean sensibility in Patrick White's *Memoirs of Many in One by Alex Xenophon Demirjian Gray*', *Australian Literary Studies*, 30: 4, pp.86–100.

Musgrave, David (2016), *Anatomy of Voice*, Melbourne: GloriaSMH Press.

Musgrave, David (forthcoming 2021), *Mishearing*, Sydney: Gorilla Books.

Perloff, Marjorie (1981), *The Poetics of Indeterminacy: Rimbaud to Cage*, Evanston: Northwestern University Press.

Scott, John A., (2020), *Shorter Lives*, Waratah: Puncher & Wattmann.

Smith, Vivian (2008), 'The higher self in Christopher Brennan's poems', review', *Australian Literary Studies*, 23, pp. 355–57.

Starobinski, Jean (1979), *Words upon Words: The Anagrams of Ferdinand de Saussure*, New Haven and London: Yale University Press.

Taylor, Andrew (1987), *Reading Australian Poetry*, St Lucia: University of Queensland Press.

Tranter, John (1979), *Dazed in the Ladies Lounge*, Sydney: Island Press.

Tranter, John (1998), 'Mister Rubenking's "Breakdown"', *Jacket*, 4. http://jacketmagazine.com/04/rubenking.html/. Accessed 27 January 2020.

Tranter, John (2009), *'Distant Voices', Doctor of Creative Arts*, Wollongong: University of Wollongong.

Tranter, John (2010), *Starlight*, St. Lucia: University of Queensland Press.

Wallace-Crabbe, Chris (2002), 'Strangled Rhetoric and Damaged Glamor: Mallarmé and John Forbes', in J. Anderson (ed.), *Australian Divagations: Mallarmé & the 20th Century*, New York: Peter Lang.

Weinfield, Henry (1994), 'Commentary', in *Stéphane Mallarmé, Collected Poems* (trans. H. Weinfield), Berkeley: University of California Press, pp. 147–256.

10

Forms of Remembrance in the Sculpted Verse of Louise Colet, Anaïs Ségalas and Some of Their Male Contemporaries

Daniel A. Finch-Race and Valentina Gosetti

'L'Image'
Moi seule puis me souvenir
De tout ce qui m'avait séduite,
Moi seule encor puis revenir
À la félicité détruite.
['Image'
I alone can turn my mind back
To what made me captivated,
I alone again can backtrack
To blissfulness terminated.]

(Siefert 2017: 108 [lines 21–24] [1869])[1]

Prelude: Remembrances of lockdown thinking

This chapter started life in 2020 with the aim of talking about Baudelaire's verse and remembrance. Then, in the autumn of the COVID-19 pandemic, we had the unexpected chance to meet to discuss matters in Lombardy – one of the areas of Italy that had been hardest-hit in the spring – during the short hiatus between the first and the second wave. The world had become a very different place since we had gathered in Sydney at the end of 2019 for the annual conference of the Australian Society for French Studies. Back then, the main topics of discussion had been bushfires and the difficulty of finding a P90 mask to filter the smoky air.

By autumn 2020 in Italy, people were having to wear surgical masks and keep a distance. Everyone had experienced lockdowns, quarantines and losses. It was not easy to find the headspace to go back to Baudelaire – we had to pause, debrief and check that we were more or less okay before we could start co-thinking. As time dilated in the midst of a global pandemic, lockdown and quarantine brought home lessons about the pressures and affordances of research.[2]

In the absence of more and more normalized constraints on unhurried reading and 'slow scholarship', we found ourselves 'loiter[ing] with intent' (Chambers 1999: 291). This providential mode of resistance led us to embrace the pressing call to #FeminizeYourCanon (Garman 2018). There is another literary history to be written and much relearning to be done – this is just a beginning, a sign, a promise. Indeed, many more voices need to be heard. Throughout this chapter, we refer to 'the male poet' in order to unmask centuries of unjust treatment of 'the female poet', who has always merited the status of 'the poet' *tout court*. As Aimée Boutin and Adrianna Paliyenko point out,

> When the Third Republic established a new curriculum to inculcate republican values [in the 1880s], gender-based expectations dictated that women writers could not be upheld as models of a national literature. [...] The number of women acclaimed as poets by the century's end notwithstanding, the Woman poet in particular did not prevail against public opinion.
>
> (2002: 78)

In the present Paris-centred volume, our loiterly move of decentralizing resistance is to divert – as much as we can – from the Baudelairean elephant in the room. We embrace different narratives of literary history and alternative temporalities along the lines of Gretchen Schultz: 'women's poetry [...] addressed existential transformations that defied the static figures found overwhelmingly in the dominant poetic tradition. Women poets employed different temporal models' (2008: 243). What can be learned from the form of their poetry in this regard?

Spurred by the invitation of Alistair Rolls and Marguerite Johnson to reflect on 'what it is about Paris that causes remembrance' and 'what it is about various kinds of remembrance that speaks to Parisianness', our goal is to explore the intricate connections between poetic form and remembrance in nineteenth-century verse. We have three questions in mind:

1. What is it about verse form that causes remembrance?
2. Can physical geographies be encapsulated within the creative limits of verse form?
3. How do poets express the changing identity of Paris without completely dismantling verse form?

The coming pages revolve around an investigation of verse by Louise Colet (1810–76) and Anaïs Ségalas (1811–93). These two contemporaries wrote poems about their impressions and remembrances of Paris from their respective positions as a provincial and a Parisian. Although we shall briefly contextualize them within an overwhelmingly male poetic canon, the main event here is a determination to *remember* through the verse of Colet and Ségalas, whose fastidious craft inspires a similarly fastidious mode of analysis. Our emphasis on key details of form will be clarified through the example of sculpture in the second half of the chapter.

The (re-)shaping of Paris

In the verse collection *Émaux et camées* (1872, *Enamels and Cameos*), the male poet Théophile Gautier's 'Nostalgies d'obélisques [Obelisks' Longings]' laments, through the personified voice of an obelisk, 'a nostalgia for the fixity of the ancient and classical city' (Kerr 2013: 75). As a precedent to 'L'Obélisque de Luxor [The Luxor Obelisk]' in the two-part poem, the first section concerns 'L'Obélisque de Paris [The Paris Obelisk]':

> Sur cette place je m'ennuie,
> Obélisque dépareillé;
> Neige, givre, bruine et pluie
> Glacent mon flanc déjà rouillé;
>
> Et ma vieille aiguille, rougie
> Aux fournaises d'un ciel de feu,
> Prend des pâleurs de nostalgie
> Dans cet air qui n'est jamais bleu.

(Gautier 1872: 65 [lines 1–8])

> [Flanks rusting in this dismal square,
> Frozen with rain, snow, mists, and frost,
> Obelisk – once a stately pair! –
> I languish now, alone and lost;
>
> And my slim shaft that once had shone
> Red in the brazier-sky of old,
> Wears a nostalgic pallor, grown
> Ashen in this air, gray and cold.]

(Gautier 2011: 79)

These opening quatrains convey a sharp sense of dissonance and decay, framed by the ruddiness of nostalgia. In contrast, Louise Colet's verse collection *Fleurs du Midi* (1836, *Flowers of Southern France*) excitedly announces the dynamism of Paris as a 'bazaar', an idea developed decades later by the male poet Tristan Corbière in the verse collection *Les Amours jaunes* [*These Jaundiced Loves*]: 'Bazar où rien n'est en pierre, | Où le soleil manque de ton [where the sun lacks tone, | A bazaar where nothing's made of stone]' (1873: 5 [lines 3–4] [1995: 19]). As Katherine Lunn-Rockliffe observes, 'the term "Bazar" suggests that Paris is both a physical site cluttered with bric-a-brac and a marketplace in which capital is the driving force. [...] [I]t is a familiar metaphor for the city as a teeming centre of activity' (2004: 120). Colet's 'Paris' celebrates the vaunted 'capital of the nineteenth century' as a 'city of marvels':

> Paris! bazar du monde, immense capitale
> Où de toute grandeur la puissance s'étale;
> Ton image, toujours, revenait dans mes nuits
> Éveiller mes désirs, apaiser mes ennuis!
> [...]
> Je ne te voyais pas, Babylone frivole,
> Telle qu'on croit te peindre avec une hyperbole:
> Je ne te voyais pas, dans la fange et le sang,
> Pousser de crime en crime un peuple frémissant:
> Phare des nations, brûlant plus qu'il n'éclaire.
> Enflammer et trahir la fureur populaire,
> Et montrer pour exemple aux vassales cités
> Les horribles tableaux de tes atrocités:
> Oh! non! je te voyais la ville des merveilles,
> À l'Europe étalant tes splendeurs sans pareilles.
>
> (1836: 97–98 [lines 1–4, 9–18])

> [Paris! Immense capital, bazaar of the world,
> Where, in all its grandeur, power is unfurled;
> Your image, so often, used to come to me at night,
> Kindling my desire, easing my plight!
> [...]
> I did not see you, frivolous Babylon,
> In the hyperbolic way that people tend to carry on:
> I did not see you mired in mud and blood,
> Driving trembling people to crimes by the flood:
> Lighthouse of nations that burns rather than illuminates.
> By turns, igniting or betraying popular fury that accumulates,

And begetting for vassal cities, as a warning sign,
Horrific tableaus of the atrocities that you enshrine:
Oh, no! I used to see you as a city of marvels,
Displaying to Europe so much that incomparably sparkles.]

As we intend to show throughout this chapter, the meaning of words is enhanced through verse form – a mindful reader remembers the ways that the *combination* of content and form deepens meaning, just as a rhyme rounds out the sense of the individual words involved. In the first two lines, the city's world-leading immensity comes to the fore through the feminine rhyme in [tal] between 'capitale' and 's'étale', as well as a syllabification of 2+22 due to enjambment and subsumed caesurae owing to elision ('monde,⫽ immense') and syntactic association ('Où […]⫽ la puissance'). Colet's Paris is a glorious place that takes on the role of 'the guarantor of national unity' (Hazareesingh 2016: 188). Personal remembrance takes pride of place in the next two lines, with emphasis in the form of the alliteration in [t] and a syllabification of 4+2+18 because of enjambment and the contrasting resonance of the caesura, marked by a comma in the first instance ('toujours,⫽ revenait') and subsumed by a liaison in the second instance ('désirs,⫽ apaiser'). The masculine rhyme in [nɥi] between 'nuits' and 'ennuis' brings out well-trodden provincial remembrances going back to canonical male poets of the mid-1500s, including Clément Marot, Pierre de Ronsard and Maurice Scève (Bellenger 1979: 46). Parisian values supercede atrocities, injustices and gloom in lines 15–16, where the *léonine* masculine rhyme in [si.te] between 'cités' and 'atrocités' – i.e. encompassing two syllables – amplifies the impact of the 24-syllable run involving enjambment and subsumed caesurae on account of elision ('exemple⫽ aux') and syntactic association ('tableaux⫽ de'). The French capital is positioned as unparalleled across the globe in the pair of lines beginning with monosyllabic interjections ('Oh! non!') that set the stage not only for the feminine rhyme in [ɛj] between 'merveilles' and 'sans pareilles' but also for subsumed caesurae due to syntactic association ('je te voyais⫽ la ville' and 'étalant⫽ tes').

The poetic gaze here has all the hallmarks of a stereotypical wide-eyed young southerner, as Colet takes her first steps towards a career involving 'wr[iting] prolifically in all genres […] and […] reign[ing] over literary Paris for many years' (Schultz 1999: 148). Colet's quasi-mythical sense of Paris as the centre of the universe is one of the strongest remnants of Revolutionary and Napoleonic-era propaganda:

Toi, que le monde entier demande pour idole,
Liberté! j'ai cherché vainement ton symbole:
Dans ce livre des temps, que Paris a gardé,
Souvent tu déchiras, et tu n'as rien fondé.

Mais, l'esprit généreux, que ton règne propage,
Promet à l'avenir une éternelle page:
Rends au siècle haletant la paix et le bonheur.
Liberté, ce sera ton monument d'honneur!

(1836: 101 [lines 53–60])

[You, whom the whole world has idolized,
Freedom! I searched in vain for your being symbolized:
In the book of time, which Paris keeps closely guarded,
You have seldom built, and too often discarded.
Yet, the generous spirit that your reign makes new
Promises a page in eternity to be found through you:
Restore this breathless century to happiness and peace.
Freedom, this will be your glorious showpiece!]

The city is to be lived in a glorious present, where every monument is a reminder of 'grandeur' that should be enjoyed in all its awesomeness, as encapsulated by the feminine rhyme in [ɔl] between 'idole' and 'symbole'. Steeped in the capital's mythos, Colet could hardly be further from the vision of a disillusioned Parisian dweller like the male poet Charles Baudelaire, whose verse collection *Les Fleurs du mal* (1857/61/68, *The Flowers of Evil*) does not embrace a presentist sense of glory. Rather, he criticizes the massive programme of arcade- and boulevard-building for destroying Paris's memory-rich sites, particularly in 'Le Cygne [The Swan]': 'Le vieux Paris n'est plus (la forme d'une ville | Change plus vite, hélas! que le cœur d'un mortel) [The old Paris is gone (the form a city takes | More quickly shifts, alas, than does the mortal heart)]' (1861: 202 [lines 7–8] [1998: 175]). Baudelaire conjures an atmosphere of instability due to rapid alterations, and feelings of irredeemable loss are firmly at play. Colet, on the other hand, gives an impression of Paris as a timeless counterpoint to a generation's actions, however destructive, not least with the masculine rhyme in [de] between 'gardé' and 'fondé', as well as the comma-marked caesura of 'temps,// que'. In lines 57–58, her alliteration in [ʀ] combines with the feminine rhyme in [paʒ] between 'propage' and 'page' to evoke the function of writing and the city as a means of transcending the scope of a human life. Adrianna Paliyenko highlights that '*Fleurs du Midi* (1836), Colet's first published volume, interweaves the poet's reflections about her craft with autobiographical notes' (2016: 29). Trust in the rewards of cultural, personal and creative constancy is brought home by the *léonine* masculine rhyme in [ɔn.œʀ] between 'bonheur' and 'honneur', reinforced by the assonance in [ɔ] around the subsumed caesura due to syntactic association ('ton# monument').

Something old, something new?

It is questionable whether the city of Paris was *ever* truly like the ideals espoused here. Colet's version – in the mode of a regional piece 'written to Paris' (Williams 2003: 489) – comes across as a post-revolutionary myth, whereas Baudelaire's *vieux Paris*, 'rather than a truthful reflection of historical Paris, became an idealized imaginary geography and a repository of dark emotions, which Haussmannian clarity (another urban myth) was to repress' (Gosetti 2016: 59). The contemporary Paris of Revolutionary grandeur is as fictional a character as the Paris of old, much like the mysterious provincial countryside so dear to the Parisians of the day. In the poetry of Colet and Baudelaire, as well as Gautier and Corbière, writing is a paradoxical way of resuscitating places that were non-places from the outset. Alistair Rolls examines this fable-inflected style of representation: 'in verse poems like "Le Cygne", [there] is the explicit co-presence in the text of Paris past (mythical, metaphorical) and Paris present (existential, real)' (2020: 72). As will shortly be discussed, all this verse presents a way of *sculpting* memories. Nothing is spontaneous in the careful chiselling of the city-poem, which is a *chantier* of (mythical) remembrances just like sites of de- and re-construction in the physical world.

With 'fake news' and alternative realities on the rise today, it is not difficult to empathize with the sorts of 'fake' memories/presents that poets were evoking in the nineteenth century – a handful of decades before a 'fake Paris' came into being near Maisons-Laffitte due to military planners' strategizing at the close of World War One to lure German air raids with wooden replicas of renowned buildings (Allen 2011). Poets' contributions to inventing and reinventing Paris for generations of Parisians, provincials and foreigners reached an apex as the 1800s advanced. The perfect excuse to rail against abrasive modernity, to long for something that almost certainly never existed, arose inexorably among people grappling with 'transformations of Paris [...] as a ceaseless struggle between the spirit of place and the spirit of time' (Hazan 2011: ix [2002]). In the form of the *préfet* Georges-Eugène Haussmann, French society was provided with a hero, an innovator, a builder of decidedly Parisian 'grandeur' and/or a culprit, a villain, a destroyer of (physical) memories – rarely has a reconstruction-minded state official been loathed or loved to such an extent. Many poets, inclined towards nostalgia, saw Haussmann as the demolisher of Paris, even of one that never was. Can he be seen as the destroyer of verse, too? Especially in the case of mid-century poetry by the likes of Baudelaire, there are *correspondances* between changes in the structures of verse akin to shifting geographies: 'alterations in the physical space of Haussmannian Paris can be linked to [...] topographic placelessness [...] paralleling the escalating flexibility of poetic forms in the latter half of the century' (Finch-Race 2015: 1025). Haussmann could be deemed the true architect of the *poème en prose*, ostensibly the form of urban modernity *par excellence*. Indeed, as Rolls explores in Chapter 1, representations of the Haussmannian era are complicated due to the simultaneous construction and destruction of landmarks in Paris.

The modern city's plasticity is widely considered to find expression in the 'noisiness' of poetry in prose, i.e. a sort of self-destructiveness that makes Baudelaire's posthumous prose collection *Le Spleen de Paris* (1869, *Paris Spleen*) a highly compelling reflection of *chantier*-Paris. The poet's pioneering perceptiveness is renowned:

> Baudelaire [...] saw that poets needed to find a way of accommodating the making of poetry to the sometimes exhilarating, but mostly prosaic and alienating, mode of existence [...] led by the inhabitants of cities. Baudelaire saw too that this effort held a crucial clue to the significance of modernity.
>
> (Chambers 2005: 101)

In the year following the appearance of 'Le Cygne', the publication of the first copy of Baudelaire's 'Le Mauvais Vitrier [The Bad Glazier]' in *La Presse* came to encapsulate the discordance of Parisian life: 'la première personne que j'aperçus dans la rue, ce fut un vitrier dont le cri perçant, discordant, monta jusqu'à moi à travers la lourde et sale atmosphère parisienne [the first person I saw in the street below was a glazier whose piercing, discordant cry rose up to me through the heavy, foul Parisian air]' (1862: 2 [2008: 16]). In the words of Aimée Boutin,

> Similarly to his [male] contemporaries Théodore de Banville, Champfleury, [Pierre] Dupont, and others, Baudelaire strove to relax classical verse by integrating some of the features of popular song, notably its verve and contrasts, as well as the liberties it took with meter and rhyme. [...] *Le Spleen de Paris* seeks to transpose a different kind of musicality.
>
> (2015: 99)

On this basis, poems in prose may be interpreted as a challenge to older pieces of verse. Echoing Barbara Johnson's work during the 1970s on Baudelaire, Sarah Gubbins reminds us how 'the early prose "doublets" of poems from *Les Fleurs du mal* seem to question the lyrical assumptions of their verse counterparts' (2018: 8). In a new era of unstable conditions, all kinds of order become subsumed to the prosaic. As the landmarks of poetry vanish, feelings of alienation and being out-of-place are amplified – the head and heart yearn for the rhythms of past centuries, akin to Baudelaire's swan. Can poetic history really be divided in terms of a quasi-lapsarian line after which everything is post-verse, though? This is the time to nuance the schema of a Before involving a familiar order, and an After where dissonance and alienation reflect the modern city's essence.

La forme d'une ville/la forme d'un poème *(and the dismantling thereof)*

The abrasive modernity of poetry in prose like *Le Spleen de Paris* is not in question, but there is no denying that verse form can be a treasure trove of creative difference and an expression of similar 'noise'. In *Les Fleurs du mal*, the groundbreaking poems in the section entitled 'Tableaux parisiens [Parisian Scenes]' express an approach that is 'à la fois une déconstruction [...] et une construction [simultaneously a deconstruction and a construction]' (Johnson 1979: 81). As Peter Broome writes,

> Form [...], in the case of the poetry of Baudelaire, *is* its modernism. It is not simply a question of an increased responsiveness to the expressive potential of verse-form or the intuitive discovery of new possibilities for pattern, though the artist of *Les Fleurs du Mal* has enlarged the poetic medium in this respect, awakened it to its latent 'selves', almost beyond recognition. [...] Perhaps not enough has been made of Baudelaire as a *lover of form* [...], regardless of the leanings of the subject-matter, creating a beauty in bleakness, tension and ugliness which is almost a redemption by form, a conversion.
>
> (1999: 10–11)

In a similar fashion, Rachel Killick stresses that 'Baudelaire's awareness of the challenges and opportunities of the way in which form and theme come together is a crucial element in his poetry, motivating an imaginative reinvigoration of prosodic convention' (2005: 52). Through verse form and content, remembrances of the everyday are transformed into a shared and imperishable human patrimony, just like antique marble sculptures or age-old paintings that still speak volumes. According to Rosemary Lloyd, 'Baudelaire's poems and criticism reveal a sharply observant eye and an analytical mind that drew its sustenance from everyday events, but transformed them into something more powerful and more universal' (2002: 3). Indeed, verse forms can connect cities, places, memories and sentiments across centuries. Think of the longing for a city that never was:

> Nouveau venu, qui cherche[s] Rome en Rome,
> Et rien de Rome en Rome n'aperçois,
> Ces vieux palais, ces vieux arcs que tu vois,
> Et ces vieux murs, c'est ce que Rome on nomme.
>
> (Du Bellay 1830: 164 [lines 1–4] [1558])

[Stranger, who look for Rome in Rome, but find
Little of what was Rome in Rome, behold!
Those arches, walls, and palaces of old
Are all that Rome, in name, has left behind.]

(Du Bellay 2002: 185)

This is one of the male poet Joachim Du Bellay's sonnets in *Les Antiquitez de Rome* (1558, *The Antiquities of Rome*), not the work of a nineteenth-century poet. In ways similar to the poems in question above, the clash between imagined and real Rome could well cause disappointment for a newcomer longing for a Rome that never existed except in literature or the imagination. To broaden the issue at stake here, is poetry an apt substitute for reality, i.e. 'all that Rome, in name, has left behind', or is it only contributing to building a literary image that future readers will long for? By the mid-1800s, the form and content of verse come to embody a cacophonous assemblage of 'arches, walls, and palaces of old'.

Conflict and dissonance are essential to nineteenth-century poetry in verse as much as prose: 'blurred identities and unexpected transformations in works by [the male poets Aloysius] Bertrand and Baudelaire entail[ing] multiplicities and antithetical constructions [...] have striking correspondences in [the male poet Arthur] Rimbaud's poetry' (Finch-Race and Gosetti 2018: 56). Verse can certainly be filled with commotion to the point of being 'noisy'. The male poet Jules Laforgue is exemplary of 'noise [...] found throughout [...] writing, suggesting a remarkable sensitivity to the soundworld of the city – industry, transport, street performers, hawkers, crowds' (Evans 2016: 58). Such poetry is a site of stratified practices, of doings and undoings, of conflicts and irresolutions. Remembrances of past and present 'noise' are fundamental to the careful crafting of a form such as the alexandrine, i.e. the twelve-syllable line that dominated French poetry from the seventeenth century to the nineteenth century. Lines from a poem like Colet's 'Paris' are structurally and thematically palimpsestic in much the same way as the city's physical geography. Indeed, a mode of expression steeped in tradition, as is the case with the alexandrine, can lead to 'noise' being doubly apparent in the case of a caesura in the middle of a syntagm/word, a rhyme of incongruous strength or a graphical feature like an ellipsis, whose dots could stand for the crumbling stone of the poem's edifice.

A superb example of such occurrences is Anaïs Ségalas's 'Les Démolitions [The Demolitions]' in the verse collection *Nos bons Parisiens* (1864, *Our Good Parisians*), which was circulated with a slightly different appearance by the literary magazine *Musée des familles* in 1854 as 'Les Démolitions de Paris [The Demolitions in Paris]', seven years before Baudelaire's 'Le Cygne' appeared in *Les Fleurs du mal*. The piece fleshes out her treatment of the French capital in

'Paris' as part of *Les Oiseaux de passage* [*The Birds of Passage*] in the year after Colet's *Fleurs du Midi*. Ségalas's 'Paris' pursues an intimately apostrophizing critique of the city's 'visage à double face [two-facedness]' – 'ton paradis est près de ton enfer [your paradise is close to your hell]' (1837: 239 [lines 22 and 29]). Besides Colet's 'Paris', the poem's hinterland includes the male poet Victor Hugo's 'Hymne [Hymn]' in the verse collection *Les Chants du crépuscule* [*Songs of the Half-Light*], from the year before *Fleurs du Midi*: 'Paris, la ville aux mille tours, | La reine de nos Tyrs et de nos Babylones [Paris, the city of a thousand towers, | The queen of our Tyres and our Babylons]' (1835: 54 [lines 15–16]). Paliyenko brings out how poetic peers became situated in male-dominated networks, with 'Gautier [...] plac[ing] Ségalas in Hugo's lineage' (2016: 86), in parallel with Baudelaire's dedication of 'Le Cygne' to Hugo. Ségalas's poem in *Nos bons Parisiens* is thematically and stylistically a construction site dominated by the figure of the stonemason – the alter ego of the poet-demiurge – as a devilish harbinger of construction and destruction:

> Quel est ce conquérant indomptable, superbe,
> Qui renverse nos murs, les fauche comme l'herbe?
> Ce vainqueur, ce César, cet Attila nouveau,
> C'est le maçon! ... il monte à l'assaut, et tout penche,
> Croule ... Il a pour armure une tunique blanche,
> > Il a pour glaive un lourd marteau.
> [...]
> Si nous voulons rentrer au foyer de famille;
> Comme le chérubin au seuil du paradis,
> Le terrible maçon nous dit: 'Sortez, maudits!'
> Faut-il vivre en oiseau, sur l'arbre ou la charmille?
> Bonnes gens de Paris, victimes du maçon,
> Enviez la tortue et le colimaçon,
> > Qui du moins gardent leur coquille.
>
> > > (1864: 165–67 [lines 1–6, 25–31])

[Who is this conqueror, untameable and bold as brass,
Who knocks down our walls, scythes through them like grass?
This victor, this Caesar, this new Attila the Hun,
Is the stonemason! ... He wages war and all is put to the test,
Crumbles ... His armour is a white vest,
    His glaive is a hammer weighing a ton.
[...]
If we want to return home, where the familial hearth awaits;

Like the cherub at Heaven's gates,
The dread stonemason tells us: 'Get out, you reprobates!'
Does it come down to living like a bird, on a tree or an arbour?
Good people of Paris, victims of the stonemason's travail,
Envy the tortoise and the snail,
    Who at least have their shell for safe harbour.]

These stanzas immortalize tattered and scattered remembrances of Paris verging on the unrecognizable. On account of the first line's syllabification of 10+2, as well as the comma-marked caesurae in the second and third lines ('murs,// les' and 'César,// cet'), the poem opens with a sense of foreboding about the capital suffering an implacable assault. Only with the exclamation in the fourth line is the culprit revealed as the construction worker, whose disturbing nature is amplified by the glut of sibilance, the syllabification of 4+5+3 around the elided caesura ('monte// à') and the masculine rhyme in [o] between 'nouveau' and 'marteau'. Éric Fournier draws attention to how 'la tendance hyperbolique consistant à transformer les chantiers haussmanniens en un maelström tellurique renforce l'association [...] entre le démolisseur et le démiurge [the hyperbolic tendency to transform Haussmannian construction sites into a telluric maelstrom reinforces the association [...] between the demolisher and the demiurge]' (2008: 36–37). Ségalas's verse graphically represents a falling-apart of the city and material memories via ellipsis, especially the one following the exclamation mark, where the alexandrine breaks into a sudden blank, a momentary vacuum in place of something expected to occupy that spot. Forces of dissonance and discombobulation are strong in the fifth line, where the visual expectation of a pause at the ellipsis is countered by the elision of 'Croule ... Il'. It is significant that the earlier version had a full stop instead of an ellipsis: 'Croule. Il a pour armure// une tunique blanche' (1854: 28) – the interceding decade saw the crumbling city-poem littered with fragments of stone.

In the fifth stanza, the disturbing encounter with the construction worker is accentuated through the unsettling of the poem's framework of six-line stanzas to include one with seven lines. Verbal, structural and memorial forms of violence come to the fore through the subsumed caesura of 'maçon// nous' due to syntactic association, along with the masculine rhyme in [di] between 'paradis' and 'maudits', which is supplemented by the internal rhyme with 'dit'. In the words of Anne Green,

> With Napoleon III's *démolisseurs* reducing great swathes of Second Empire Paris to rubble, and with Haussmann's new buildings rising all around, the emotional impact of domestic ruins was evident to all. [...] Poets [...] were sensitive to the symbolic resonance of the modern ruin [...] articulating a sense that the past

was being obliterated and history rewritten. [...] Ségalas deplores [...] the fact that buildings associated with major figures from France's cultural heritage have been torn down.

(2013: 150–51)

In effect, a mixture of unsettling absences and nostalgia-inducing physical remainders defined the emotional and physical geographies of Paris in the 1860s. To this end, a second mention of the troubling 'maçon' after a gap of just 28 syllables packs even more of a punch because of the *léonine* masculine rhyme in [ma.sɔ] between 'maçon' and 'colimaçon' that is initiated at the end of a balanced alexandrine with a comma-marked caesura ('Paris,// victimes') pointing up the distress heaped on Parisians.

Why spend time grappling with form?

What is the value of attending to the subtleties of poetic structures? In the second part of the nineteenth century, poetry in prose is supposedly *the* exciting novelty, which means that verse tends to be viewed as less 'modern'. In fact, verse is equally a site of myriad variations, as we have sought to show. Form remains highly relevant, even in an age dominated by the novel and thematic modes of reading. Today, in the wake of a move away from unflinchingly technical structuralist and post-structuralist reflections, the decision to focus on stylistic aspects such as rhymes and syllabification might come across as bold: 'when discussing a poem, asking questions about the meter or rhyme scheme seems an academic distraction from the interpretive question of what the poem means, but [...] they are unavoidable' (Culler 2010: 92). Indeed, formal analysis is a skill that educators often seek to foster, especially in the French tradition of the *commentaire composé*, which starts from an early age (Fourcaut 2010).

Why should someone care about Colet's caesurae or Ségalas's punctuation? A sculptural example is instructive here. How would these three works be described without addressing their form or shape, i.e. in purely thematic terms? Perhaps like this: Figure 10.1 is the biblical persona David with the severed head of the Philistine giant Goliath; Figure 10.2 is the biblical persona David with a slingshot; Figure 10.3 is the biblical persona David using a slingshot. Space could also be devoted to the theological context, the male artists' biographies, the commissioning process behind the sculptures and their reception by contemporaries and posterity. There would be no mention of materials, colours, pose, use of tools, namely what makes these three statues different from each other. This far-fetched notion points to the fact that any analysis of sculpture lacking references to form would be widely considered

FIGURE 10.1: Donatello, 1440

FIGURE 10.2: Buonarroti, 1504

FIGURE 10.3: Bernini, 1624

absurd. In large part, a comparative analysis of the three Davids would dwell on differences in technique, material, etc.

The syllabification of a line of verse is the equivalent of the slabification of a statue. Like the material of a sculpture, a poem's stanzaic arrangement is noteworthy (is it a sonnet? A ballad?). Given the rivers of ink that have been spilled – rightly! – to describe an element such as the disproportionate size of David's hand in Michelangelo's version, why not insist on the importance of something like a rhyme scheme? These attributes deserve to be considered as a matter of proportions. To a large degree, the strength of a poem comes not from what it says, but *how* it says it. Details such as punctuation and enjambment make a poem unique, regardless of the extent to which it touches on recurrent themes including love, death and Paris.

As in the case of marble, a manifestation of language involves a practice of shaping form, especially where a poem in verse is concerned. According to Caroline Levine,

> Things take forms, and forms organize things. [...] [F]orms travel across time and space in and through situated material objects. [...] Literature is not made of the material world it describes or invokes but of language, which lays claims to its own forms – syntactical, narrative, rhythmic, rhetorical – and its own materiality – the

REMEMBERING PARIS

spoken word, the printed page. And indeed, each of these forms and materials lays claim to its own affordances – its own range of capabilities.

(2015: 10)

Poets are experts in sculpting language in verse or prose – they are the all-mighty *maçons* of construction and deconstruction. In fact, the figure of the construction worker appears prominently in mid-nineteenth-century poetry, including Bertrand's *fantaisie* on 'Le Maçon [The Stonemason]' in his posthumous prose collection *Gaspard de la Nuit* (2000: 117 [1842]). Processes of sculpting come to the fore with Gautier, who is deeply attuned to the crafting of memory as much as verse. At the end of *Émaux et camées*, 'L'Art [Art]' offers a palette of creative tools for poets wishing to tackle the plasticity of language as if it were a raw material akin to marble:

Oui, l'œuvre sort plus belle
D'une forme au travail
   Rebelle,
Vers, marbre, onyx, émail.
[...]
Tout passe. – L'art robuste
Seul a l'éternité.
   Le buste
Survit à la cité.
[...]
Les dieux eux-mêmes meurent.
Mais les vers souverains
   Demeurent

Plus forts que les airains.
Sculpte, lime, cisèle;
Que ton rêve flottant
   Se scelle
Dans le bloc résistant!

(Gautier 1872: 223–26 [lines 1–4, 41–44, 49–56])

[Yes, fair-wrought verse shuns pliant
Form; beauty craves the touch
   Defiant:
Marble, onyx, and such.
[...]
Nothing will last [...] All must

202

Pass on, save art, strength-rife:
    The bust
Survives this earthly life.
[...]
The gods themselves die; still,
Princely, poems shall reign
    And will
Stronger than brass remain.

Sculpt, chisel, file, and let
Your flotsam dream, wind-blown,
    Be set,
In the resisting stone!]

(Gautier 2011: 263–67)

Here, the fundamental parallel between poetry and sculpture relates to the prospect of immortality for an artwork in contrast to the transient nature of cities and humans ('The bust | Survives this earthly life'). Martine Lavaud and Paolo Tortonese make clear that 'l'interpénétrabilité de l'art et de la réalité obsède une bonne part de la production poétique et narrative de Gautier [the interpenetrability of art and reality dominates a large part of Gautier's poetic and narrative production]' (2018: 11), but it is not just a question of the writer being enamoured with the plastic arts. As conveyed by Giovanna Bellati, intermediality is significant regarding poetry breathing life into the everyday, and *vice versa*: 'le travail de ciseleur du poète-peintre [...] des "émaux et camées" [...] choisit des sujets de la vie commune pour les rendre précieux par le soin formel, découvrant la beauté intime et la vie secrète des choses [the sculptural undertaking of the poet-painter [...] of the "enamels and cameos" [...] takes up subjects from everyday life in order to render them precious through a care for form, discovering the intimate beauty and secret life of things]' (2014: 95). As in the case of chipping away at a block of marble, the poet elevates certain parts of 'the real' to become art, with other fragments assigned to the scrap heap. This *plastic* understanding of all forms of art encourages reflections on the capacity of well-sculpted verse to encapsulate something beyond a moment in time and space. Patrick McGuinness emphasizes how

that [...] great manifesto poem, 'L'Art', [...] puts forward an aesthetic of hardness and force: language is there to be melted, smelted, fired, sculpted [...]. Poetry is not plucked from the air or drawn from the soul to be laid into ready song, but hewn from the undifferentiated mass of language that means nothing and is in itself nothing.

(2015: 9–10)

Indeed, whenever dexterous poets like Colet and Ségalas sculpt verse around/in/ through Paris, *le vers survit à la cité* – stanzas surpass an earthly life – with much of the transient urban everyday left unsculpted outside the scope of a historical artefact.

The alexandrine as a chantier of remembrance

The process of detecting poetry's idiosyncrasies involves time travel – what makes a poem unique in a certain moment, location or readerly experience? This is an exercise in stylistic remembrance. For Luca Pietromarchi, it is amply worth teasing out the significance of 'la configuration de la ligne, saisie dans toutes ses potentialités dynamiques et graphiques, [...] relevant toutes de l'ordre du poétique [the configuration of the line, understood in all its dynamic and graphic possibilities [...] that altogether pertain to the order of the poetic]' (2013: 83). As we have looked to exemplify through excerpts from Colet and Ségalas in particular, context is not the only matter at stake in situating a poem. Given how a chosen form at a certain juncture can speak volumes, the key responsibility of a critic, reader or translator is to engage with the How and What of a poet's work in chiselling the marble of language into shape. Such is the opportunity to experience 'the *longue durée* of artistic forms' (Kliger and Maslov 2016: 21). Like walking in a city and stopping to admire a stuccoed building or a statue's curvature, dwelling on poetic forms of remembrance is an act of loiterly resistance to the incessant bustle of modernity.

Despite the excitement caused by poetry in prose midway through the nineteenth century, the alexandrine is hard to escape. The apparent absence of alexandrines from a 'poème en prose' might even lead to longing for something that becomes the elephant in the room – in the words of the male poet Stéphane Mallarmé's 'Crise de vers [Crisis of Verse]', 'l'absente de tous bouquets [what is absent from every bouquet]' (1897: 251 [2007: 210]). David Evans goes as far as evoking 'the tyranny of the alexandrine', rooted in 'regular, predictable rhythms [...] with [a] limited, mechanical stock of rhyme words' (2015: 171). Critics today often use the language of verse to analyze poems in prose: not only does Graham Robb refer to Bertrand's *Gaspard de la Nuit* in terms of 'bits of the alexandrine hung like broken strings' (2000: 6), but also 'alexandrins-hors-les-vers [alexandrines-beyond-verse]' are heard everywhere (Contini 2013: 181 [1983]), and paragraphs are called 'stanzas'.

For readers of French poetry, the rhythms of the alexandrine – so familiar as to be reassuring – can be taken as a fundamental waypoint. To the extent that such an element stimulates remembrance of verse encountered throughout a life, a poem's form inevitably results in longing. As Clive Scott points out, 'in a lineal landscape which looks preordained and publicly owned, [there are] factors which release, which are designed to release, in the reader, moments of subjectivity, or personal memory and self-discovery' (2002: 121). In essence, a reader's experience of a structure like the sonnet carries the weight of sonnets going back to the time of Petrarch's creations in the fourteenth century. The same is true of the alexandrine, which has a French pedigree dating to the early twelfth century, constituting a landmark in the identity of poetry. By the nineteenth century, the alexandrine was 'the culturally loaded symbol of centuries-old French values of order, clarity and harmony' (Evans 2010: 80). The Paris-centrism of national values meant that the alexandrine became the symbol of a certain Paris, crystallized in the *bon usage* determined by the Académie française. Yet, creativity had not been stopped from thriving within such constraints, as we have seen. The alexandrine was constantly being repurposed from within. This heritage is what causes remembrance. The art of sculptors of the alexandrine like Colet and Ségalas articulates experiences of the physical geographies of their age within the creative limits of verse form. Indeed, the modern city's conflicting identities find their place in memory without form being completely dismantled; rather, it is a question of language being fastidiously worked, crafted, chiselled and polished.

A concluding coup de dés: *Demolition time*

As a way of bringing this exploration to a close, what happens if we undertake the quasi-Haussmannian move of demolishing lines of verse and scattering their remains all over the page? Figures 10.4 and 10.5 are word clouds derived from Colet's 'Paris' and Ségalas's 'Les Démolitions'. Here, the size of a word relates to how often it features

FIGURE 10.4: Colet's 'Paris'

FIGURE 10.5: Ségalas's 'Les Démolitions'

in the poem in question. It is striking that abstract terms such as 'gloire [glory]' prevail for Colet, whereas concrete terms like 'murs [walls]' are the crux of Ségalas's poem. A new form draws attention to different kinds of features: rhyming pairs are shattered, as is punctuation, but some syntactic networks clamour more loudly in the throng. This demonstrates how lines of verse conceal as much as they reveal within a delicate orchestration where each syllable counts. Every sound is key to this urban (dis)harmony, whether consciously embraced or not. Certain noises resonate long after a poem is finished – such are our forms of remembrance.

NOTES

1. Uncredited translations are by Finch-Race and Gosetti.
2. Valentina is the recipient of an Australian Research Council Discovery Early Career Award for 'Provincial Poets and the Making of a Nation', funded by the Australian Government (DE200101206). As #TeamFinchetti, we thank the participants in our session at the Australian Society for French Studies conference on 'Dis/connexion' on 3 December 2020, including Associate Professor Chris Andrews (Western Sydney University), Professor Natalie Edwards (University of Adelaide), Dr Chris Hogarth (University of Southern Australia) and Dr Heather Williams (University of Wales). We also express our appreciation to the new network 'Women in French: Australia', headed by Dr Christie Margrave (Australian National University).

REFERENCES

Allen, Peter (2011), '"Second Paris" Built towards End of First World War to Fool Germans', *The Telegraph*, 9 November, www.telegraph.co.uk/news/worldnews/europe/france/8879053/

Second-Paris-built-towards-end-of-First-World-War-to-fool-Germans.html. Accessed 13 December 2020.

Baudelaire, Charles (1861), *Les Fleurs du Mal*, Paris: Poulet-Malassis & De Broise.

Baudelaire, Charles (1862), 'Petits poèmes en prose', *La Presse*, 26 August, pp. 1–2.

Baudelaire, Charles (1998), *The Flowers of Evil* (trans. J. McGowan), Oxford: Oxford University Press.

Bellati, Giovanna (2014), 'Images de Paris dans la poésie de Théophile Gautier', *Studi francesi*, 172, pp. 89–99.

Bellenger, Yvonne (1979), *Le Jour dans la poésie française au temps de la Renaissance*, Tübingen: Günter Narr.

Bernini, Gian Lorenzo (1624), *David*, Rome: Galleria Borghese. [*Wikimedia Commons*, 2015.]

Bertrand, Aloysius ([1842] 2000), *Œuvres complètes* (ed. H. H. Poggenburg), Paris: Champion.

Boutin, Aimée (2015), *City of Noise: Sound and Nineteenth-Century Paris*, Urbana: University of Illinois Press.

Boutin, Aimée and Paliyenko, Adrianna M. (2002), 'Nineteenth-century French women poets: An exceptional legacy', *Women in French Studies*, 10: 2, pp. 77–109.

Broome, Peter (1999), *Baudelaire's Poetic Patterns: The Secret Language of 'Les Fleurs du Mal'*, Amsterdam: Rodopi.

Buonarroti, Michelangelo (1504), *David*, Florence: Galleria dell'Accademia. [*Wikimedia Commons*, 2011.]

Chambers, Ross (1999), *Loiterature*, Lincoln: University of Nebraska Press.

Chambers, Ross (2005), 'Baudelaire's Paris', in R. Lloyd (ed.), *The Cambridge Companion to Baudelaire*, Cambridge: Cambridge University Press, pp. 101–16.

Colet, Louise (1836), *Fleurs du Midi*, Paris: Dumont.

Contini, Gianfranco ([1983] 2013), 'Sans rythme' (trans. S. Miglierina), *L'Année Baudelaire*, 17, pp. 179–92.

Corbière, Tristan (1873), *Les Amours jaunes*, Paris: Glady.

Corbière, Tristan (1995), *These Jaundiced Loves* (trans. C.Pilling), Calstock: Peterloo Poets.

Culler, Jonathan (2010), 'Teaching Baudelaire, teaching translation', *Profession*, 34, pp. 91–98.

Donatello (1440), *David*, Florence: Museo Nazionale del Bargello. [*Wikimedia Commons*, 2015.]

Du Bellay, Joachim ([1558] 1830), 'Sonnet', in G. de Nerval (ed.), *Choix des poésies de Ronsard, Du Bellay, Baïf, Belleau, Dubartas, Chassignet, Desportes, Regnier*, Paris: Bureau de la Bibliothèque choisie, p. 164.

Du Bellay, Joachim (2002), *Lyrics of the French Renaissance* (trans. N. R. Schapiro), New Haven, CT: Yale University Press.

Evans, David (2010), 'Creating the island imaginary: Corsican poetry in French (1870–1960)', *Modern and Contemporary France*, 18: 1, pp. 67–91.

Evans, David (2015), 'Discordant harmonies and turbulent serenity: The ecopoetic rhythms of nature's – and art's – resistance', *Dix-neuf*, 19: 3, pp. 167–86.

Evans, David (2016), 'Malfunctioning music and the art of noise: The prepared pianos of Jules Laforgue', *Dix-neuf*, 20: 1, pp. 45–65.

Finch-Race, Daniel A. (2015), 'Placelessness in Baudelaire's "Les Sept Vieillards" and "Les Petites Vieilles"', *Modern Language Review*, 110: 4, pp. 1011–26.

Finch-Race, Daniel A. and Gosetti, Valentina (2018), 'Destabilizing the other in Baudelaire-Bertrand-Rimbaud', *L'Esprit créateur*, 58: 1, pp. 48–58.

Fourcaut, Laurent (2010), *Le Commentaire composé*, Paris: Armand Colin.

Fournier, Éric (2008), *Paris en ruines: Du Paris haussmannien au Paris communard*, Paris: Imago.

Garman, Emma (2018), 'Feminize your canon: Olivia Manning', *The Paris Review*, 13 June, www.theparisreview.org/blog/2018/06/13/feminize-your-canon-olivia-manning.

Gautier, Théophile (1872), *Émaux et camées*, Paris: Charpentier.

Gautier, Théophile (2011), *Selected Lyrics* (trans. N. R. Schapiro), New Haven, CT: Yale University Press.

Gosetti, Valentina (2016), *Aloysius Bertrand's 'Gaspard de la Nuit': Beyond the Prose Poem*, Oxford: Legenda.

Green, Anne (2013), *Changing France: Literature and Material Culture in the Second Empire*, London: Anthem.

Gubbins, Sarah (2018), 'Generic baggage: Encountering other people in "À une passante" and "Les Veuves"', *L'Esprit créateur*, 58: 1, pp. 8–16.

Hazan, Éric ([2002] 2011), *The Invention of Paris: A History in Footsteps* (trans. D.Fernbach), London: Verso.

Hazareesingh, Sudhir (2016), *How the French Think: An Affectionate Portrait of an Intellectual People*, London: Penguin.

Hugo, Victor (1835), *Les Chants du crépuscule*, The Hague: Vervloet.

Johnson, Barbara (1979), *Défigurations du langage poétique: La Seconde Révolution baudelairienne*, Paris: Flammarion.

Kerr, Greg (2013), *Dream Cities: Utopia and Prose by Poets in Nineteenth-Century France*, Oxford: Legenda.

Killick, Rachel (2005), 'Baudelaire's versification: Conservative or radical?', in R. Lloyd (ed.), *The Cambridge Companion to Baudelaire*, Cambridge: Cambridge University Press, pp. 51–68.

Kliger, Ilya and Maslov, Boris (2016), 'Introducing historical poetics: History, experience, form', in I. Kliger and B. Maslov (eds), *Persistent Forms: Explorations in Historical Poetics*, New York: Fordham University Press, pp. 1–36.

Lavaud, Martine and Tortonese, Paolo (2018), 'Avant-propos', in M. Lavaud and P. Tortonese (eds), *Théophile Gautier et la religion de l'art*, Paris: Classiques Garnier, pp. 7–14.

Levine, Caroline (2015), *Forms: Whole, Rhythm, Hierarchy, Network*, Princeton, NJ: Princeton University Press.

Lloyd, Rosemary (2002), *Baudelaire's World*, Ithaca, NY: Cornell University Press.

Lunn-Rockliffe, Katherine (2004), 'Paris as bazaar: Tristan Corbière's poetry of the city', *Nineteenth-Century French Studies*, 33: 1–2, pp. 120–34.

Mallarmé, Stéphane (1897), *Divagations*, Paris: Eugène Fasquelle.

Mallarmé, Stéphane (2007), *Divagations* (trans. B. Johnson), Cambridge, MA: Belknap.

McGuinness, Patrick (2015), *Poetry and Radical Politics in 'fin de siècle' France: From Anarchism to 'Action française'*, Oxford: Oxford University Press.

Paliyenko, Adrianna M. (2016), *Genius Envy: Women Shaping French Poetic History, 1801–1900*, University Park: Pennsylvania State University Press.

Pietromarchi, Luca (2013), 'Baudelaire et la ligne qui danse', *L'Année Baudelaire*, 17, pp. 83–96.

Robb, Graham (2000), 'Three strings of a damaged violin', *The Times Literary Supplement*, 20 October, p. 6.

Rolls, Alistair (2020), 'Saving Paris from nostalgia: Jumbling the urban and seeing swans everywhere', *Australian Journal of French Studies*, 57: 1, pp. 66–77.

Schultz, Gretchen (1999), *The Gendered Lyric: Subjectivity and Difference in Nineteenth-Century French Poetry*, West Lafayette, IN: Purdue University Press.

Schultz, Gretchen (2008), 'Through the looking glass: Reflections of ageing women in the poetry of nineteenth-century France', *Romance Studies*, 26: 3, pp. 233–48.

Scott, Clive (2002), *Channel Crossings: French and English Poetry in Dialogue*, Oxford: Legenda.

Ségalas, Anaïs (1837), *Les Oiseaux de passage*, Paris: Moutardier.

Ségalas, Anaïs (1854), 'Les Démolitions de Paris', *Musée des familles*, 22, pp. 28–29.

Ségalas, Anaïs (1864), *Nos bons Parisiens*, Paris: Magnin, Blanchard & Co.

Siefert, Louisa ([1869] 2017), 'L'Image', in V. Gosetti, A. Bedeschi, and A. Marchetti (eds), *Donne: Poeti di Francia e oltre – Dal Romanticismo a oggi*, Borgomanero: Giuliano Ladolfi, p. 108.

Williams, Heather (2003), 'Writing to Paris: Poets, nobles and savages in nineteenth-century Brittany', *French Studies*, 57: 4, pp. 475–90.

Contributors

FELICITY CHAPLIN teaches in French studies at Monash University. She is the author of two books, *Charlotte Gainsbourg: Transnational and Transmedia Stardom* (Manchester UP, 2020) and *La Parisienne in Cinema: Between Art and Life* (Manchester UP, 2017) and is a contributor to the forthcoming edited collection *Refocus: The Films of François Ozon* (Edinburgh UP, 2021). Felicity has written extensively on cinema, stardom, celebrity, fashion, French female identity and cultural histories of Paris. Her work appears in *French Screen Studies*, *Australian Journal of French Studies*, *Celebrity Studies*, *Metro*, *Screening the Past* and *Senses of Cinema*. Felicity is also a film reviewer for the *Australian Book Review*.

CHRISTOPHER FALZON is a conjoint senior lecturer at the University of Newcastle, Australia, and visiting fellow in philosophy at the University of New South Wales. He has published widely on twentieth-century French philosophy, especially Sartre and Foucault, and on philosophy and film. He is the author of *Foucault and Social Dialogue* (1998), *Philosophy Goes to the Movies* (3rd edition, 2014) and *Ethics Goes to the Movies* (2018), and co-editor of *Foucault and Philosophy* (2010) and the Blackwell *Companion to Foucault* (2013).

DANIEL FINCH-RACE, FHEA is a research fellow in the Center for the Humanities and Social Change at Università Ca' Foscari in Venice, following teaching/ research fellowships in Southampton, Durham, Edinburgh and Bristol. His solo publications include articles in *Interdisciplinary Studies in Literature and Environment*, *Modern Language Review* and *Romance Studies*, as well as an issue of *Nineteenth-Century Contexts* about 'Poetics of Place' in 2019. As co-editor, he worked with Jeff Barda on *Textures* (Peter Lang, 2015), with Stephanie Posthumus on *French Ecocriticism* (Peter Lang, 2017), and with Julien Weber on issues of *Dix-neuf* and *L'Esprit créateur* about 'Ecopoetics' and 'French Ecocriticism' in 2015/17. During 2019-20, he was the treasurer of the Society of Dix-Neuviémistes, and the founding co-chair of a special interest group for early career academics within the University Council of Modern Languages.

VALENTINA GOSETTI is a poetry translator, an Australian Research Council DECRA Fellow, and senior lecturer in French at the University of New England (Australia), following her Kathleen Bourne Junior Research Fellowship in French and Comparative Literature at St Anne's College, University of Oxford. She authored *Aloysius Bertrand's "Gaspard de la Nuit": Beyond the Prose Poem* (Legenda, 2016), co-edited *Still Loitering: Australian Essays in Honour of Ross Chambers* (Peter Lang, 2020) with Alistair Rolls, and co-edited and co-translated the bilingual anthology *Donne: Poeti di Francia e oltre* (Ladolfi, 2017) with Adriano Marchetti and Andrea Bedeschi. Her articles appear in *Australian Journal of French Studies*, *Dix-neuf*, *French Studies Bulletin*, *L'Esprit créateur*, *La Giroflée*, *PMLA*, *Revue Bertrand* (with E. J. Kent), and *Romantisme* (with Antonio Viselli).

As #TeamFinchetti, Finch-Race and Gosetti co-authored an article in *L'Esprit créateur* in 2018, received grants from the Arts and Humanities Research Council's Open World Research Initiative for public events on multilingual poetry translation in Bristol and Sydney in 2019, and co-edited a double issue of *Dix-neuf* about 'Ecoregions' in 2019.

MARGUERITE JOHNSON is professor of classics at the University of Newcastle, Australia. Her research expertise is predominantly in the area of ancient Mediterranean cultural studies, particularly in representations of gender, sexualities and the body. She is especially interested in the ways in which the ancients write about women. She also works in classical reception studies, including later receptions of Sappho and other ancient poets.

DAVID MUSGRAVE has published six collections of poetry and one novel, *Glissando*. In 2005 he founded the literary publishing house Puncher & Wattmann, which takes its name from Beckett's *En attendant Godot*, and which is Australia's leading publisher of poetry. He has published widely on Australian poetry, Menippean satire and the grotesque. In 2013 his monograph *Grotesque Anatomies: Menippean Satire since the Renaissance* was published by Cambridge Scholars Publishing. He teaches creative writing at the University of Newcastle, Australia.

ALISTAIR ROLLS is associate professor of French studies at the University of Newcastle, Australia. His interests include twentieth-century author Boris Vian, post-war French crime fiction and, increasingly, twentieth-century intertextual references to Baudelaire's poetry. His books on Paris include *Paris and the Fetish: Primal Crime Scenes* (Rodopi, 2014), and *Origins and Legacies of Marcel Duhamel's Série Noire* (Brill, 2018), which he co-wrote with Clara Sitbon and Marie-Laure Vuaille-Barcan.

CLIVE SCOTT is professor emeritus of European literature at the University of East Anglia and a fellow of the British Academy. He was president of the MHRA

2014-2015. His principal research interests lie in French and comparative poetics (*The Poetics of French Verse: Studies in Reading*, 1998; *Channel Crossings: French and English Poetry in Dialogue 1550-2000*, 2002); in literary translation, and in particular the experimental translation of poetry (*Translating Baudelaire*, 2000; *Translating Rimbaud's Illuminations*, 2006; *Literary Translation and the Rediscovery of Reading*, 2012; *Translating the Perception of Text: Literary Translation and Phenomenology*, 2012); and in photography's relationship with writing (*The Spoken Image: Photography and Language*, 1999; *Street Photography: From Atget to Cartier-Bresson*, 2007). Translation and photography combine in his *Translating Apollinaire* (2014). His most recent book is *The Work of Literary Translation* (2018). He is at present working on the application of the concepts of dialogue, movement and ecology to literary translation.

Index

A

Alcy, Jeanne d' 94
Allen, Woody 136
Andersen, Nathan 117–18
Anderson, Jill 173, 182n
Andreadis, Harriette 56n
Andrew, Dudley 122
Andrews, Chris 10–11, 18n
Apollinaire, Guillaume 182, 184n
Aragon, Louis 37n
Archibald, J. F. 165
Arnold, Matthew 175
Ashbery, John 175
Atget, Eugène 160
Athenaeus 56n

B

Bailly, Edmond 169
Baldick, Robert 144, 145n
Balducci, Richard 117
Balides, Constance 93, 95
Banville, Théodore de 82, 157
Barnes, Katherine 170–71
Barney, Natalie Clifford 5, 10, 59–68, 72, 72n, 73n, 74n
Barnouw, Erik 95, 104n
Baron Cohen, Sacha 97
Barthes, Roland 8, 23, 29–30, 37n, 147n, 178
Baudelaire, Charles 1–18, 19n, 21–34, 35n, 36n, 39–54, 55n, 59–60, 62–64, 66, 73n, 78–85, 87–89, 90n, 93, 96, 102–04, 106n, 107n, 129–40, 142, 144, 145n, 146n, 147n, 148n, 150, 152–63, 163n, 164n, 167, 176, 182, 187–88, 192–97
Bazin, André 111, 114
Beaudouin, Valérie 18n
Beauvoir, Simone de 108–09, 111, 124, 129, 140, 145n
Becker, Jacques 80
Bellati, Giovanna 203
Belmondo, Jean-Paul 111, 113
Benjamin, Walter 32, 40, 42, 45, 52, 60, 77–78, 80–81, 84–85, 87–89
Bens, Jacques 18n
Benstock, Shari 72n
Bergson, Henri 77–78
Berti, Eduardo 18n
Bertrand, Aloysius 202, 204
Betz, Mark 84
Bogart, Humphrey 111, 116, 120, 122–23
Boulanger, Gustave 55n
Boutin, Aimée 188, 194
Boyer, Philoxène 48
Boym, Svetlana 41
Brainard, Joe 11–12, 19n
Brecht, Bertolt 118
Brennan, Christopher 165–73, 175–77, 182, 182n
Bresson, Robert 112
Breton, André 95, 184n

215

Brody, Richard 123
Brooks, Romaine 72n
Brooks, Shelton 146n
Broome, Peter 195
Buñuel, Luis 93, 95–99, 101, 103–04, 105n, 107n
Butterfield, Asa 96

C
Calvino, Italo 145n
Camus, Albert 34n
Céline, Louis-Ferdinand 35n, 140, 145n
Chabrol, Claude 108, 111
Chambers, Ross 2, 6–7, 13, 16–17, 18n, 26–29, 33, 36n, 62, 129–31, 133–36, 138, 173, 176
Choiseul-Praslin, Charles de 4
Choquette, Leslie 50–51, 72n
Clark, Axel 167–69, 173
Clayson, Hollis 47
Cohen-Solal, Annie 145n, 146n
Colet, Louise 18, 189–93, 196–97, 199, 204–06
Colin, Armand 169
Conway, Kelley 83, 86–87
Corbière, Tristan 190, 193
Corrozet, Gilles 2–3, 18n, 41
Courbet, Gustave 49
Coutard, Raoul 113
Covin, Michel 22–24, 27, 30, 32, 35n, 37n
Crane, Sheila 61

D
Dalí, Salvador 93, 95, 98, 105n
Daumier, Honoré 32
Davray, Dominique 80
Degas, Edgar 56n
DeJean, Joan 65
Delacroix, Eugène 55n
Delannoy, Jean 112
Delerue, George 82

DeRoo, Rebecca 80
Derrida, Jacques 175
Deschanel, émile 48
Dilts, Rebekkah 74n
Domarchi, Jean 119
Dorf, Samuel 62, 72n
Douchet, Jean 119
Dreyfus, Hubert 120–21
Du Bellay, Joachim 196

E
Edison, Thomas 105n
Edwards, Chris 173, 176–78, 182, 184n
Eisenstein, Sergei 114
Eliot, T. S. 172
Erinna 74n
Estienne, Robert 4
Evans, David 204

F
Fabre-Serris, Jacqueline 74n
Faderman, Lillian 73n
Fagan, Kate 176–77
Fairfax, Daniel 111
Farrell, Michael 166, 172
Felman, Shoshana 2
Ferguson, Priscilla Parkhurst 41
Ferlinghetti, Lawrence 12–14
Ferrier, Claude-Marie 55n
Fitch, Toby 175, 184n
Fitzgerald, Ella 139
Flaubert, Gustave 167
Flem, Lydia 18n
Flitterman-Lewis, Sandy 84
Forbes, Jill 79, 82
Fournel, Victor 86
Fournier, éric 198
François I (King) 41
Fränkel, Hans 70
Freud, Sigmund 77–78, 97, 99–100

INDEX

G

Gallimard, Gaston 140
Gandy, Matthew 53
Garréta, Anne 18n
Gautier, Théophile 167, 189, 193, 202–03
Gérôme, Jean-Léon 48, 55n
Gibb, Dirk 92, 104n
Glavey, Brian 11–12, 19n
Glick, Elisa 73n
Gluck, Mary 35n, 147n
Godard, Jean-Luc 4, 108, 111–18, 120–23
Gourmont, Rémy de 72n
Gouvard, Jean-Michel 21, 23–28, 35n, 36n
Grandville, Juliette 49
Green, Anne 198
Grosz, Elizabeth 52–53
Gubbins, Sarah 194
Guest, Stephanie 177
Guy, Constantin 84, 159, 164n

H

Hall, Radclyffe 72n
Harvey, David 22
Haussmann, Georges-Eugène 1, 5, 13, 15, 23, 25, 31, 33, 40–41, 53–54, 55n, 62, 155–56, 193–94, 205
Hawke, John 166, 168
Hawkes, Howard 116
Hawthorne, Melanie 72n
Heller, Nathan 117
Hendrycks, Eric 19n
Henkel, Arthur 184n
Hiddleston, J. A. 150
Hitchcock, Alfred 116, 118
Hobsbawm, Eric 66
Hodges, Elizabeth 2, 41
Homer 43
Hooper, Barbara 53
Horace 67

Houssaye, Arsène 24, 48, 155
Hughes, Randolph 182n
Hugo, Victor 36n, 40–41, 55n, 82, 197
Humphreys, Karen 49
Husserl, Edmund 146n
Huyssen, Andreas 41

I

Ingold, Tim 153
Irigaray, Luce 74n

J

Johnson, Barbara 23, 26, 30, 104, 106n, 194
Johnson, Marguerite 188
Johnston, Claire 100, 106n
Jollivet, Simone 140
Jouet, Jacques 18n

K

Killick, Rachel 195
Kingsley, Ben 94
Kirkpatrick, Peter 166
Kohan, Martin 18n
Kopp, Robert 35n
Kozhevnikova, Evgeniya 19n
Kristeva, Julia 19n
Krueger, Cheryl 17

L

Lacan, Jacques 100
Laclos, Pierre Choderlos de 145n
Laforgue, Jules 196
Langlois, Henri 111
Lanzoni, Rémi Fournier 95, 104n
Larkin, Brian 136–37
Lavaud, Martine 203
Lefebvre, Henri 153
Le Tellier, Hervé 18n
Levine, Caroline 201

Lewis, Ted 139
Lindon, Mathieu 18n
Lloyd, Rosemary 195
Louÿs, Pierre 73n
Lumière, Auguste and Louis 108
Lunn-Rockcliffe, Katherine 190

M

McCrory, Helen 94
McGowan, James 102–03, 145n
McGuinness, Patrick 203
McMillan, James 56n
Mallarmé, Stéphane 15, 146n, 166–77, 182, 182n, 183n, 204
Manet, édouard 33, 150
Marchal, Bertrand 183n
Marie, Michel 105n
Marot, Clément 191
Martin, Walter 102–03, 106n
Marville, Charles 154
Mathews, Harry 18n
Méliès, Georges 3, 92–96, 101–02, 104n, 105n
Melville, Jean-Pierre 112, 119
Mennel, Barbara 116, 121
Meschonnic, Henri 153
Metz, Christian 102
Michelangelo 201
Miller, Cristanne 72
Miller, J. Hillis 5
Mogador, Céleste 49–51, 56n
Moncan, Patrice de 37n
Monet, Claude 33
Monnet, Nadja 12
Montrichard, Christian de 18n
Moreton, Lionel de 49
Morrissey, Jim 84–85
Mouton, Janice 84, 87–88
Murray, Les 169
Muybridge, Eadweard 161

N

Nadar (G.-F. Tournachon) 32, 37n
Neymark, Gustave 168
Niemeyer, Katharina 36n, 92, 104, 148n
Nora, Pierre 2
Nymphadorus/Nymphis 56n

O

O'Reilly, Dowell 168, 170, 183n
Ovid 39, 43–46
Owen, Hugh 55n

P

Pagès, Nicolas 18n
Paliyenko, Adrianna 188, 192, 197
Parent-Duchâtelet, Alexandre 49, 51, 53, 56n
Paul, R. W. 105n
Péguy, Charles 55n
Perec, Georges 9–12, 14, 19n
Perkins, V. F. 115
Petrarch 205
Pietromarchi, Luca 204
Pliny 56n
Poiccard, Michel 123
Porphyrio 67
Pound, Ezra 172
Powrie, Phil 87
Preminger, Otto 116
Prévert, Jacques 9, 12–14, 19n
Propertius 64
Proust, Marcel 77, 151

Q

Queneau, Raymond 19n
Quillen, Christophe 18n
Quinney, Anne 128

R

Ray, Chelsea 63
Ray, Nicholas 116

INDEX

Redon, Odile 183n
Renoir, Jean 112, 121
Renoir, Pierre-Auguste 33
Riffaterre, Michel/Michael 5, 130–31, 138
Rimbaud, Arthur 173, 182, 183n, 184n
Rivette, Jacques 108, 111, 119
Robb, Graham 204
Robert, Élias 55n
Roditi, Édouard 146n
Rodriguez, Suzanne 74n
Rohmer, Éric 108
Romney, Jonathon 119
Rolls, Alistair 80–81, 188, 193
Ronsard, Pierre de 191
Rosewarne, Lauren 33, 147n
Rossellini, Roberto 114
Rouch, Jean 117
Rubenking, Neil J. 175
Ruddick, Lisa 67
Ryan, Judith 48

S

Sanyal, Debarati 55n
Sappho 5, 10, 39, 44–51, 56n, 59–72, 73n, 74n
Sartre, Jean-Paul 3, 27–28, 34, 36n, 37n, 108–12, 119–20, 122, 124, 127–44, 145n, 146n, 147n, 148n
Saussure, Ferdinand de 183n
Scève, Maurice 191
Schlossman, Beryl 44, 79–80, 90n
Schöne, Albrecht 184n
Schultz, Gretchen 188
Schweitzer, Anne-Marie 146n
Scorsese, Martin 3, 92–96, 101
Scott, Clive 15–17, 102–03, 137–38, 204
Scott, John A. 184n
Seberg, Jean 111, 113, 124
Ségalas, Anaïs 18, 189, 196–99, 204–06
Sherman, Antoinette 72n

Sicard, François-Léon 165
Sidney, Philip 177
Signoret, Simone 80
Skinner, Marilyn 72
Slessor, Kenneth 166
Smith, Alison 80
Solomon, Simeon 74n
Sontag, Susan 86, 88
Starobinski, Jean 183n
Stein, Gertrude 59, 66–68, 71–72, 74n
Steiner, George 156
Stephens, A. G. 165–66, 169–70
Sterrit, David 117, 121–22
Swinburne, Algernon Charles 74n
Sydney, Viscount 182

T

Taylor, Andrew 167–68, 183n
Thorsen, Thea 56n
Toklas, Alice 67–68
Tortonese, Paolo 203
Tranter, John 171, 173–76, 182, 183n
Troubridge, Una 72n
Truffaut, François 108, 111–12, 116
Tucker, Sophie 139, 146n

U

Ungar, Steven 78, 83, 85, 87, 89
Usher, Phillip John 113

V

Valéry, Paul 77–78
Van Laerhoven, Bob 26, 35n
Varda, Agnès 17, 77–89, 108
Varèse, Louise 35n
Verne, Jules 96, 105n
Vian, Boris 11
Vilallonga, José Luis de 81
Virgil 39, 42–43, 55n
Visconti, Luchino 114

219

Vivien, Renée 5, 61, 63, 65–66, 72, 72n, 73n, 74n

W
Wallace, Jennifer 84, 86
Wallace-Crabbe, Chris 166
Walters, Ethel 139
Weinfield, Henry 172, 175
Wells, Amy 66, 68, 73n
White, Patrick 184n
Wilde, Oscar 72n
Williams, Linda 26, 93, 97–101, 103, 105n, 106n

Willis, Ika 55n
Winning, Joanne 61
Wolfe, Elsie de 61
Wood, James 128, 145n
Wratislaw, Theodore 15
Wright, Edgar 18n, 138
Wright, Judith 166

Z
Zola, Émile 147n

Ingram Content Group UK Ltd.
Milton Keynes UK
UKHW032227060423
419773UK00011B/769